SOVIET CONDUCT IN WORLD AFFAIRS

SOVIET CONDUCT

IN WORLD AFFAIRS

*A SELECTION OF READINGS
COMPILED BY ALEXANDER DALLIN*

GREENWOOD PRESS, PUBLISHERS
WESTPORT, CONNECTICUT

Library of Congress Cataloging in Publication Data

Dallin, Alexander, comp.
  Soviet conduct in world affairs.

  Reprint of the ed. published by Columbia University
Press, New York.
  Includes bibliographical references.
  CONTENTS: Dallin, A. Introduction.--Bell, D. Ten
theories in search of reality.--Ideology and power
politics; a symposium: Hunt, R. N. C. The importance of
doctrine. Sharp, S. L. National interest. Lowenthal,
R. The logic of one-party rule. [etc.]
  1. Russia--Foreign relations--1917-   --Addresses,
essays, lectures. I. Title.
[DK266.D23 1975   327.47   75-31359
ISBN 0-8371-8511-4

Acknowledgments

The compiler is eager to express his gratitude to the several publishers and authors for permission to reprint their materials in the present volume. He hereby acknowledges appreciation to the *Antioch Review*, for permission to republish Alex Inkeles' "The Challenge of a Stable Russia"; to Bertram D. Wolfe and *Commentary*, for permission to republish "The Durability of Soviet Despotism"; to *Foreign Affairs*, for permission to republish Historicus' "Stalin on Revolution" and X's "The Sources of Soviet Conduct"; to the Free Press of Glencoe, Illinois, for permission to republish the prologue of Nathan Leites' *A Study of Bolshevism*; to Harvard University Press, Cambridge, Massachusetts, for permission to republish Chapter 17 of Barrington Moore's *Soviet Politics: Dilemma of Power*; to the *New Leader*, for permission to republish Michael M. Karpovich's "Russian Imperialism or Communist Aggression?"; to *Problems of Communism*, for permission to republish the symposium "Ideology and Power Politics"; to the RAND Corporation, for permission to republish Robert C. Tucker's "The Psychology of Soviet Foreign Policy"; to Henry L. Roberts and the *Texas Quarterly*, for permission to republish "Soviet-American Relations: Problems of Choice and Decision"; to the World Peace Foundation, Boston, for permission to republish Philip E. Mosely's "Some Soviet Techniques of Negotiation"; to *World Politics*, for permission to republish Daniel Bell's "Ten Theories in Search of Reality" and Marshall D. Shulman's "Changing Appreciation of the Soviet Problem."

The compiler also wishes to record his sincere thanks to Professor Henry L. Roberts and Miss Louise Luke, of the Russian Institute, for their encouragement, substantive interest, and valuable assistance in seeing this collection from blueprint to publisher.

Contents

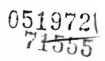

Introduction

The present selection of readings is not intended to remedy the absence of a satisfactory textbook on Soviet foreign policy. Its purpose is neither to present new facts nor to offer a novel hypothesis.

These readings were originally compiled in response to the interest of, and as a convenience for, students of the Russian Institute at Columbia University, who, seeking their own conclusions, were eager to acquaint themselves with the various interpretations of Soviet policy that have been advanced. The compilation now appears in book form for the use of others who may have felt a similar need.

To gain an understanding of Soviet foreign policy and Soviet conduct, the student must reach out beyond the confines of the immediate diplomatic setting. He must consider the motives of Soviet policy-makers, the trends of Soviet development, domestic as well as foreign, and the implications of these for United States (or generally 'Western') attitudes and policies.

The articles and chapters here presented express a variety of views, often incompatible with one another. They raise, from different fields of specialization and in different perspectives, some of the key problems inherent in an inquiry into Soviet behavior. While Soviet analyses are also essential for a study of Soviet policy, they are not included in this volume, for they are uncritically unanimous in their apologia for Soviet performance.

Many of the selections refer primarily to the Stalin era, inasmuch as few systematic papers have as yet been developed on the Khrushchev period. On the other hand, insight into the mainsprings of Soviet conduct in earlier years should provide a better basis for judging to what extent the very real changes which the Soviet Union has witnessed since Stalin's death have or have not involved an abandonment of the fundamental assumptions and objectives prevailing in Moscow prior to 1953.

These pieces do not exhaust the available interpretations, but they seem to me representative of the most challenging thinking in this field. Among the other studies which the inquisitive student may wish to add to those offered in this collection are the following:

Max Beloff, "The Principles of Soviet Foreign Policy," which is Chapter 15 in Volume II of his *Foreign Policy of Soviet Russia* (New York, 1949).

David J. Dallin, "Foreign Policy," which is Part III of his *Changing World of Soviet Russia* (New Haven, 1956).

Diplomaticus, "Stalinist Theory and Soviet Foreign Policy," *Review of Politics*, October 1952.

Raymond L. Garthoff, "Strategic Concepts and Doctrine for the Nuclear Age," which is Chapter 4 of his *Soviet Strategy in the Nuclear Age* (New York, 1958).

William A. Glaser, "Theories of Soviet Foreign Policy," *World Affairs Quarterly*, July 1956.

Henry L. Roberts, *Russia and America: Danger and Prospects* (New York, 1956).

Hugh Seton-Watson, "Communism, Social Classes, and Power," which is Chapter 16 of his *From Lenin to Malenkov* (New York, 1953).

Jan F. Triska, "A Model for Study of Soviet Foreign Policy, " *American Political Science Review*, March 1958.

Adam Ulam, "Soviet Ideology and Soviet Foreign Policy," *World Politics*, January 1959.

Nor do the pieces presented here eliminate the requirement to study and know the facts. But I hope that they may stimulate some additional reflection about the patterns and significance of the evidence.

Columbia University   ALEXANDER DALLIN
August 1959

Ten Theories in Search of Reality: The Prediction of Soviet Behavior in the Social Sciences

DANIEL BELL

Surely, more has been written about the Russian Revolution and the ensuing forty years of Soviet rule than about any comparable episode in human history. The bibliography of items on the French Revolution occupies, it is said, one wall of the Bibliothèque Nationale. A complete bibliography on the Soviet Union—which is yet to be compiled and may never be because of the geometric rate at which it multiplies—would probably make that earlier cenotaph to scholarship shrink the way in which the earlier tombs diminished before the great complex at Karnak.

And yet how little of this awesome output has stood the test of so short a span of time! If hell, as Thomas Hobbes once said, is truth seen too late, the road to hell must now be paved twice over with the thousands of books claiming to discover the 'truth' about Russia—while the tortures of the damned are reserved for those, diplomats especially, who committed the fates of millions in the confident belief that they could predict correctly the way in which the Soviet rulers would respond.

In the last ten years there has been, presumably, a new sophistication, and an extraordinary amount of research and writing on Soviet society, particularly in the United States. Some of this research has come from Russian defectors; most of it has been done in special institutes set up by government or foundation research grants in an effort to obtain reliable knowledge about Soviet behavior. We have seen, too, the entry of new disciplines—anthropology, sociology, and psychiatry—into the study of political phenomena. In some instances these newer approaches have claimed to provide a total understanding of Soviet

Published in *World Politics* (April 1958).

Daniel Bell, author of several studies of socialism and labor problems, is Associate Professor of Sociology at Columbia University.

behavior; in others, to supplement existing explanations. So thick and heavy is this research that an outside observer, seeking to push his way through the marshes, often finds himself mired (as that wonderful Russian onomatopoetic evocation has it) in *splosh*'. And one is bogged down further by the fact that much of this newer research is couched in a special jargon which owes allegiance to other modes of discourse than the common tongue. (As R. P. Blackmur has said of the 'New Criticism,' the terminology rigidifies in the course of time and the "normal pathology of a skill becomes a method, and the method a methodology.")

In this article, the writer has attempted a description and, in representative cases, a detailed assessment of these methodologies. This is not a 'national estimate' of Russian capabilities and weaknesses, social, military, or economic, such as is made by the National Security Council. Nor is it a 'survey' of empirical research. The writer has sought to distinguish ten approaches in social theory, each of which, despite some shading or overlap, represents a coherent judgment of Soviet behavior. It is hoped that by 'reading' each against the other, some sense of the crucial differences, analytical or methodological, may emerge. Beyond that, such a reading may aid in the formulation of the two judgments which are essential in any stocktaking: (1) Which theories or approaches have 'stood up' in explaining events, and which have not? (2) If one were a policy-maker, which research would one underwrite in the future, and why?

Enter Pirandello

Hegel once said that what was reasonable was real. Each of the theories to be discussed seems reasonable, yet not wholly real. Something may be wrong with Hegel, the theories, or both. The reader will have to be the judge.

CHARACTEROLOGICAL THEORIES

(1) *Anthropological*. Beginning with the work of Ruth Benedict, and taken up by Linton and Kardiner, Margaret Mead, and Clyde Kluckhohn, contemporary anthropologists have developed the concept of 'culture and personality.' The argument is that members of a given

culture share certain common, sufficiently distinct ways of handling emotional drives and regulating social conduct which form a unique life style that differs, often markedly, from the life style of other cultural groups. The 'norms' of the group specify how an individual must manage the key tensions generated in social living (attitudes to authority, frustration of impulses, aggression, and so forth) and how the social controls against violations of those norms (mechanisms of guilt and shame, disposal of repressed hate, and so forth) operate.

Margaret Mead,[1] Geoffrey Gorer and John Rickman,[2] and Henry V. Dicks[3] have sought to apply these 'culture and personality' concepts to Russian behavior. Gorer, particularly, has gained a certain notoriety for what skeptics have dubbed 'diaperology.' Together with the late John Rickman, a respected British psychiatrist who had lived in Russia during World War I, Gorer argued that the maternal practice of tightly swaddling the Russian infant produces a privation-gratification cycle. This predisposes the 'Great Russian' national character to pendulum swings of submissiveness and violent eruption, of apathy and diffuse persecutory anxiety, of 'oral' greed and abstinence.[4] This accounts, too, for the willingness of the Russian adult to submit to brutal authority.

Dicks's work is more specific. A British psychiatrist at the Tavistock Institute (he set up the War Office Selections Boards), Dicks's generalizations are based, principally, on long interviews with Russian defectors. The outstanding trait of Russian personality, says Dicks, is its ambivalence. On one side is the omnivorousness, the tendency to rush at things and to 'swallow them whole,' the need for quick and full gratification, the spells of manic omnipotence, the anarchic demand for abolition of all bounds and limitations. On the other, the melancholy

---

[1] Mead, *Soviet Attitudes to Authority* (New York, 1951).

[2] Gorer and Rickman, *The People of Great Russia* (London, 1949).

[3] Dicks, "Observations on Contemporary Russian Behavior," *Human Relations*, V, No. 2 (1952), 111-75.

[4] A dichotomy, like an atom once split, can seemingly be multiplied indefinitely. Thus Dinko Tomasic in his study of *The Impact of Russian Culture on Soviet Communism* (Glencoe, Illinois, 1953) finds that Russian national character is a bisect of two contrasting influences, that of the "power-seeking and self-oriented nomadic horsemen of the Eurasian steppes" and of the "anarchic and group-oriented [Slavic] tillers of the land." One can also point to antinomies, such as Gordon Wasson's discovery that Russians are mycophiles and Anglo-Saxons are mycophobes.

closeness and suspicion, the anxious and sullen submissiveness, the "moral masochism and grudging idealization of a strong and arbitrary authority which is thought of as the only safeguard against the excesses of Russian nature." Authority, thus, if it is to be *authority*, must be hard, deprivational, arbitrary, and capricious; if the *vlast'* were weak, nobody would obey it.

Against the traditional untidiness, lack of system, and formlessness of the Russian masses is the contrasting behavior of the elite. It has to be puritanical, in full control of all sentimentality and self-indulgence, and strong enough to renounce the gratifications which 'traditional' Russian character seeks. At important points there are congruities. The people expect and the elite satisfies the image of authority as severe, arbitrary, and fickle. The system, further, permits the most authoritarian fraction of the population "to act out their introjected bad-object relations"—to step into the shoes of a hated, yet, deep down, secretly identified-with father figure (tsar, landlord). "By this hypothesis," says Dicks, "I would explain the rise in Soviet Russia of a rigid, gold-braided, intensely status-conscious, and anxious bureaucracy, which is winning in the struggle against the very tendency originally successfully attacked by the new system and its founders during the Revolution."

But this very transformation of goals, on a conscious or an unconscious level, provides the 'salient' divergence between the Soviet system and the traditional Russian culture-pattern. For the elite, faced with the need of quickly producing a new type of technological and managerial personality, "is using the impetus of its own imperfectly assimilated and conflict-laden goal-drives to force and mold the people into a new cultural norm." Since the greater the pressure the more intensive the inner conflicts, the elite "projects its own compulsive and sadistic authoritarian dominance needs on to foreign outgroups." Thus it creates a psychological situation of 'encirclement' and attributes all failures to the work of the external enemy.

It is difficult to estimate [says Dicks] how much of this paranoid behavior is the result of conscious design and how much is the effect of an inner compulsion due to cultural-psychological forces into which the top leaders have little insight. In this respect, I can only refer to the amazing discovery of the psychiatric pictures presented by a comparable power clique whom we were able to study: Hitler's entourage. We had assumed a cynical and coldblooded exploitation of this paranoid dynamic by people like Goebbels and Himmler—and we found they were its victims.[5]

The acceleration of industrialization, says Dicks, will increase the tensions between the elite and the people. The coercions are "resented and stored up against the regime," the deprivations in the name of some ultimate and impersonal good are interpreted as "withdrawal of love and nurturance." But such unconscious rage also leads to a sense of guilt for having defied authority, and this becomes projected onto the elite (that is, creates a feeling, at all levels, that the elite is angry at the masses and wants to punish them), leading to an increase in the atmosphere of "persecutory anxiety and diffuse fear (*strakh*)." The guilt thus also reduces a tendency to strike out at, or oppose, the regime.

(2) *Psychoanalytic.* An attempt to analyze not Russian but Bolshevik character structure, particularly as exemplified in the Politburo, has been made by Nathan Leites, in his RAND study, underwritten by the U.S. Air Force.[6] But Leites' work goes beyond the mere codification of behavior in operational terms. In guarded, almost esoteric fashion, Leites undertakes a psychoanalytic explanation which is fairly breathtaking in its attempt. Bolshevik elite behavior is seen in contrast to that of the nineteenth-century intelligentsia. The latter were moody, nervous, soul-searching, brooding, introspective. 'The Bolshevik' is rigid, suspicious, unyielding, ever-aggressive. This character is stamped in the primal image of Lenin, and is derived, psychoanalytically speaking, as a 'reaction-formation' to fears of death and latent homosexual impulses. (Since Leites' massive work—639 pages—is the most ambitious attempt yet to read an 'operational code' of Bolshevik behavior, particularly in international strategy, a more detailed exposition of the theory is undertaken below.)

SOCIOLOGICAL THEORIES

(3) *The Social System.* This socio-psychological theory, developed at Harvard in the Russian Research Center, and expressed most concisely in the recent book by Raymond A. Bauer, Alex Inkeles, and Clyde

[5] Dicks, p. 171.

[6] Leites, *A Study of Bolshevism* (Glencoe, Illinois, 1954).

Kluckhohn,[7] seeks to identify the functionally relevant 'operating characteristics' of the Soviet system—for example, the overcommitment of resources to particular objectives, 'storming,' the refusal to allow independent concentration of power—and the effect of these behavior patterns on the various social groups. In this fashion, the authors seek to locate the points of strain in the Soviet system. (Because it is the summary volume of the largest single research project on Soviet behavior, it is discussed in greater detail below.)

(4) *Ideal Types.* This approach, exemplified largely in the writings of Barrington Moore, Jr., at Harvard[8] (though it has influenced the thinking of W. W. Rostow at MIT and Henry Dicks at Tavistock), sets up a number of models for the organization of power in a society and seeks to establish how far any society, and the Russian in particular, can go in its commitment to one or another of these forms.

According to Moore, power and position in a society are held in one of a combination of three ways: (a) *traditional:* power and position are transmitted through the family or kinship system, from father to son; (b) *rational-technical:* power and position are attained by an individual on the basis of skill and technical ability, regardless of the status of one's parent; (c) *political:* power and position are awarded on the basis of loyalty to a political leader, party, or clique.

The use of any one criterion limits the range of workable alternatives for the solution of other problems. Rationality emphasizes that technical competence should be the criterion for employment. But the nature of power struggles demands that jobs should go to the faithful, to the commissar rather than the manager, while purges, the most drastic expression of politics, remind individuals that obedience is the first law of the Soviet system. Meanwhile, traditionalism is still the 'natural' mode of the peasantry, and, *sub rosa,* within large sections of Soviet industry, for family and informal ties have become a necessary means of protection against arbitrary orders.

The political criterion of power in Russia (for example, the commissars in the army, the control functions of the Party in relation to in-

---

[7] Bauer, Inkeles, and Kluckhohn, *How the Soviet System Works* (Cambridge, Massachusetts, 1956).

[8] Moore, *Terror and Progress— USSR* (Cambridge, Massachusetts, 1954) and *Soviet Politics: The Dilemma of Power* (Cambridge, Massachusetts, 1950).

dustry) has been employed too ruthlessly, says Moore, at the expense, even, of sacrificing large classes of technicians and experienced army officers (the *Ezhovshchina*).[9] The power of the dictator to intervene arbitrarily at any point in the administrative hierarchy creates a level of insecurity which an ongoing system may find difficult to maintain. The choice now, Moore feels, lies between 'creeping rationality' and traditionalism, or in some combination of both.

Since the Soviet Union is intent on industrialization, the rationalizing elements are likely to become more deeply embedded in the society. This would mean that technical criteria would replace political decisions, jobs would be allocated according to skill, career expectations would have a higher degree of stability, family privileges could be passed on to the children. In turn, the power and prestige of the industrial manager, the engineer, and the technician would rise, and the share in power and prestige held by the 'control' apparatus—the Party and the secret police—would decline.

An alternative evolution in a traditionalist direction, which Moore finds politically 'somewhat more plausible,' would mean that the Party and military elements would retain control, but arbitrary intervention would diminish as personal cliques and machines within the bureaucracy become the focal point of loyalties. Such a development would also imply a rise in local autonomy and a resistance to innovation and change.

Plausible as these alternatives seem, if there is any sense to Khrushchev's vast 'decentralization' scheme, it would seem to mean the reassertion of a political criterion, rather than economic rationality, in the handling of economic affairs. Genuine economic decentralization, as Richard Lowenthal points out,[10] would leave the Party as a parasitic appendix to the economy. Despite the absorption of managers into the Party, the division of function between managers and Party whips has been a source of conflict; and this was utilized by Malenkov, speaking for the managerial group. What Khrushchev, whose strength has been in the Party secretariats, has now done is to create a union of function, whereby the Party secretaries, at the republic and regional levels, will

[9] [The 'Great Purges' of 1936-1938.—A.D.]
[10] "The Permanent Revolution Is On Again," *Commentary*, XXIV, No. 2 (August 1957), 105-12.

8   DANIEL BELL

be responsible for the economic performance of the plan. As Lowenthal concludes: "It is the 'irrational' Khrushchev with his party bosses, and not the 'rational' Malenkov with his managers and economic administration, who has won the latest round; and the reason is to be found precisely in the logic of self-preservation of the Party regime."[11] If Moore is correct, such logic may yet lead to economic crises; but that remains to be seen.

POLITICAL THEORIES

(5) *Marxist.* Expressed most directly by Isaac Deutscher, this approach sketches a theory of Soviet development based on the proposition that the level of productive power always acts as a constraint on the possibilities of action. It argues that the Stalinist dictatorship was a historically 'necessary' stage, therefore, in overcoming the resistance of the masses to industrialization, but that once this social stage has been achieved, the dictatorial apparatus will 'come into social conflict' with the requirements of the new, higher stage of economic development.[12]

As developed by Deutscher—agreement can be found in the writings of E. H. Carr—the year 1920 represented the crossroads of the revolution:[13] the working class was exhausted, demoralized, shrunken to half its size, anxious for relaxation; in a free election the Bolsheviks would have been ousted; only the iron will of the Bolshevik leadership saved the revolution, at the expense of putting down democracy in the Party (suppressing the Workers' Opposition faction, the 'levelers or Utopian dreamers'). The result was an anomaly, a workers' revolution without working-class support. The rationale for this paradox was 'historical necessity'—that nationalized property represented a higher stage of social development and therefore had to be defended, even against the workers.

The theory, *sans* Stalinist apologetics, had its origin in Trotsky's *The New Course* (1923) and later *The Revolution Betrayed* (1937). There Trotsky argued that in the growth of bureaucracy Russia faced a crisis: either the release of productive forces from the heavy hand of

[11] *Ibid.*, p. 109.
[12] Deutscher, *Russia: What Next?* (London, 1953).
[13] Deutscher, *The Prophet Armed: Trotsky, 1879-1921* (New York, 1954).

bureaucracy, or a 'Thermidor,' a return to some capitalist form, state or otherwise. Deutscher, at this point, feels otherwise. The backwardness of the peasant masses and their reluctance to make the sacrifice for industrialization, he says, required the harsh measures and iron discipline of Stalinism. But with the progress that was achieved in the 1930s, says Deutscher, the Stalinist terrorism and 'primitive magic' had outlived their 'usefulness' and were coming into conflict with the 'new needs of Soviet society.' Industrialization, he believes, "tends to awaken the democratic aspirations of the masses," while the "phenomenal growth of Soviet wealth . . . tends to soften class privileges, and the orthodoxy, the Iron Curtain, and the elaborate mythology of Stalinism tend to become socially useless. . . . Stalinism is untenable in this expanding society at its present level of productive forces."[14]

This theme, with a greater emphasis on the working class as a "political power of a magnitude hitherto unknown in Russian history," has been expanded by Deutscher in a recent publication.[15] The post-Stalin reforms, he notes, are reforms from 'above,' intended largely to provide some security for the bureaucracy. But the working class, particularly the skilled elements in engineering (which employs about one third of Russia's industrial manpower), is now displaying long-suppressed egalitarian aspirations. This is evident in the revision of the old 'progressive' piece-rate system, the narrowing of wage differentials, the introduction of a new pension scheme, and the abolition of all tuition fees in education.

This egalitarian drive—which is reinforced by the formal ideology that the workers are the ruling power in the country—says Deutscher, must come into conflict with the bureaucracy, which will seek to maintain its privileges and to preserve the *status quo*. And such an impending conflict must create a problem for a regime. With the power of the secret police diminished, there is only the army as the guardian of the order. But the army, rather than keeping order for the benefit of the Party, sooner or later will do so on its own account. "In other words," concludes Deutscher,

the strains and stresses caused by a stormy revival of mass move-

---

[14] Deutscher, *Russia: What Next?* pp. 123, 125.
[15] Deutscher, "Russia in Transition," *Universities and Left Review*, I, No. 1 (Spring 1957), 4-12.

ments lacking leadership and clear political purpose may lead to the establishment of a dictatorship of the Bonapartist type. All the more so as the military could hardly view with indifference a situation in which they must see a threat to Russia's positions of power and to all the strategic gains she won in the last war.[16]

It is highly debatable whether industrialization leads to a striving for *freedom* (even though it may lead to a demand by workers for a greater distributive share of wealth) or whether the expansion of wealth tends to diminish class privileges. *Relative* scarcities in the Soviet Union are bound to exist for a long period, however 'phenomenal' the growth of Russian productivity. And the congealing of class privileges may become the real brake on any relaxation of the dictatorship, although key social groups at the top may win a measure of security. Certainly, in the downfall of Zhukov, the military has, for the time being at least, once again come under the control of the Party. Deutscher clearly underestimated the role of the Party, and in *Russia: What Next ?* (published in 1953) failed even once to mention Khrushchev —so remote was he from the inner-elite struggles. What is relevant, however, for this presentation is that in Deutscher's scheme of analysis there is a clearly determinable sense (whether substantively right or wrong) of a mainspring of change; and thus it focuses attention on the question which all social theory must confront—the sources of change in social systems.

(6) *Neo-Marxist.* Leading out of Trotsky's discussion of the nature of Soviet society, a group of theorists argued that Russia, despite nationalized property, was no longer a workers' state, but a new social form, namely, 'bureaucratic collectivism.'[17] The distinction has been

---

[16] *Ibid.*, p. 12.

[17] The first book to insist that Russia was a new class state—calling it 'bureaucratic collectivism'—was that of Bruno R., *La Bureaucraticisation du Monde* (Paris, 1939). The theme was debated in the Menshevik press in the early 1940s, with the late Theodor Dan arguing in *Novy put'* that Russia was still a workers' state, and Rudolf Hilferding and Solomon Schwarz arguing the contrary in *Vestnik*. (Dan, following the invasion of Russia, gave qualified support to the Russian regime.) Hilferding's argument, a classic statement of the neo-Marxist position, was printed in the *Modern Review*, I, No. 4 (June 1947), 266-71, under the title "State Capitalism or Totalitarian State Economy." Schwarz's data appeared later in his article "Heads of Russian Factories," *Social Research*, IX, No. 5 (Sep-

important for the political orientations of the Marxist parties and sects. The orthodox Trotskyites, for example, claimed that Russia, although a 'degenerated' workers' state, was, because of nationalized property, 'historically progressive' and therefore worth defending in the event of a conflict with capitalist powers. The dissident Trotskyites, claiming that a new exploitative class society had been established, took a 'neither-nor,' 'third camp' position. Analytically—that is, in terms of its predictive utility—the scheme is of less value. The neo-Marxists, in their analysis of the future course of events in the Soviet Union, would tend to use the same terms as the Marxist analysts.

(7) *Totalitarian.* Expressed most forcefully in the categories of political philosophy by Hannah Arendt,[18] this theory argues that a radically new social form, different from tyranny, dictatorship, or authoritarianism, was created in Germany and exists now in Russia. The essentially new fact of totalitarianism is that all intermediate or secondary institutions between the leader and the 'masses' have been eliminated, and that the ruler, unrestrained by legal or political checks, rules by terror. The theory, as applied to the Soviet Union by Bertram D. Wolfe, holds that no essential change in the nature of the regime is possible and that totalitarianism, through an inner 'ideo-logic' of its own, can never relinquish its combative posture vis-à-vis democratic societies.

This argument was developed by Wolfe in his paper prepared for the Oxford Conference and published in the August 1957 issue of *Commentary.* Since his paper was subject to detailed challenge by Raymond Aron at the conference, it was not discussed in my paper as originally prepared. But in terms of my frame of reference, one point can be noted—as a 'working tool' to explain specific political situations,

tember 1942), 315-33, and in his collaborative effort with Gregory Bienstock and Aaron Yugow, *Management in Russian Industry and Agriculture* (New York, 1944). The debate was carried over into the Trotskyite press in the 1940s, principally in the *New International* and the *Fourth International* in New York. Trotsky's last argument is contained in the collection entitled *In Defense of Marxism (Against the Petty-bourgeois Opposition)* (New York, 1942). The revisionist position can be found in James Burnham's *The Managerial Revolution* (New York, 1941) and Max Schactman's introduction to the revised edition of Trotsky's *The New Course* (New York, 1943).

[18] Arendt, *The Origins of Totalitarianism* (New York, 1951); published in England as *The Burden of Our Times.*

the theory of totalitarianism, which Mr. Wolfe draws from Karl Witt-fogel's *Oriental Despotism* (New Haven, 1957), is too sweeping. From such heights the terrain of politics, its ridges and gullies, become flat-tened and the weary foot-traveler finds few guides to concrete problems. Even on a simpler, intuitive basis, one can question the basic assump-tion of the theory, namely, that society becomes completely atomized and rule is anomic and direct. In a *crisis* situation, a state can fragment all social life and through terror, perhaps, mold a people to its will. But can a society live in permanent crisis? Can it hold such a rigid posture, without either exploding into war or relaxing? The basis of all social life requires not only a minimum of personal security but the reasonable expectation by parents that their children will be educated, develop careers, and so forth. To that extent, a tendency toward 'normalization' is at work in any crisis state.

(8) *Kremlinological.* These speculations, identified principally with the writings of the late Franz Borkenau and of Boris Nicolaevsky, focus primarily on the power struggle within the core elite and seek to identify the shifting coalitions ("who is doing in whom") within the Kremlin as a basis for predicting political events. While open to easy satire, it is the supercilious who mock it at their peril, as the *New York Post* once learned when it scoffed at the speculations arising from the fact that all the Bolshevik leaders *but* Beria had appeared en masse at the Bolshoi Ballet. "Perhaps Beria doesn't like ballet," said the *Post* archly. Perhaps he didn't, but we never had the opportunity to find out, for two days later came the announcement that Beria had been arrested as a traitor.

In one form or another, Kremlinology is practiced today by every foreign office and by most journalists. Its emphasis is largely on per-sonality and power groups, and less on the social systems and the way such systems can or cannot constrain these leaders. (There is an en-largement of this discussion below.)

HISTORICAL THEORIES

(9) *Slavic Institutions.* Represented in an earlier generation by Nicholas Berdayev, Sir Bernard Pares, and Sir John Maynard, and today to some degree by Edward Crankshaw, Ernest Simmons, and Werner Philipp (of the Free University of Berlin), this school states

that much of contemporary Russian behavior can be accounted for by traditional Slavic character and institutions. "Too often we forget," said Professor Ernest Barker, in introducing Maynard's *The Russian Peasant and Other Studies* (London, 1942), "that Russia, with all her changes, still largely remains the same." The theme is elaborated in Sir John's book: "All Russian regimes have been sudden and arbitrary." "Old Russia was always rough, with its Siberian exiles." "Planning . . . a characteristic feature of the new regime, is not as new as at first glimpse it looks to be." "Even the 'Party'—that misnomer of the vocation of leadership—is not really new, but rather a new application of an ancient institution: the priesthood." And so on, and so forth.

One finds a similar argument in the November 1951 lecture by Professor Werner Philipp on the "Historical Presuppositions of Political Thought in Russia," inaugurating the Osteuropa Institute of Berlin.[19] As a reviewer summarizes Professor Philipp's argument:

Conditions and traditions have produced a definite political mentality in Russia which goes back for several centuries. . . . The Russian distrust of the West, the cult and consciousness of the precedence of the community over the individual, the recognition of the unlimited power of governmental authority over society, and the discrepancy between political reality and the professed ideal aim—all these phenomena of Soviet thought and life have their roots in conditions which developed in Russia between the beginning of the thirteenth and the end of the sixteenth century.[20]

The theme of an 'eternal Russia' is propounded, too, by Crankshaw in his *Cracks in the Kremlin Wall* (New York, 1951).

To argue that the roots of Soviet life go down deep in the Russian past is not, of course, to justify those practices (although the argument lends itself sometimes to apologetics, and in the 1930s and 1940s apologists like Bernard Pares or Maurice Hindus did justify Russian behavior in such terms). But like the characterological theories ('parallel travelers,' one might call them), the Slavophile theory argues in effect that, since Soviet institutions were shaped by historical social forms

---

[19] Horst Jablonowski and Werner Philipp, eds., *Forschungen zur osteuropäischen Geschichte*, Vol. I (Berlin, 1954).

[20] Hans Kohn in the *Russian Review*, XIV, No. 4 (October 1955), 373.

and since they are deeply rooted in the traditions of the people, they will change only slowly.

(10) *Geopolitical.* This school, which had some vogue during World War II (Nicholas Spykman at Yale, and William T. R. Fox's *The Super-Powers*, New York, 1944) and still has some supporters, holds that Russian foreign policy is dictated primarily by long-range strategic interests deriving from its position as a great land-mass power, and that its contemporary political aspirations (for example, in the Middle East) reflect the historic drives of Great Russian policy. The school generally tends to minimize ideology (as in Walter Bedell Smith's introduction to the Marquis de Custine *Diaries*, New York, 1951) and to see Russian policy primarily as a function of strategic power position. To some extent, the policy views of George Kennan (see his Princeton University lectures, *Realities of American Foreign Policy*, Princeton, 1954) and those of Henry Kissinger are shaped by these considerations.

Kto-Kogo—*The Id and Ego of Bolshevism*

During the truce negotiations in Korea a slim book, *The Operational Code of the Politburo*, by Nathan Leites, was used by the American negotiators as a tactical manual. Leites' research, embodied in the larger *Study of Bolshevism*, was sponsored by the U.S. Air Force's Project RAND. The fact that RAND has given strong support to the pioneering method of Leites (which is now being applied to the study of French politics) makes a more detailed examination of his work worthwhile.

Leites begins by attempting to define 'Bolshevik character' as a type distinct in social history. The attempt to define historic character is not unique—we have the image, somewhat overworked these days, of the 'inner-directed Protestant.' What makes Leites' work unique are the novel categories he chooses and, above all, his method. There is no observation of behavior. Like Max Weber, who drew his 'Protestant ethic' from the writings of Luther, Calvin, Baxter, and others, Leites scans the writings of Lenin and Stalin to infer similar norms which guide the Bolshevik Party. He reads the Bolshevik character as a 'reaction' to the Oblomovs, who slept away their lives;

to the Rudins, the high-flown talkers but never-doers; to the indecisive, soul-sick, moody students. The Bolshevik, as Boris Pil'niak put it, is "against the old peasant roots of our old Russian history, against its aimlessness, its non-teleological character . . . against the philosophy of Tolstoy's Karataev." The moral training of the Russian intelligentsia stressed both the prohibition against egotism and the prohibition against 'dirtying oneself.' Chekhov once said, "If all socialists are going to exploit the cholera for their own ends, I shall despise them." But for the Bolshevik, refusal to use bad means is merely an expression of sentimentality and stupidity; in Bolshevik doctrine, the worst egotist is precisely he who refuses to soil his hands. The Party strives for humanity, and 'purity' lies not in a personal refusal to act immorally but in dedication to the Party. In such dedication the individual finds his defense against both egotism and personal impurity.

In contrast to the Russian intelligentsia, who spoke of ultimate things and sacred values, the Bolsheviks maintain silence about the sacred. Against the vice of outpouring emotion, the Bolsheviks uphold the virtue of reserve. Against the older Russian tendency to depressed passivity, introspection, nervous impressionability, and excited babbling, against the protracted searching for metaphysical truths and the posing of unanswerable questions--against all these, there is the determinism of history, the certainty of purpose, the commitment to action, the ability to avoid taking personal offense, the 'masculinity' of action. Against the fear of a life with nothing to strive for, a life filled with uncontrollable, impulsive gratifications which arouse anxiety and guilt and thus lead to the famous Russian flirtation with death—Gorky tells how in his youth boys would lie immobile on a railroad track while trains passed over them—against this there are the constant goals of work and the Party. Death is merely the point at which one has outlived one's *usefulness*. Of the suicide of Marx's son-in-law, Paul Lafargue, Lenin wrote: "If one cannot work for the Party any longer, one must be able to look truth in the face and die like the Lafargues."

Out of such elements of ethics and moral temper emerges, in Leites' view, the 'operational code in politics.' For Bolshevism, all politics is summed up in the formula *kto-kogo*—literally, 'who-whom,' but in its most radical sense, 'who kills whom.' Political relations are between dominators and dominated, between users and used. There can be no neutrals. If politics is *kto-kogo*, then all political strategies are guided by this fundamental rule: one pushes to the limit, one refuses to be provoked, one acts when one is ready, and so on.

. . . .

The political consequence of this analysis is inescapable—if politics is *kto-kogo*, then 'coexistence' as a sustained *modus vivendi* is impossible. Leites sums it up flatly: "A 'settlement' in Western terms, with outside groups—an agreement sharply and indefinitely reducing the threat of mutual annihilation—is inconceivable, [although] agreements with them, codifying the momentary relationship of forces, must always be considered and often concluded."[21] But the Party "maintains a full awareness of the basic conflict," and at the strategic moment presses forward again. Promises, as Lenin said, are like pie crusts, "made to be broken."

But let us now look more closely at Leites' use of psychoanalytic insight, for the novelty of his book lies there. To say, as Leites does, that the sources of Bolshevik character lie in a reaction to the extreme temper of the Russian intelligentsia in the nineteenth century is still to write history without the help of Freud; Lenin and his co-workers were perfectly *conscious* of their attempts to reverse traditional patterns of Russian character, to overcome Karataev and Oblomov. But when Leites speaks of the Bolshevik character as a 'reaction-formation' to *unconscious*, overwhelmingly powerful wishes, he is approaching politics in a way that was impossible before psychoanalysis.

Two principal drives, according to Leites, explain Russian intellectual character: preoccupation with death, and latent passive homosexual impulses. (Tolstoy, for example, could not endure the idea of death or sex.) The Russian intellectual displayed a fascination with death that is terrifying to the Bolshevik. Against that fascination, the Bolshevik defense is to minimize death by work and, more important, to express a kind of personal omnipotence through the dissolution of the self into the all-embracing, undying Party. Thus, Leites writes, "the earlier Russian feeling that life is empty because of death has been

---

[21] Leites, *A Study of Bolshevism*, p. 527.

replaced by the Bolshevik feeling that death is empty and small and unable to interfere with life."[22]

. . . .

The theme of latent homosexuality, lying deep in the arcanum of psychoanalysis, is seen as a pervasive yet repressed element of Russian intellectual desire. In Dostoevsky, the utmost demonstration of emotion by the usually overwrought and emotionally charged characters is to embrace and clasp one another. To Bolshevism, the fantasy of men embracing each other is repulsive and frightening. When Lenin described those once close to him who had now made common cause with his enemies, he would say that they 'kissed' and 'embraced' one another. ("The Scheidemannites kiss and embrace Kautsky." "The followers of Bernstein are impudently blowing kisses to [Plekhanov].")

To Leites, a further significant clue lies in the number of Lenin's intimate friendships which ended in violent ruptures. These included Struve, a close collaborator in the 1890s; Potresov, an early *Iskra* associate; Plekhanov, Lenin's 'ambivalently loved master,' who 'capitulated' to the Mensheviks; Aleksinskii, perhaps Lenin's most intimate associate in the years after 1905, who later denounced him as a German agent; and Malinovskii, the Bolshevik whip in the Duma, of whom Lenin said, "He will not be another Aleksinskii," and who turned out to be a police agent.

"One might speculate," says Leites

—the data discussed here allow no more than that—whether the Bolshevik insistence on, in effect, killing enemies and being killed by them is not in part an effort to ward off fear-laden and guilty wishes to embrace men and be embraced by them. This hypothesis is consistent with the existence of certain pervasive Bolshevik trends described in this study: the fear of being passive, the fear of being controlled and used, the fear of wanting to submit to an attack. Once one denies one's wish to kiss by affirming one's wish to kill, this is apt to reinforce one's belief in the enemy's wish to kill by virtue of the mechanism of projection, probably heavily used by the Bolsheviks.[23]

On the basis of what documentation can one make such sweeping inferences? Even if we fully accept the psychoanalytic theories, how

[22] *Ibid.*, p. 137.   [23] *Ibid.*, pp. 403-4.

does one validate these judgments without putting the Bolshevik leaders on the couch, so to speak? Leites' method is to examine the imagery, fantasy, and characteristic literary metaphors employed by Bolshevik leaders, and the fictional models in Russian literature with which the Bolsheviks identify, or those they assail. Russian literature and the Russians' attitude toward it seem to make this possible. In few cultures have fictional characters become such sharply defined national types: Dostoevsky's gallery—the Karamazovs, Raskol'nikov, Myshkin, Verkhovenskii—Turgenev's Rudin, Gogol's Chichikov, Goncharov's Oblomov, Chekhov's multifarious characters. These are all models which are accepted or rejected by Russians as psychological masks.

Taking off from these literary sources, Leites draws on Freudian theory to highlight the latent meanings of specific imagery. For example, fear of impotence, fear of being beaten (in Stalin's famous speech to the managers of Soviet industry in 1931, the image of beating or being beaten occurs eleven times in a single paragraph), fear of contamination, of embraces, of annihilation, jokes about 'cleaning out' the Party, fear of being used as a 'tail,' and so forth. As chief evidence for his theories Leites relies on the marshaling of images, in a vast profusion.

. . . .

What Leites is arguing is that any view held with stubbornness, exaggeration, and intensity—as all Communist views are held—and which violently rejects all rational tests, raises the presumption that it may constitute a defense against strong unconscious wishes or fears which stand in contradiction to the idea. To follow a pronouncedly masculine profession like soldiering does not label a man as a 'latent homosexual,' but, if we find him compulsively, violently, and beyond reason insisting on his military posture, 'common sense' permits us to suspect that he may be afraid of being less a man than he would like to appear.

Granting even the validity of the psychoanalytic method in the study of personality, we must still ask whether it can legitimately be extended into the analysis of politics.

Erich Fromm has argued, in *Escape from Freedom* (New York, 1941), that the sado-masochistic character, typical of the German middle

class, found an outlet in the Nazi Party. T. W. Adorno and his associate authors of *The Authoritarian Personality* (New York, 1950) have
pointed to the rigid, compulsive individuals who seek authoritarian
values. Harold Lasswell, in the early *Psychopathology and Politics*
(Chicago, 1930), sought to show how the political arena acts as a dis-
placement of personal needs. . . .

Leites' view, however, goes beyond this. He says, in effect, that
character determines politics. Since the mainspring of Bolshevism is
action, the movement, by impressing its character on others, transforms
all politics and, in the end, the social structure itself as well. . . . For
ideologies are, in effect, attempts to unite ideas, behavior, and character; they demand a hardening of commitment. The Communist (or
the Fascist, or the kibbutznik, or the 100 per cent American) is not
only supposed to believe certain things; he is supposed to act, to *be*
something, and, in acting, to fix his character. If one is 'serious,'
one 'lives' one's ideology. Thus ideology may be said to presuppose
character.[24]

. . . .

Leites, it seems to me, would be forced to argue that the Bolshevik
pattern was a product of will. Further, if he is to be consistent with the
psychoanalytic approach, he would have to argue that *it was the character of Lenin, the 'primal father,' which shaped the Party* (his followers
did call themselves Leninists) *rather than the Party organization and the
environment which shaped Lenin* and the other Bolsheviks. And it was
the will of Lenin alone which altered the Party's politics, as in the crucial decisions in April and July 1917. The Bolshevik Party, more than
any other party in history, has demonstrated the nature of will. It
was, and is, one of the most highly self-conscious movements in history.
Its patristic writings are not only canonical; they are also 'training
documents' in the tempering of a 'hard core' party membership.
Individuals may join from a variety of motives, but all must be stamped
in the mold or driven out. The splits and expulsions (becoming blood
purges after power is achieved) which characterize Communist parties

[24] This may explain the intensity of the feelings of ex-Communists toward the
Party. Though they are free of the ideology, the rigid personality pattern remains.

may thus be seen not as mere ideological or even power fights but as *a process of personality selection*.

With the Leites study we come full circle in the theories of history and politics. It was the fashion a hundred years ago to ascribe historical change to 'great men' and the force of their personalities. Subsequently we interpreted history in terms of abstract 'social forces'—for instance, population pressure, search for markets—which somehow, but never fully understandably, translated themselves through individual actors into tangible events. The glaring inadequacies of these deterministic theories have led to the reintroduction of psychological and, through Freudian influence, of characterological explanations.

. . . .

Leites' theory deals with the dynamics of Bolshevism in the process of its formation, but once Bolshevism has come to birth, the model, as he presents it, is static. Take, for example, the initial turning on Stalin by Khrushchev and company. One could say that this, in turn, represents a reaction to the overbearing, almost paranoid Stalin; or there may be more 'rational' explanations, for instance, the need to win mass support. Further, how are we to explain the seeming 'openness' and marked vulgarity of Khrushchev's character? We have no guide in the model itself to the possibility or the nature of the change.

The static quality of the model comes in part from its methodology. The basic outlines of Bolshevik character are drawn not from the empirical world of action but from the abstract canons of Bolshevik doctrine. In itself this is not too great a fault, since the doctrine itself is evident. The greater fault of the theory—and, paradoxically, its strength—lies in the fact that, starting from static doctrine, it posits a static force called 'character' and then gathers all human action into that one hedgehog force.[25] But how often in social action does character or will actually impose itself on events? People live largely in social systems, and they are 'chained' to one another in complex ways. All of us, no doubt, would like to impose our 'character' on the world, but in practice we find ourselves forced to modify our demands to

[25] As George Ivask has said, if all men may be divided into foxes and hedgehogs, they may also be divided, following the satire of Saltykov-Shchedrin, into boys with pants and boys without pants. If Lenin wore pants, is Khrushchev without them?

conform with *possibilities*. Leites may thus be claimed to have given his concept of 'character' a false autonomy, and in applying this concept to politics—which is par excellence a phenomenon of change within possibilities—to have falsified the nature of the subject.

How the Harvard System Works

To turn now to the sociological approach, the study by three Harvard social scientists—Raymond A. Bauer, Alex Inkeles, and Clyde Kluckhohn—is the best that contemporary sociology offers, and on this score alone merits attention. Their book, *How the Soviet System Works*, is a revised presentation of a report, *Strategic Psychological Strengths and Vulnerabilities of the Soviet Social System*, that was prepared for the U.S. Air Force, the agency which commissioned and paid for the five years' research that went into the study. In one respect, the study illustrates the hazards of such sponsored research, since the authors found themselves under pressure to produce a 'popular' book which the Air Force sponsors could show to their own controllers. The result is not a happy combination; 'theses' are condensed and presented with only partial documentation, and the book is written in an attempted vernacular style which just does not come off. The project, based on systematic interviewing of defectors, drew data from 329 extended life-history interviews, including detailed personality tests; 435 supplementary interviews; almost 10,000 questionnaires on special topics; 2,700 general questionnaires, and 100 interviews and psychological tests, administered for control purposes, to a matched group of Americans. In all, 33,000 pages of data were accumulated. These, together with the list of over fifty specialized unpublished studies and thirty-five published articles on which the authors drew in preparing the book, indicate how rich their source materials were.

Economic and political matters were not considered to be within the scope of the project. The key concept was that of the 'social system,' and this is the heart of the Harvard contribution. A social system is simply the characteristic ways in which societies, or subgroups, organize their activities to achieve specific goals. Since the resultant institutions or behavior patterns are linked, in meaningful fashion, presumably variations in one area are accompanied by regular—and determinate—variations in others. (Thus, for example, a change in the rate of capital accumulation, one of the fundamental determinants of an economic system, must precipitate changes in the rate of consumption.) In the social system, reorganization of the structure of authority in the factory would presumably entail corresponding changes in the organization of the school system, the family, and so forth. For example, when Stalin introduced one-man rule and tight labor discipline in the factories in 1931, one could imagine a manager, confronted with a disrespectful student from a 'progressive' school, asking, "What kind of a hooligan is this?" and insisting that school methods be changed so that students would learn obedience. The educational commissars, however, confronted with 'wild' children from broken homes, would be forced to demand that the family be strengthened and divorce be made more difficult. And so, in linked fashion, we find the reintroduction of older, traditional forms of authority.[26] Yet such social change may become self-defeating, for, as repression in the factory becomes pervasive, individuals need to find protection and do so in close family ties. And thus, after a while, the regime begins to complain about undue familialism. This example oversimplifies a social process, but it is not unjust.

The Harvard group has concentrated, however, not on locating change in the conventional institutions of society—family, political system, education, industry—but on the typical adaptive patterns of behavior which regulate the life of the ruled. Such 'central patterns' are the need to conform to an explicit ideology, the refusal to allow independent sources of power, the centralization of all planning and control, the overcommitment of resources to particular objectives, the use of terror and forced labor, 'storming' as a method of reaching objectives, the tolerance of evasions which fulfill the plan—for instance, *blat* (the network of informal deals). On the basis of these 'operating characteristics,' the Harvard group seeks to identify the general strengths and weaknesses of the *system*. Weaknesses: there are no orderly processes of succession in office; economic growth in heavy industry is disproportionate to that in consumer industries; there are constant purges and insecurities. Strengths: the atomization of resistance, the

---

[26] The example has been adapted from Alex Inkeles, "Understanding a Foreign Society: A Sociologist's View," *World Politics*, III, No. 2 (January 1951), 269-80.

Russians' ignorance of the realities of the outside world, the deep loyalties to the system on the part of the managerial groups.

One trouble with this approach is that one does not know, actually, which of these 'operating characteristics' are central and which are not, for the Harvard group seems to lack an organizing principle which determines the selections. Is 'forced labor,' for example, an 'inherent' aspect of the system, or a fortuitous element which got out of hand and may be discarded? And, if the latter, how is the judgment made? On the basis of the fact that the terror has become self-defeating or that it is uneconomic, or because of moral disapprobation from the outside, or what? Moreover, if one seeks to forecast the "likely responses . . . of various segments of the Soviet leadership" in order to gauge the degree of loyalty and disaffection among the major social groups, the 'central patterns' may be of less importance than an accurate definition of the different interests of such segments and of their power vis-à-vis other interest groups. The question is, what do we look for in a mode of analysis?

A mode of analysis is a function of the particular categories one uses to group together related characteristics. In political theory, one can classify regimes, as Aristotle did, as monarchies, oligarchies, or democracies; or, as Max Weber did, as traditional, rational, and charismatic. One's purpose dictates one's perspectives. The danger is that one tends to think of categories as realities rather than as theoretical constructs. This error has been appallingly true of Marxist thought, which in rudimentary fashion first employed the concept of a social system. Since in a simple Marxist model of capitalism, classes are formed in relation to the means of production, to the simple-minded Communist there could be no exploitation in Russia since the 'people' owned the factories and there were, therefore, no exploiting classes. Hence, too, the fierce doctrinal debates as to whether Russia was a 'workers' state,' a 'degenerated workers' state,' or what.

But, given all these pitfalls, the gain in trying to define the *essential* nature of a system is that one can locate the causal factors (in modern jargon, the independent variables) the changes in which affect all other parts of the system. (To Marx, for example, the essential nature of capitalism is the compulsion to accumulate and reinvest. Crises are deemed inevitable because of ensuing gaps between consumption and production, because of overproduction, and because of the falling rate of profit, which is a function, presumably, of high capital and low labor inputs.)

The Harvard group, however, shrinks from seeking to specify the motor forces in the social system as they have conceived it. "It is difficult, if not impossible," they say, "to assign a rank order of importance to those operating characteristics since they constitute an interlocking system in which each has implication for the other."[27] Apart from the fact that one may question the 'tightness' of such 'interlocks' (what, for example, is the link between 'storming' and 'forced labor' as characteristics of the system?) or even the congruence of the different 'operating characteristics,' *is it so difficult to single out the factor of prime importance?* Is it not quite clear, really, that the Soviet system is characterized, essentially, by the centralized control of political power, that it is a *command* system, with few institutional checks, and that all other aspects of the system—the refusal to allow independent power, the overcommitment of resources, and so on—derive from that fact?

But, once that is admitted, a large element of indeterminacy has to be admitted as well. For, in such a command system, the decisions of a few men—and, in the case of Stalin, of one—become decisive in changing the nature of the system. If Bukharin, rather than Stalin, had won, would not Russia be a different society? Or if Malenkov, rather than Khrushchev, had kept power, would not the profile of Russia be somewhat different today? The development of Soviet society depends thus on the nature of Soviet political developments.

If this be true, then, in seeking to understand the Soviet Union we are back to Kremlinology, the endlessly fascinating and often exasperatingly occult game of charting the petty protocol at the dinner table or seeing who is called on to speak at the Supreme Soviet, and in what sequence, in order to guess who is 'on first.'

The essential fact is that the Harvard system, lacking a sense of motor, cannot locate the sources of change in the system. While it is important to know the 'limits' of social action (for example, how far one can push recalcitrant peasants before offering new incentives, or which groups have the greatest potential for independent action),

[27] Bauer, Inkeles, and Kluckhohn, p. 20.

in *politics* one has to know who composes a ruling group, how the group arrives at a decision, how the claims of subordinate groups are adjudicated, and so on. For in a society like Russia, where institutional and behavior patterns are not autonomous, a 'social system' has no meaning unless it can be defined within the context of politics.

Who Eats before Whom

The basic assumption of Kremlinology is that every move at the Russian *verkhushka* is shot through with the struggle for protocol, prestige, and power. Thus the manifest need to decentralize the Russian economy because of the increasing inability of a single center to direct the operation of 300,000 enterprises becomes a problem as well of whose power is increased and whose power reduced by such a shift. Thus, not in the final analysis, but in the immediate one, all rational-technical criteria bow to the political. And thus, in analyzing any move of Russian policy, we are forced to thread our way through the Byzantine intrigues which are spun in such power fights.

The real problem arises, first, in the definition of the contending power groups and, second, in the way we identify the alignments of individuals, particularly subordinates. One approach has been to define power groups in 'functional' terms—Party, army, secret police, state bureaucracy—and to locate spokesmen for those groups from the positions they hold.

. . . .

A difficulty arises from mechanically countering bloc with bloc. While it is true that there are often interest conflicts between functional groups, the very nature of a political power struggle carried on by small cliques and coteries requires the power figure to have his allies within *all* groups. Thus the fight may not be simply 'managers' *vs.* 'Party,' or 'army' *vs.* 'Party,' but may cut across these groupings. Is the army, for example, a unitary interest group (united on what interests?) or does Zhukov line up with X and Konev with Y and Vasilievskii with Z? From what we know of armies elsewhere, certainly such internal conflicts and differing outside alliances take place—for example, in the U.S. Army, the Marshall-Eisenhower group *vs.*

MacArthur. The problem, then, is to locate those issues on which the army would stand united and those on which its top officers would divide. And, in so doing, one faces the problem of determining what it is that ties cliques and coteries together: school affiliation, loyalties to one who has made promotion possible, differences in generation, common wartime or service experiences, and so on, and so forth.

Nor can one say that ideology determines alignments, for on key policy issues—consumer goods *vs.* heavy industry, tough or soft line toward the West, tough or soft line toward the satellites—there may be no unitary ideology which dictates a consistent attitude toward such issues. Malenkov may have wanted relaxation at home so as to be more tough with the West. Moreover, a top figure will often switch ideological sides opportunistically in a bid for support. Certainly Stalin's history is instructive in this regard. (The question is often put: Does Khrushchev represent the 'Stalinist' faction or does Malenkov? The difficulty with these formulations is that what we are observing is the break-up of a faction and, in such a highly personal situation, few of the formal sociological criteria for charting allegiances seem to hold.)

Even greater difficulties are faced in the task of locating the links of support down the line. Every foreign office and propaganda organization maintains extensive biographical dossiers on members of the Soviet elite in an effort to keep track of the shifting personnel as a means of measuring the relative strength of the contenders at the top. And often... the method is highly tenuous. How far one can go with this detailed, yet mechanical, scoring is open to question. . . .

And sometimes the same event—in this instance, the appointment of one F. R. Kozlov to the key post of candidate member of the Party Presidium—is interpreted in diametrically opposite fashion. Harrison Salisbury, in *The New York Times* of February 16, 1957, reported that Kozlov was a member of a group to which Mr. Pervukhin belonged, and was "probably an adherent of Mr. Malenkov." Kozlov, said Salisbury, was one of the authors of the key propaganda documents of the 'doctors' plot' of 1953; and one can surmise, therefore, in line with the logic of Kremlinology, that Malenkov was one of the directors of the plot. But Richard Lowenthal commented a day later in the *London Observer*: "Mr. Khrushchev's inner-party position has been reinforced not only by Mr. Shepilov's return to the Party Secretariat, but by the promotion of Frol Romanovich Kozlov, the first secretary of the Leningrad region, to candidate membership of the Party Presidium. . . . Having returned to obscurity during the early Malenkov era, he was at the end of 1953 promoted by Khrushchev's personal intervention to take the place of Malenkov's protégé, Andrianov, as head of the Leningrad Party organization." And, by equal logic, since Kozlov had signaled the campaign of vigilance at the start of the 'doctors' plot,' Khrushchev was thus tied to the execution of the plot.

This is not to say that the method is wrong, but that someone's information is inadequate. . . .

Consider, too, the dilemma of the Kremlinologist in having to make spot interpretations of a major change in the status of leading personnel when the announcement of the change itself offers no clue as to its meaning. Thus, the day after a terse announcement appeared that Marshal Zhukov had been relieved of his post, Harry Schwartz, the *New York Times* specialist, began his story in this fashion: "Two principal possibilities have emerged from Marshal Georgi K. Zhukov's removal yesterday as Soviet Defense Minister: a substantial decline in his real power or a step toward his promotion in the Soviet hierarchy" (October 27, 1957).

One can sympathize with these occupational hazards. Henry Adams, in his *Autobiography*, remarks that when he was in London during the American Civil War, serving as secretary to his father, the United States Minister, he was making reports on the splits in British Cabinet opinion —reports which became the basis of American policy (for example, the Mason-Sliddel affair), and which, he felt, were based on firsthand information. Twenty years later, when the Cabinet papers were opened, he found to his dismay that his reports had been completely wrong. Shortly after the revolt in Budapest, Hugh Gaitskell raised the question in the House of Commons whether the Russians had been emboldened to intervene because of the news of Eden's action at Suez. The question, even if Gaitskell intended it only to press a political advantage, was not an unfair one. It would be important to know if this were so. Is there an answer? We have no access to sources.

But one *can* raise a question regarding method, at least as to the way in which Kremlinology has been applied. Put most simply, Kremlinology often becomes the obverse side of the Bolshevik mentality—that is, it becomes overdeterministic. The characteristic fact about Bolshevik mentality is its refusal to admit of accident and contingency. Everything has a reason, a preordained motive. Hence the sinister refrain in Bolshevik rhetoric, "It is no accident, comrade, no mere *accident*, that . . ." or "Why at this time, why at *this particular moment*, does the enemy choose . . . ?" And so all such questions lead, with insidious intent, to the ultimate question, *kto-kogo*, who is using whom?

. . . .

One sometimes finds a similar logic among the Kremlinologists. Every move—both of personnel in the power conflicts within, and of policy in the international arena without—is seen as a carefully plotted, conspiratorially conceived, predetermined plan whose every consequence is anticipated; every move has a secret meaning which detailed charting of protocol and word counting can uncover. But from what we know of every chancellery in the world, few campaigns in political (or even military) affairs are ever calculated with such precision. And the analyst who fails to consider contingency runs the same risk as the Bolshevik in overdetermining the political game.

And with one more step we come full circle. Whatever the importance of power at the top, no group of power figures, however absolute their rule, can wield infinite power. The problem with the Kremlinological approach is the same as with that of Leites. Every attempt to impose one's will has to take into account the finite limits of natural resources and the recalcitrance of human institutions—but how?

The One Road and the Many—Exit Pirandello

Now that we have investigated many roads, are there some which can lead us to reality better than others? (Says a passage in the Talmud: "If you don't know where you are going, any road will take you there.") Perhaps a few distinctions—and questions—are in order.

THE DIFFERENT MOMENTS

There should be a clear distinction between the types of change which take place: between changes in Soviet society (the social system) and in Soviet politics, although in crucial moments one is dependent on the other. The difference is one of distinguishing between a process and an event, or, to revive an old distinction of the crusty sociologist William Graham Sumner, between *crescive* and *enacted* change.

Crescive changes are those which surge, swell, go on willy-nilly, and develop with some measure of autonomy. They variously derive from organic growth of tradition, or from changes in values (for example, the decision of people to have fewer children or more), or from technical imperatives, once a key decision has been taken (the need for training more engineers, once a country industrializes).

Enacted changes are the conscious decisions or intents of legislators or rulers (the declaration of war, the collectivization of agriculture, the location of new industry). Those who enact change have to take into account the mores of the people and the resources at their disposal, but these serve only as limiting, not determining, factors.

Sociological analysis is most sure when it deals with crescive changes. These can be identified, their drift charted, and, like iceberg floes, their course and even their break-up specified more readily than others. But sociological analysis often fails in predicting political decisions. There are in history what Hegel called the 'unique moments,' and, in calling the turn, not pure reason but practical judgment (that unstable compound of information, intuition, and empathy) has to take hold. Bolshevism has been par excellence a movement minutely conscious of the past and supremely aware of the tactical and strategic nuances of events. It has been this constant awareness of 'unique moments' (the 'revolutionary situation,' as Lenin first conceived it) and its ability to adapt its timing to the changing situation that have given Bolshevism its unique political advantage in the past.

THE PROBLEM OF PREDICTION

The nature of the changes which one describes conditions the kinds of prediction one can make. One can define, and predict, the limits of broad crescive changes (if one knows the resource pattern of the Soviet Union—amount of arable land, minerals, manpower—one can make a guess about the slowdown in the rate of economic growth), but in predicting the short-run policy turns one comes up against the variabilities of accident, folly, and simple human cantankerousness. The situation is reminiscent of two radicals in the 1920s debating the future course of Soviet politics. "The objective situation," said one, "requires that Trotsky do so and so and so and so." "Look," replied the other, "you know what Trotsky has to do, and I know what Trotsky has to do, but does Trotsky know?"

One of the key problems in the analysis of power is the mode of succession. In the Soviet system, as opposed to a constitutional regime, there seems to be no formal definition of legitimacy, and no system of investiture of power. In seeking to duplicate Stalin's rise, Khrushchev used the Party secretariat as a power lever. But in doing so he was taking a big gamble. In the war years and after, Stalin had emphasized his governmental and military titles rather than his Party position. At the time of his death in 1953, Stalin was only one of nine Party secretaries, but was, uniquely, the Chairman of the Council of Ministers of the USSR. Malenkov relinquished his post as Party secretary, when forced to make a choice, and sought to legitimize his authority through the post of Premier and the Council of Ministers. It is the measure of Khrushchev's shrewdness that he assumed correctly that, despite the rise of the technical and military classes, the mechanics of political power had not changed essentially since the 1930s. Yet can we assume that these 'laws of mechanics' will hold in the naming of Khrushchev's successor? How do we define the balance of forces and predict the direction in which they will tip?

And yet, given all these problems and pitfalls, it would be a forward step in the social sciences if a group of Soviet experts were, at regular intervals, to make predictions at different levels of probable Soviet developments and state the reasons for their inference. (Bauer, Inkeles, and Kluckhohn, for example, stated that the collegial system of power in Russia *could* stabilize itself; Rush said that it would not, and predicted Khrushchev's bid for power.) By systematic review of the predictions, the successes and failures, one could probably obtain a more viable operational model of Soviet behavior.

THE ROLE OF THE IRRATIONAL

In social theory the weight of analysis has always been thrown on the side of the rational explanation. The presumption (see Moore, Rostow, Deutscher, Aron) is that a society ultimately makes its choices on the basis of the rational alternatives which confront it. But how much meaning can one make of the role of pique (Tito's anger, as reported in the Dedijer biography, at the fact that "we were treated like Komsomols,"[28] or Khrushchev's resentment at being forced by Stalin to dance the *gopak*) in explaining the precipitateness or intensity of political acts? And, taking into account the researches of Leites, what weight can be given to the role of emotional components, conscious or unconscious, as a clue to political stance? Is it simply that rationality dictates the political course, and emotions the choler, or what?

MYTH AND MONOLITH

One difficulty with analysis in social science is that it deals with categories, not people. In recent analyses of the Communist movement, particularly in the United States, the movement has been seen as a monolith, with each adherent a disciplined soldier or a 'true believer' ready always to follow orders of 'the Party.'

To some extent the West itself has been seduced by the very image of 'the Bolshevik' with which the Communist rulers have sought to mold the 'new' Soviet man. For, like any human group, the Communists have not been immune to personal rivalries and, more important, they have not been immune to the inherent factionalism which besets all radical movements. In fact, one might argue that factionalism, if only the need at times to chop off a 'left' wing or a 'right' wing, has been necessary in order for the party to maintain a myth of inviolate correctness. Certainly, however, the strains and factions of earlier years (the defections of Levi, Ruth Fischer, Brandler, Thalheimer, Souvarine, Rappaport, Rosmer, Bordiga, Silone, Cannon, Lovestone, Wolfe) have had their counterparts—although the struggles were more hidden and suppressed—in the defections and expulsions and murders of Marty, Tillon, Lecœur, Hervé, Cucchi, Magnani, Reale, Tito, Petkov, Gomulka, Rajk, Nagy, and thousands of others. In fact, not monolithism but factionalism has been a basic law of the Communist movement. And we have failed to see this and exploit it. For from general political experience—whether it be in the trade-union movement or political parties—we know that ruling groups rarely collapse, but fall through the defection of key power figures who control sub-

[28] Vladimir Dedijer, *Tito* (New York, 1953), p. 327.

stantial followings. This was the experience of the CIO with the 'Communist problem' in the United States, and the meaning of Tito, Nagy, and (perhaps) Gomulka in the international Communist movement.

But more than a tactical inability to exploit the fissures and cracks is involved. In the character approach, and in Kremlinology, too, there has often been a 'false concreteness.' One saw all Communists as 'the enemy,' as 'the Bolshevik,' and any unrest, particularly in the satellites, purely as power conflicts between rival leaders. But there was more than this. There was also the simple recalcitrance and the simple decency of the human being which lay underneath. Who becomes the *apparatchik*, seduced by sadism and power, and who does not; who the bureaucrat and who the lurking idealist; who the Rakosi and who the Gyulya Hay—this question is not, as we saw in Poland and Hungary in 1956, a closed book.

We can now see, in retrospect, the real meaning of the first Nagy regime in 1954-55, how the momentum gathered when people were able to communicate with each other, exchange experiences, and realize that some hope of change was possible.[29] But why did almost all the specialists in Soviet affairs fail to catch the significance of those clues in 1954-55? Was it because they were so mesmerized by the thought of 'power' alone as the singular clue to the meaning of social conflict as to forget its impact on people?

Having said this, we must also recognize that political events do not return in the same trajectory. Having failed to catch the 'unique moment,' we are apt to forget that the moment may not return. The lesson of the last few years, from East Berlin to Budapest, is that a 'thaw' breaks up glaciers and log jams, creates rifts and fissures, and sends massive floes down the sea of history. But have not the Rus-

[29] We realize, too, the profound wisdom of de Tocqueville: "It is not always when things are going from bad to worse that revolutions break out. On the contrary, it oftener happens that, when a people which has just put up with an oppressive rule over a long period of time without protest suddenly finds the government relaxing its pressure, it takes up arms against it. . . . Patiently endured so long as it seemed beyond redress, a grievance comes to appear intolerable once the possibility of removing it crosses men's minds. For the mere fact that certain abuses have been remedied draws attention to the others, and they now appear more galling." Alexis de Tocqueville, *The Old Regime and the French Revolution* (New York, 1955), pp. 176-77.

sians—who are more sensitive than most to the lessons of history—
seen this as well and, learning from these events, may they not have
decided that, if they can help it, there will be no more thaws?

THE WORD AND THE DEED

Every society, every social organization, lives for certain goals which,
in considerable measure, are dictated by its ideology. We know—to
use an example from modern trade-union experience—that many individuals act quite pragmatically when their doctrinaire ideological
goals conflict with the ongoing reality, and they compromise accordingly.
Yet, when called upon to take a stand on issues far removed from their
immediate experience, the only vocabulary, the only rhetoric, the
only categories of analysis or even simple formulae available to them
are the old ideological banners. They use them and become trapped,
for ideology is a hardening of commitment, a freezing of opinion.

Since the Bolshevik ideology is the only formal canon of Soviet intentions that we have, an answer to this question is of prime importance:
To what extent are the Soviet leaders committed to the formal Bolshevik ideology (the incompatibility of compromise, the attribution
to capitalism of inherent imperialist aims, and so on), and to what
extent are they prepared to modify it on the basis of experience and
reality?

The answers are contradictory : (1) If one accepts the 'characterological evidence' (Dicks, Leites), compromise is precluded. The rigid
psychological postures and even paranoid suspicions of the Soviet
rulers make it difficult for them to appraise realistically the changes
in the Western world. (2) An extreme Kremlinologist might say that
the Soviet rulers are cynical and regard the ideology simply as a necessary myth for the masses. (3) A geopolitical theorist, taking a
completely rationalist view, would argue that strategic interests rather
than ideology determine the behavior of Soviet rulers. (4) The weight
of some evidence (see pages 29-35 of the Bauer, Inkeles, and Kluckhohn
book) is that ideology, even though cynically used by the Soviet rulers, is
a real factor in the way they think and in the formulation of their goals.

But all this was before Khrushchev. While in the fields of literature
and the arts the Party has moved to reassert *partiinost'* (ideological
control), in other fields practical considerations rather than ideology seem

to determine policy. Soviet economists, for example, in conformity with the Marxist theory of value, could not admit of the productivity of capital, or utilize the interest rate to measure the rational allocation of capital. But even under socialism capital scarcities exist, and, if cost economies were to be achieved, some disguised techniques had to be created in order to carry out the functions of the interest rate. After the war, these evasions of dogma were attacked by the ideologists. "In the hot debate which followed," writes Robert Campbell,

the conflict between the very real problem of the planners and the demand of purity in doctrine was made quite clear. The Soviet leaders faced an impasse; one of the central assumptions of Marxist economic theory had been proved wrong by their own experience, and they were faced with a painful choice between ideology and rational expediency. . . . So long as Stalin was alive, no official line emerged to break the deadlock. About a year after his death, however, the Gordian knot was cut, and cut in such a way as to constitute a surrender of orthodoxy to reality.[30]

In the field of agriculture, Khrushchev has taken the dramatic, drastic step of abolishing the machine and tractor stations, which, in the Stalinist scheme, represented a giant step forward in the elimination of the peasantry, and is turning their equipment over to the kolkhozes. And we can surmise that, in the fields of nuclear physics and other strategic specializations, the pressure to squeeze all theories into the ritualistic formulae of dialectical materialism has diminished.

And yet, at some point—but where?—some essential aspects of the regnant ideology—but which?—must be maintained, for without a central belief system with some continuity, disintegrative opinions begin to spread (as in Poland). Nothing demonstrates better the incalculable effects of such opinion—and of the role of single events in politics—than the corrosive effects of the Khrushchev speech denigrating Stalin. Once the charade is exposed, how can the large masses of people—particularly the youth—retain any belief, when the leadership itself has destroyed the moral and psychological basis of believing? Paradoxically, this may lead the rulers to an even more intensive effort to assert the validity of the central features of the ideology. A movement is

---

[30] Robert W. Campbell, "Some Recent Changes in Soviet Economic Policy," *World Politics*, IX, No. 1 (October 1956), 8.

never more fanatical than 'when prophecy fails,' or when hypocrisy is exposed, for in an effort to still the panicking doubts of the believers, it redoubles its efforts to assert the fundamentals of the faith.[31] And however cynical a ruling group may become about the 'myths' that are necessary for the masses, in such situations they may find themselves psychologically trapped by the verbal formulae they employ and act as if the ideology were real.

FOREIGN AND DOMESTIC

In the past a determining factor in the behavior of foreign Communist parties, and in the policy of the Soviet government, has been the internal power struggles in the Soviet Party. But one can argue now that the primary motives of internal Soviet development (for example, the continued emphasis on heavy industry) are in reflex to the tense world situation. In any assessment, how do the Soviet rulers weigh these considerations?

Both the characterological and the geopolitical approach state, in effect, that whatever the internal developments in the Soviet Union, Soviet policy will be combative and expansionist and that internal and external calculations affect only the timing of aggressive moves. But this leads, with deliberate intent, to the question which is the purpose of this visit: To what extent is the Soviet system a qualitatively new phenomenon, subject to its own laws and indestructible from within? To what extent can the Soviet Union evolve gradually from within into a more stable, normal society?

The approaches broadly labeled characterological, Kremlinological, and totalitarian would argue the former, while the sociological (including Aron's variant in the paper presented to the Oxford Conference) and the neo-Marxist, plus some of the historical school, would argue the latter proposition.

Derivative questions immediately arise: Was Stalin an aberration, or does communism, by its very nature (vanguard party, dictatorship of the proletariat, Bolshevik ideology), take one through a period of the Stalinist type even without a Stalin? Can Communist regimes in Europe, and especially in Asia, 'leap directly' to a mellowed phase

[31] In this connection, see the interesting study *When Prophecy Fails* by Leon Festinger, Henry W. Riecken, and Stanley Schacter (Minneapolis, 1956).

without going through the type of upheaval which Russia experienced?
Are the repressive phases merely a function of forced industrialization?
At this stage the author, like Pirandello pursuing the illusion of reality,
is tempted, almost, to repeat the ten theories which first set him off
in search of reality. But, except for a coda, the play is done.

There is one large variable which these theories, in the nature of
things, cannot adequately take into account—the behavior of the
free world, which is the most important 'reality factor' limiting the
freedom of action of the Communist leaders. Here the role of social
science becomes characteristically ambiguous. For the theories we have
been discussing are designed to shape the behavior of the free world in
its opposition to communism, but in so doing they set up the risk of a
self-confirming hypothesis whereby we, because of our judgment of
how the Communists may be expected to act, adopt policies forcing
them to confirm or negate that judgment (just as the Russians force us
into similarly prefigured molds). This is always a danger, but we can
minimize it if we remember that, no matter how far our social science
sophistication has come, it cannot take the place of that practical flexibility which is demanded by two necessary humilities: an awareness of
the limitations of our knowledge, and of the openness of history.

Ideology and Power Politics : A Symposium

The three papers following were published in *Problems of Communism* in the issue of March-April 1958, in an attempt to sharpen the arguments and differences in one of the major debates on Soviet foreign policy—concerning the relative weight of ideology and power politics in Moscow's dealings with the world abroad. The editors of the magazine invited each of the contributors to the symposium to acquaint himself with the articles of, and take issue with, the other analysts.

This symposium is to be reprinted, with some revisions, in an anthology entitled *Communism after Stalin*, consisting of articles from *Problems of Communism*.—A.D.

The Importance of Doctrine

R. N. CAREW HUNT

The term ideology is one which is more often used than defined. As the present study will be concerned with what the Russian Communists, and Communists in general, mean by it, a definition taken from a Soviet source is in order. The *Filosoficheskii slovar'* [Philosophical Dictionary], 1954 edition, calls ideology "a system of definite views, ideas, conceptions, and notions adhered to by some class or political party," and goes on to say that it is always "a reflection of the economic

R. N. Carew Hunt, who died in 1959, was on the faculty of St. Antony's College, Oxford University. Author of *Marxism Past and Present* and *A Guide to Communist Jargon*, he was a leading British analyst of Soviet affairs.

system predominant at any given time." In a class-divided society the ideology will be that of one or another of the struggling classes, but under socialism, when there is no longer any class division, it will be that of society as a whole. A quotation from Lenin is added to the effect that there can be no 'middle way' between the ideology of the bourgeoisie and that of the proletariat. The one is false and the other true.

Such a summation, albeit neat, is not altogether satisfactory. Broadly speaking, Marx was right in contending that the ideology of a society —the complex of ideas which determine its 'way of life'—will be that of its dominant class, that is, of those whose abilities (whether used rightly or wrongly is irrelevant in this context) have raised them above the common herd. But this sociological fact applies equally to the Soviet Union, where the Party certainly constitutes such a class and indeed is assigned the duty of fertilizing the masses with its ideas. Undoubtedly the current Soviet ideology is intended to strengthen the Party and reinforce its claim to rule. But one must probe further to explain why the Party should have adopted the particular body of doctrine that it has. The fact is that the ideology has been largely determined by the type of collective society which has been established in the Soviet Union.

The authors of the October Revolution were Marxists, and were thus committed to abolishing the capitalist system and replacing it by a nationwide planned economy. For a brief period the experiment of allowing the workers to take charge was tried out, but, when this led to chaos, the Party assumed control and has ever since retained it.

If a Communist regime is to be set up in a backward country, the first prerequisite, as Lenin saw, is industrialization; this is likely to be carried out as rapidly as possible since the quicker the country is developed, and particularly its war potential, the stronger will be the position of its rulers. The execution of such a program of necessity demands the centralization of power in the hands of a small group of leaders, along with the adoption of such unpopular measures as the fixing of wages, the direction of labor, and the prohibition of strikes. And as large-scale planning geared to an expanding economy is impracticable if the plan is liable to be upset at any moment by a vote in a popular assembly, it is not to be expected that the planners will long tolerate any opposition. Furthermore, they will be tempted to interfere in one branch of human activity after another, seeing that all can be so manipulated as to assist the execution of their grand design.

All this has happened in the Soviet Union, and the outcome has been an ideology which derives from the logic of collectivism. Its basic principles are to be found in Marx's revolutionary doctrine, the implications of which were spelled out by Lenin and Stalin when confronted with the practical problem of setting up the type of social order Marx had advocated. Communist literature and propaganda have made us familiar with the doctrine, and there is no need to analyze it here even if space permitted. The issue to be decided is what role ideology plays today, and how far it influences Soviet policy.

Myths and the Masses

Virtually all analysts would agree that in the years of struggle before the October Revolution the Bolsheviks took the theory which lay behind their movement in deadly earnest; there is also general agreement that in the 1920s the doctrine acted as a stimulus to the workers, who took pride in building up their country. In the 1930s, however, the situation changed. Stalin assumed absolute power. The machinery of the state and of the secret police was greatly strengthened, and all prospect of establishing a genuine classless society disappeared. With the Stalin-Hitler pact, if not before, the Soviet Union entered an era which can plausibly be represented as one of naked power politics, perpetuated after World War II in the aggressive and obstructive policies pursued by the regime. Hence it is sometimes argued that Communist ideology has now ceased to possess any importance; that it is simply a top-dressing of sophistries designed to rationalize measures inspired solely by Soviet interests; and that apart from a few fanatics, such as may be found in any society, no one believes in the doctrine any longer, least of all the leaders themselves.

Yet such unqualified assertions are erroneous. Consider, first, the outlook of the ordinary Soviet citizen vis-à-vis the ideology. Day in, day out, he is subjected to intensive and skillfully devised propaganda through every known medium, designed to demonstrate that the ideology on which the Soviet Union is based makes it the best of all possible worlds and that on this account it is encircled with jealous enemies bent on its destruction. The Soviet leadership has always considered it essential that every citizen possess as deep an understanding of Communist principles as his mind is capable of assimilating, and those holding positions of consequence are obliged recurrently to pass through carefully graded schools of political instruction.

It is significant that whenever the leaders feel themselves in a tight corner—as in the recent aftermath of de-Stalinization and the intervention in Hungary—their invariable reaction is to intensify indoctrination in an attempt to refocus public attention on 'first principles.' As hard-headed men they would certainly not attach such importance to indoctrination if they did not know that it paid dividends—and experience has proved that the persistent repetition of a body of ideas which are never challenged is bound to influence the minds of their recipients. Of course, the present generation does not react to the formal ideology with the same fervor as did its forebears who made the revolution, and there are doubtless those who view official apologetics with a large degree of cynicism. But between total commitment and total disillusionment there are many intermediate positions; it is quite possible for a man to regard much of what he is told as nonsense while still believing that there is something of value behind it, especially if he identifies that 'something' with the greatness of his country as 'the first socialist state' and believes in its historic mission.

Leadership Credence—a Hope or a Habit?

More significant, in the present context, than the attitude of the ordinary citizen is that of the ruling elite which is responsible for policy. What its top-ranking members believe is a question which no one, of course, can answer positively. But before surmising, as do some analysts, that the Soviet leadership cannot possibly believe in the myths it propounds, we should remind ourselves that no class or party ever finds it difficult to persuade itself of the soundness of the principles on which it bases its claim to rule.

The Soviet leaders are fortified in this conviction by the very nature of their creed. They have been nurtured in it from birth, and it would be strange indeed if they had remained unaffected. It has become second nature to these men to regard history as a dialectical process —one of incessant conflict between progressive and reactionary forces which can only be resolved by the victory of the former. The division of the world into antagonistic camps, which is an article of faith, is simply the projection onto the international stage of the struggle within capitalistic society between the bourgeoisie, which history has condemned, and the proletariat, whose ultimate triumph it has decreed. The leaders seem to be confident that history is on their side, that all roads lead to communism, and that the contradictions of capitalism must create the type of situation which they can turn to their advantage.

Democratic governments desirous of recommending a certain policy normally dwell upon its practical advantages. But in the Soviet Union this is not so. Any important change of line will be heralded by an article in *Pravda*, often of many columns, purporting to show that the new policy is ideologically correct because it accords with some recent decision of a Party congress, or with Lenin's teaching, or with whatever other criterion may be adopted. How far the policy in question will have been inspired by considerations of ideology as opposed to others of a more mundane nature can never be precisely determined. This, however, is not an exclusive feature of the Communist system; in politics, as for that matter in personal relations, it is seldom possible to disentangle all the motives which determine conduct. The policies of any party or government are likely to reflect its political principles even if they are so framed as to strengthen its position, and there is no reason why the policies adopted by the Soviet leaders should constitute an exception.

Analysts of the 'power politics' school of thought hold that the Kremlin leaders are concerned solely with Soviet national interest, and merely use the Communist movement to promote it. Yet here again the difficulty is to disengage factors which are closely associated. The future of the Communist movement cannot be disassociated from the fortunes of the Soviet Union. If the Soviet regime were to collapse, that movement would count for little, and whether it would long survive even in China is doubtful. Recognizing this, non-Russian Communist parties generally have remained subservient to Moscow even when threatened with large-scale defections of rank-and-file members in the face of particularly odious shifts in the Moscow line.

The 'Separate Paths' Issue

The quarrel between the Soviet and the Yugoslav Communist parties —which an intergovernmental agreement of June 1956 has failed to resolve—is a good example of the interpenetration of ideological and non-ideological factors in policy determinations. The immediate occasion of the quarrel was Tito's unwillingness to allow the spread of Soviet influence through the presence of Soviet military officers and technological experts on Yugoslav soil. As a result Stalin determined to crush Tito and resorted to various political and economic measures in an unsuccessful attempt to do so. It was at least a year before the struggle was extended to the ideological plane. But that it should have been was inevitable. One may well sympathize with Tito's desire for independence and hope that other national leaders will follow his example. Yet from the Communist point of view, if the movement is to be an international one, it must have an international center, and upon historical grounds alone Moscow has a strong claim to the mantle. Ever since Communist parties were formed, it was in fact to Moscow that their internal disputes were referred for settlement, just as it was Moscow which directed their general policy. Whether this role was performed well or ill is beside the point.

Hence the principle of 'separate paths to socialism,' approved by the Twentieth CPSU Congress for tactical reasons, is one which Moscow can accept only with reservations. If it means merely that in establishing communism in a given country consideration must be given to local conditions and that every country's experience adds to the common store, then it is not only unobjectionable but is a salutary corrective to the earlier dogmatism which insisted on the universal applicability of the Russian experience. Such is the attitude nowadays expressed by Soviet theoreticians, though they insistently stress the dangers of exaggerating the importance of national characteristics, denying 'the common laws of socialist development,' or playing down the October Revolution. The official Soviet position is best expressed in an article in *New Times*, March 1956, which states that "while *serving as an example* to other working class parties, the CPSU *draws upon their experience and formulates it in general theoretical principles* for the benefit of all working class parties."

Clearly the Soviet leaders are on the defensive in this matter. They recognize that concessions must be made, but will make no more than they can help. The desire to perpetuate their own power doubtless influences their stand, but considering the fact that communism professes to be a world movement, it would be unreasonable to conclude that either national or personal interests are the sole factors motivating them.

Inefficiency—an Index of Ideology

Indeed, if the analysis given earlier in this article of the genesis of the Communist ideology is correct, the attitude of the Soviet leaders *must* be attributed, at least in part, to the theoretical principles which distinguish Communist regimes from other forms of dictatorship. Certainly the leaders shape and phrase their domestic and foreign policies to fit the general framework established by these principles, and the latter often do not allow much room for maneuver. In fact, their application may sometimes weaken rather than strengthen the country.

To take a simple example, much waste would be avoided if small traders were permitted to operate on a profit basis; the fishmonger, for instance, would have an incentive to put his fish on ice, which he frequently fails to do, to the discomfort of the public. Allowance of profits, however, would constitute a return to private enterprise, which cannot be tolerated.

Similarly, in the Communist view it has long been regarded as indefensible to subordinate a higher to a lower form of socialized enterprise. Thus, while it has been apparent for years that Soviet agriculture would be more efficient if the Machine Tractor Stations were handed over to the collective farms, the issue has been consistently dodged, because the MTS are fully state-owned organs and therefore 'higher' than the farms, which still belong in part to the peasants. When the economist Venzher advocated this measure some years ago, he was slapped down at once by Stalin, the fact that it had already been adopted in Yugoslavia only making his suggestion the more objectionable. Just two years ago Khrushchev launched an extensive program to strengthen the organization and power of the MTS. Very recently, however, he indicated that the regime was—at long last—prepared to yield to practical necessity on this point; in a speech on farm policy, he advocated the transfer of farm machinery to the collectives, and although his proposals are not yet legalized, it would appear that a number of MTS have already been dissolved.

The principle of hierarchy has not been repudiated, however, and still governs other aspects of agricultural organization—for example, the relative status of the two forms of agricultural enterprise. From the standpoint of productive efficiency the collective farms are bad, but the state farms are worse. Nonetheless, the latter represent a 'higher type' of organization, and thus the present virgin lands campaign has been based upon them.

Dogmatism in Foreign Policy

The same point can be scored by examining the Soviet Union's treatment of its satellites. Poland affords a good example. With the country at its mercy after World War II, the Soviet regime decided, among other measures, to integrate the Polish economy with its own. Now had Poland been regarded merely as a colony to be exploited, the operation would have been viewed primarily as a business proposition, and due attention would have been paid to such questions as the nature of the country's resources and the aptitudes of its people. The need to proceed with caution was very evident. The traditional hostility of the Poles to everything Russian should have been taken into account, as well as the fact that the Polish Communist Party had no public support (due in part to the liquidation of its established leaders during the great purges). Yet it was decided that the country must pass through, in shorter time intervals, precisely those stages of development which the Soviet Union had traversed. The result was a serious disruption of the economy through the erection of a top-heavy industrial structure on the basis of a depressed agriculture. This policy cannot be attributed to Stalin alone as it was continued after his death. It proved disastrous, and is only intelligible on the assumption that it was primarily motivated by ideological considerations.

The argument can be carried further. By its behavior throughout its history, the Soviet Union has incurred the hostility, or at least the suspicion; of the entire free world. Yet there was no practical reason why it should have done so. After the October Revolution the Bolshevik regime was faced with appalling domestic problems, and it had nothing to gain by courting the animosity of the West. The Soviet leaders might well have built up their country in accordance with the principles to which they were committed without exciting such widespread hostility. What governments do at home is commonly regarded as their own affair. Fundamentally, the regime in Yugoslavia is as Communist as that of the Soviet Union, and was established with an equal ruthlessness. But Tito, having asserted his independence from Moscow, has muffled his attacks on the West, and in turn the Western governments have demonstrated their desire—albeit tempered with caution—to believe in his good faith.

What no country will tolerate is the attempt, deliberately engineered by a foreign power, to overthrow its form of government; this has been the persistent aim and effort of the Soviet regime in defiance of its express diplomatic guarantees of noninterference. It is hard to see how this strategy has assisted the development of Soviet Russia, and that it has never been abandoned cannot be dissociated from those messianic and catastrophic elements in the Communist creed which influence, perhaps impel, the Soviet drive for world power.

In conclusion, it is frequently stated that communism has created an ideological cleavage between the West and the Soviet bloc. Yet this statement would be meaningless if the issue today were, as some believe, simply one of power politics. An ideology is significant only if it makes those who profess it act in a way they would not otherwise do. The fact that large numbers of persons accept communism would not constitute a danger if it did not lead them to support policies which threaten the existence of those who do not accept it. It is true that many people, especially in backward countries, call themselves Communists without having any clear idea of what it means. Yet the movement would not be the force it has become were there not in every country men and women who sincerely believe in the ideas behind it, which form collectively what we call its ideology.

To represent this ideology as a species of opium with which the

Soviet leaders contrive to lull the people while taking care never to indulge in it themselves is to attribute to them an ability to dissociate themselves from the logic of their system—an ability which it is unlikely they possess. For the concepts which make up that system, fantastic as many of them appear to be, will be found on examination to be interrelated, and to be logical extensions of the basic principles to which all Communists subscribe.

To turn it the other way around, Communists claim a theoretical justification for the basic principles in which they believe. But these principles must be translated into appropriate action; and action, if directed by the rulers of a powerful country like the Soviet Union, will take the form of *Realpolitik*. There is no yardstick which permits a measure of the exact relationship between power politics and ideology in the policies which result, but surely neither factor can be ignored.

National Interest : Key to Soviet Politics

SAMUEL L. SHARP

An enormous body of Western research and analysis focuses on Marxist-Leninist ideology as a clue to understanding Kremlin policy. This extensive and intensive preoccupation with matters doctrinal is, at least in part, the result of a rather widely circulated belief that the democratic world was guilty of neglect when it refused to take seriously the 'theoretical' writings and pronouncements of Adolf Hitler. It has been alleged that these writings later guided Hitler's actions and that a ready key to his conduct was thus overlooked.

When, at the end of World War II, the Soviet Union appeared on the international scene as a power—and a menace—of the first order, led by a group consistently claiming its adherence to a body of doctrine

Samuel L. Sharp, Professor of International Relations at American University, Washington, D.C., has written extensively on the Soviet orbit.

as a guide to action, legions of experts began to dissect that body in a search for a key to Soviet behavior, current and future. The material at hand was certainly more promising than the intellectually scrawny homunculus of Nazi or Fascist 'ideology.' After all, Marxism has its not entirely disreputable roots in legitimate Western thought. Even in terms of sheer bulk there was more to operate on, what with Lenin's and Stalin's additions to and modifications of the original scriptures and the voluminous exegetic output of a generation of Soviet propagandists.

The massive study of Communist ideology has had one happy result in that some serious scholarly output has been provided to counterbalance Party-line apologias, thereby destroying a number of primitive notions concerning the Soviet system and what makes it tick. At the same time, in this writer's view, preoccupation with the search for a formula of interpretive and predictive value has produced its own distortions. These distortions seem to be the composite result of cold-war anxieties, faulty logic, and disregard of some of the elementary principles and practices of international relations. To these causes must be added the human tendency to look beyond the simple and obvious for the complicated and mysterious in attempting to explain any condition which is exasperating and which is therefore perceived as strange and unique. Baffled by the Soviet phenomenon, millions in the Western world have found a negative consolation of sorts in the famous statement by Winston Churchill that Russian policy is 'a riddle wrapped in a mystery inside an enigma.' But how many have bothered to read the qualifying words which followed? Having disclaimed ability to forecast Soviet actions, Churchill added: "*But perhaps there is a key. That key is Russian national interest.*"[1]

Clearly implied in this observation was the logical supposition that the policy-makers of the Soviet Union act in what they believe to be the best interest of the state over whose destinies they are presiding. In this sense the Soviet Union is to be looked upon as an actor, a protagonist, on the stage of international politics; and, in this writer's view, its actions can be interpreted most fruitfully in terms of behavior

---

[1] Radio broadcast of October 1, 1939, reprinted in Churchill, *The Gathering Storm* (Boston, 1948), p. 449. Author's italics.

germane to the practice of international politics. Without denying the possible pitfalls of this approach, the writer proposes to argue its usefulness as a key to understanding a phenomenon which the non-Communist world can ill afford to envelop in a fog of self-generated misinterpretation.

The Doubtful Art of Quotation

Whenever the suggestion is made that the concept of national interest be applied as an explanation of Soviet behavior on the international scene, objections are raised in many quarters. The most vigorous protests come, of course, from Soviet sources. It is a standard claim of Soviet spokesmen that their state is by definition something 'different' (or 'higher') and that the foreign policy of this entity is different in principle (*printsipial'no otlichna*) from that of other states because the latter are capitalist and the former is socialist.[2] It would seem that only uncritical adherents of communism could take such statements seriously. Yet non-Communists very often cite them as a convenient *ipse dixit* in support of their own claim that the Soviet Union is indeed 'different,' though not in the way Soviet propaganda wants one to believe. The claim is that the Soviet Union is, at best, 'a conspiracy disguised as a state' and cannot be viewed as a 'normal' member of the world community of nations. There is no attempt to explain on what basis some Soviet statements are to be taken as reliable indices of regime motivations, while other statements, no less abundantly scattered throughout the Marxist-Leninist scriptures, are rejected as lie and deception.

It is surely dubious scholarship to collect quotations (sometimes reduced to half a sentence) from Lenin and Stalin without regard to the time, place, circumstances, composition of the audience, and, whenever ascertainable, immediate purposes of such utterances. What results from such compilations, no matter how laboriously and ingeniously put together, is, as a thoughtful critic has pointed out, "a collection of such loose generalizations and so many exceptions and

---

[2] To cite just one recent source, see V. I. Lisovskii, *Mezhdunarodnoe pravo* (Kiev, 1955), p. 397.

contradictions that few readers can find much guidance in it."[3] Stalin, for example, can be quoted as once having said that "with a diplomat words must diverge from facts" and that "a sincere diplomat would equal dry water, wooden iron"; yet this not too astute observation was made in 1913 in an article dealing with bourgeois diplomacy written by an obscure Georgian revolutionary who probably had never met a diplomat. His view in this instance is identifiable as a variant of the classic image of the diplomat as "an honorable gentleman sent abroad to lie for his country." This image may very well have stayed with the congenitally suspicious and pessimistic Stalin in later life, and thus might indeed afford us a clue to his 'real' nature. However, sound scholarship would seek to reconstruct the attitudes of the Kremlin ruler out of words and deeds of a more relevant period of his life rather than from this loose piece of Djugashvili prose torn out of context.

The Vital Factor of Feasibility

Some objections to the interpretation of Soviet policies in terms of national interest are rooted in the aforementioned line of analysis which conjures up the ghost of Adolf Hitler. The democracies erred, did they not, in initially looking upon Hitler's aims as an expression of 'legitimate' (we will return to this phrase in a moment), however distasteful, national aspirations, only to discover later that they were dealing with a maniac whose appetites were unlimited. Since it is generally agreed that Soviet policy, like Hitler's, belongs to the total-

[3] Marshall Knappen, *An Introduction to American Foreign Policy* (New York, 1956). The quote is from the chapter entitled "Capabilities, Appeal, and Intentions of the Soviet Union" and refers specifically to the well-known effort by Nathan Leites in *A Study of Bolshevism* (Glencoe, Illinois, 1953) to construct, out of thousands of quotes from Lenin and Stalin bolstered with excerpts from nineteenth—century Russian literature, an 'image of Bolshevism' and an 'operational code' of the Politburo. See also the remarks on "Difficulties of Content Analysis" and "The Problem of Context" in John S. Reshetar, Jr., *Problems of Analyzing and Predicting Soviet Behavior* (New York, 1955). In all fairness to Leites and his prodigious undertaking it must be pointed out that he was aware of a 'spurious air of certainty' in his formulations, which were intended to be only 'guesses about the mind of the Soviet Politburo' (Leites, p. 27).

itarian species, would it not be impardonable to repeat the same
mistake by looking upon the aims of the Soviet leaders as the expression of the aspirations of a 'normal' nation-state?

Two points should be made here. First, Hitler bears comparison
with no one; there is no other leader in history who has combined his
precise mental make-up with his enormous concentration of power.
He was, as his biographer Allan Bullock pointed out, a man 'without
aims,' that is, without *limited* and therefore tractable aims.[4] At one
point in his career Hitler began to disregard the cardinal rule of politics
—the necessity of aligning ambitions with capacity to translate them
into reality. He broke the barrier of the *feasible*, motivated by what
could most likely be diagnosed as the death-wish. Whatever else may
be said about the Soviet leaders, no one, including people who suspect
them of ideological self-deception, has denied them the quality of
caution. Far from seeking self-destruction, they are lustily bent on
survival. This in itself, even in the complete absence of scruples, makes
their aims *limited*.

Mr. Carew Hunt argues elsewhere in these pages that there are
"messianic and catastrophic elements in the Communist creed which
influence . . . the Soviet drive for world power." While there may
indeed be a degree of messianism in the Soviet leadership's view of
its mission, the 'catastrophic' tendency seems to be held carefully
in check. Hitler was propelled by the absurd notion that he had to
accomplish certain aims before he reached the age of sixty—an arrogant
and, from the point of view of German national interest, totally irrelevant assumption. Granted that the Soviet leaders aim at 'world
power' (a concept which in itself should be defined more explicitly
than it usually is), they have long since decided not to fix any specific time limit for the achievement of this ultimate aim. Certainly
the present generation of leaders has acted to modify (perhaps 'refine'
is a better word) the aggressive drive for power abroad at least to an
extent which will allow some enjoyment at home of the tangible fruits
of the revolution this side of the Communist heaven. Even back in
the early days of Bolshevik rule, Lenin, though at times carried away
by expectations of spreading revolution, never sacrificed practical

[4] Allan Bullock, *Hitler—A Study in Tyranny* (New York, 1953).

caution to missionary zeal; repeatedly he warned his followers to look after the 'bouncing baby' (the Soviet state), since Europe was only 'pregnant with revolution' (which it wasn't).

An Applicable Concept of Interest

The second point to be made is a crucial one. Reluctance to analyze Soviet aims in terms of national interest is due, in part, to the aura of legitimacy which surrounds the 'normal' run of claims of nation-states, giving rise to the notion that the term itself infers something legitimate. However, suggesting that Kremlin moves can best be understood in terms of what the leaders consider advantageous to the Soviet state by no means implies subscribing to their aims or sympathizing with them. In international relations the maxim *tout comprendre c'est tout pardonner* does not apply. The concept of national interest, by focusing attention on the *objective sources of conflict*—that is, those which *can* be explained rationally as issues between nations—permits us to view the international scene in terms of a global problem of power relations rather than a cops-and-robbers melodrama. We can then perceive which are the *tractable* elements in the total equation of conflict, and devote our energies to reducing or altering these factors.

This approach seems to the writer to be indispensable both to the scholar and to the statesman. The scholar who accepts the 'natural' (in terms of the nature of international politics) explanation for Kremlin behavior is not likely to violate the 'law of parsimony' by unnecessarily piling up hypotheses which are unprovable and which in any case simply confuse the issue, insofar as dealing practically with the Soviet Union is concerned. The statesman finds that he is coping with a phenomenon which he knows how to approach both in accommodation and in opposition, rather than with some occult and other-worldly force.

Those who object to the framework of analysis here proposed would say, as does Mr. Hunt, that there are many cases on record when the Soviet leaders have acted in a way clearly inconsistent with the Russian national interest and intelligible only in terms of ideological dogmatism. The answer to this argument is simple: it does not matter what

Mr. Hunt—or anybody else—considers to be the Russian national interest; as the term is defined here, the only view which matters is that held by the Soviet leaders. By the same token it is a rather fruitless thing to speak of 'legitimate' *vs.* 'illegitimate' Soviet interests. One of the essential attributes of sovereignty (and the Soviet leaders are certainly jealous where their own is involved !) is that it is up to the sovereign to determine what serves him best.

Yet doesn't this reasoning render pointless the entire conceptual approach proposed? If Soviet national interest is what the Soviet leaders take it to be, and if one agrees—as one must— that their view of the world is derived largely from their adherence to Marxism-Leninism, isn't this another way of saying that Soviet behavior is the result of ideological conditioning? Not quite. The point at issue is whether the 'pure' Soviet view of the world is important *as a guide to action,* whether the *ultimate* aims of the Communist creed are operative in policy determinations. In the present writer's view they are not; the fault of the opposing line of analysis is that, in dwelling on the supposed impact of ideology on the leadership, it tends to ignore the degree to which the pursuit of ultimate goals has been circumscribed in time and scope by considerations of the *feasible.* In simple arithmetic, doctrine minus those aspects which are not empirically operative equals empirically determined policy. If a policy action is called 'revolutionary expediency,' it is still expediency. Why then introduce into the equation an element which does not affect the result?

A supporting view in this respect is W. W. Rostow's characterization of Soviet foreign policy as a series of responses to the outside world which, especially before 1939, "took the form of such actions as were judged most likely, *on a short-range basis,* to maintain or expand the national power of the Soviet regime." Despite the Soviet Union's vastly greater ability to influence the world environment in the postwar era, says Rostow, "there is no evidence that the foreign policy criteria of the regime have changed."[5] If some instances of Soviet behavior appear to have produced results actually detrimental to the

---

[5] W. W. Rostow *et al., The Dynamics of Soviet Society* (New York, 1952), p. 136. Author's italics.

Soviet interest, we must not only refrain from applying our view of Soviet interest but also—as Rostow's viewpoint suggests—judge the policy decisions involved in terms of their validity at the time they were made and not in the light of what happened later (remembering, too, that mistakes and miscalculations are common to all policy-makers, not just those who wear 'ideological blinders').

The words 'on a short-range basis' have been underscored above to stress that the term policy, if properly applied, excludes aims, ambitions, or dreams not accompanied by action visibly and within a reasonable time capable of producing the results aimed at or dreamed of. In the case of the Soviet leaders, concentration on short-range objectives and adjustment to political realities has, in the brilliant phrase suggested by Barrington Moore, Jr., *caused the means to eat up the ends.*[6]

The objection will still be raised that the Soviet leaders mouth every policy decision in terms of ideological aims. Enough should have been said on this score to obviate a discussion here. As able students of the problem have pointed out, the Soviet leaders' claim to rule rests on their perpetuation of the ideology and their insistence on orthodoxy; they have no choice but to continue paying lip service to the doctrine, even if it is no longer operative. The liberal mind somehow balks at this image of total manipulation, of an exoteric doctrine for public consumption which has no connection with its esoteric counterpart—that is, the principles or considerations which really govern Kremlin behavior. Yet allowance must be made for this possibility.

Moscow and International Communism

One serious argument of those who reject the image of the Soviet Union as a 'legitimate' participant in the balance-of-power game played in the arena of international politics is that the Soviet leaders consistently violate the rules of the game by enlisting out-of-bounds help from foreign Communist parties. This point invites the following brief observations:

[6] Barrington Moore, Jr., *Soviet Politics : The Dilemma of Power* (Cambridge, Massachusetts, 1950).

1) Early in its history the Communist International was transformed into a tool of Soviet foreign policy, at a time when few other tools were available to Moscow.

2) As soon as the Soviet state felt at all sure of its survival (after the period of civil war, foreign intervention, and economic chaos), it reactivated the apparatus of foreign policy along more traditional lines.

3) Under Stalin the Third International was reduced to a minor auxiliary operation. An index of his attitude toward it is the fact that he never once addressed a Comintern congress. Probably the International was kept up in the interwar period because it seemed to produce marginal dividends in terms of nuisance value. Moreover, Stalin could hardly have divorced himself from it officially at a time when he was jockeying for total power inside Russia, since this would have helped to confirm his opponents' accusations that he was 'betraying the revolution.' But he certainly did everything to show his belief in the ineffectiveness of the organization and its foreign components as against the growing power of the Soviet state.

4) When the entire record of Soviet success and failure is summed up, the achievements are clearly attributable to Soviet power and diplomacy with no credit due to the international Communist movement. Furthermore, the ties between the Soviet Union and foreign parties have never deterred Moscow from useful alliances or cooperation with other governments—including, from one time to another, the astutely anti-Communist Turkish government of Atatürk, the more brutally anti-Communist regime of Adolf Hitler, and, during World War II, the Western powers. That the Soviet leaders, by virtue of their doctrine, entertained mental reservations about the durability of friendly relations with these governments can hardly be doubted. But it is equally clear that the cessation of cooperation was due in each case to the workings of power politics rather than Soviet ideological dictate—that is, to the historical tendency of alliances to disintegrate when what binds them (usually a common enemy) disappears.

5) Finally, it might be argued that the Soviet appeal to foreign Communist parties is not dissimilar to the practice of various governments of different periods and persuasions to appeal for support abroad on the basis of some sort of affinity—be it Hispanidad, Slav solidarity,

Deutschtum, or Pan-Arabism. The Soviet appeal is admittedly broader and the 'organizational weapon' seems formidable, but is importance should not be exaggerated. Actually, there is no way at all to measure the effectiveness of the appeal *per se* since Communist 'success' or 'failure' in any situation always involves a host of other variables—including military, geographical, social, political, or economic factors. In the last analysis, virtually every instance where Moscow has claimed a victory for communism has depended on Soviet manipulation of traditional levers of national influence.

An Exception to Prove the Rule

There remains one area of Soviet 'foreign policy' where the Soviet leaders have supplemented power politics—or more accurately in this instance naked force—with an attempt to derive special advantage, a sort of 'surplus value,' from claiming ideological obeisance to the Soviet Union as the seat of the secular church of communism. This area is the so-called Soviet orbit in Eastern Europe.

The term foreign policy is enclosed in quotation marks here because Stalin obviously did not consider areas under the physical control of Soviet power as nations or governments to be dealt with in their own right. He was clearly impatient with the claim of at least some Communist parties that their advent to power had changed the nature of their relationship to Moscow, and that the party-to-party level of relations must be separated from the government-to-government level (as Gomulka argued in 1948). In Stalin's thinking, especially after 1947, the East European regimes were not eligible for more real sovereignty than the 'sovereign' republics of the Soviet Union. He attempted to extend the principle of *democratic centralism* (a euphemism for Kremlin control) to these countries, allowing them only as much of a façade of sovereignty as was useful for show toward the outside world.

One need not necessarily dig into doctrine to explain this attitude; in fact, doctrine until recently said nothing at all about relations between sovereign Communist states. The explanation lies to a large extent in Stalin's personal predilection for total control, plus the need to tighten Moscow's bonds to the limit, by whatever means or arguments possible, in the face of the bipolarization of global power after World War II.

Stalin's successors began by pressing the same claims of ideological obeisance from the satellites. But rather strikingly—in the same period that their foreign policy has scored substantial successes in other areas in traditional terms of diplomatic advances and manipulation of the economic weapon[7]—they have failed in the one area where they attempted to substitute the ties of ideology for the give-and-take of politics. Communist parties in power, it turned out (first in the case of Yugoslavia, while Stalin still reigned, and later in Poland, not to mention the very special case of China), claimed the right to be sovereign—or at least semi-sovereign—actors on the international scene. Whether or not this makes sense ideologically to the Soviet leaders is unimportant; they have recognized the claim.

It is not necessary to review here the post-Stalin history of fluctuating Soviet relations with Eastern Europe which began with the B. & K. pilgrimage to Belgrade. Let us take only the most recent attempt to reformulate the nature of relations between the USSR and other Communist countries—the interparty declaration issued on the occasion of the fortieth anniversary of the Bolshevik revolution. On the surface, the declaration, published in the name of twelve ruling Communist parties, seems to reimpose a pattern of ideological uniformity as well as to recognize the special leadership position of the Soviet Union.[8] However, the circumstances of the gathering and the internal evidence of the declaration, together with the reports of some of the participants, show a far more complex situation.

The following aspects of the conference deserve attention: First, the very fact that the parties representing governments of sovereign countries were singled out for a special meeting and declaration instead

[7] Samuel L. Sharp, "The Soviet Position in the Middle East," *Social Science*, National Academy of Economics and Political Sciences, XXXII, No. 4 (October 1951).

[8] The text of the declaration, adopted at a meeting held on November 14-16, 1957, was published in *Pravda* on November 22. A separate 'peace manifesto' issued in the name of all of the Communist parties present at the congregation appeared in *Pravda* a day later.

of being lumped together with the mass of parties (many of them illegal, some leading no more than a paper existence) is a significant departure from past practice. Secondly, the Yugoslav party, though represented at the festivities, refused to sign the declaration, apparently after long negotiations. Thirdly, attempts to revive in any form an international, Moscow-based organization resembling the Comintern were unsuccessful. Gomulka's report on the meeting made it clear that the Polish party opposed both a new Comintern (for which it nevertheless had a few good words) and a new Cominform (for which it had nothing but scorn).[9]

Perhaps most significant for the purposes of the present discussion was a statement by Mao Tse-tung, who next to Khrushchev and Suslov was the main speaker at the meeting of the 'ruling' parties and was billed as co-sponsor of the declaration. Mao bolstered his argument for the recognition of the leading position of the Soviet Union in the 'socialist camp' with the remark that "China has not even one fourth of a sputnik while the Soviet Union has two."[10] Now, the possession of a sputnik is a symbol of achievement and a source of prestige for the Soviet Union, but certainly not in terms of ideology. It was Soviet national power to which Mao paid deference.

In sum, the entire circumstances of the gathering indicate a disposition on the part of the Soviet Union to substitute—wherever it has to—the give-and-take of politics for its former relationship with the orbit countries, which relied on naked power to enforce demands of ideological subservience.

From all the foregoing, it should be clear that the task of the non-Communist world is not to worry itself sick over the ultimate goals of the Soviet leadership or the degree of its sincerity, but to concentrate on multiplying situations in which the Soviet Union either will be forced or will choose to play the game of international politics in an

[9] Gomulka's report was published in *Trybuna Ludu* (Warsaw), November 29, 1957.

[10] Cited in Friedrich Ebert's report to the East German party (SED), published in *Neues Deutschland* (East Berlin), November 30, 1957, p. 4.

essentially traditional setting. How the Kremlin leaders will square
this with their Marxist conscience is not really our problem.

The Logic of One-Party Rule

RICHARD LOWENTHAL

To what extent are the political decisions of the Soviet leadership
influenced by its belief in an official ideology, and to what extent are
they empirical responses to specific conflicts of interest, expressed in
ideological terms merely for purposes of justification? The phrasing
of the question at issue suggests the two extreme answers which are
prima facie conceivable—on the one hand, that ideology provides the
Kremlin with a ready-made book of rules to be looked up in any situation; on the other, that its response to reality takes place without
any reference to ideology. Yet any clear formulation of this vital
issue will show that both extremes are meaningless nonsense.

A ready-made book of rules for any and every situation—an unvarying road map to the goal of communism which the Soviet leaders
must predictably follow—cannot possibly exist, both because the situations to be met by them are not sufficiently predictable and because
no government which behaved in so calculable a manner could conceivably retain power. On the other hand, empirical *Realpolitik*
without ideological preconceptions can exist as little as can 'empirical
science' without categories and hypotheses based on theoretical specu-
lation. Confronted with the same constellation of interests and pressures, the liberal statesman will in many cases choose a different course
of action from the conservative—and the totalitarian Communist's
choice will often be different from that of either.

It seems surprising, therefore, that at this late stage of discussion
Professor Sharp is apparently in earnest in defending the extreme of
the *Realpolitik* interpretation and in denying completely the relevance
of Communist ideology for the formation, and hence the understanding,
of Soviet foreign policy. The latter, he assures us, can be adequately

Richard Lowenthal, a veteran writer on communism, is East European correspondent of the London *Observer*.

understood in terms of national interest, just as with any other state. When reminded by Mr. Carew Hunt of certain irrational features of Soviet foreign policy, he replies that what matters is not any outsider's concept of Soviet interests, but the Soviet leaders' own. Yet this reduces his thesis to a tautology: he 'proves' that national interest motivates Soviet foreign policy by the simple device of labeling whatever motivates it 'national interest.'

Surely Professor Sharp cannot have it both ways. Either there are objective criteria of national interest, recognizable by the scholar —and then the view that these interests explain Soviet actions is capable of proof or refutation; or else it is admitted that different statesmen may interpret national interest in different but equally 'legitimate' ways—and then the concept of a self-contained study of international relations collapses, because a consideration of the internal structures of different national communities and of the 'ideologies' reflecting them becomes indispensable for an understanding of their foreign policies.

. . . .

The Function of Doctrine

Assuming, then, that the Soviet leaders' ideology is relevant to their conduct, the real problem remains to discover which are the actual operative elements in it and in what way they affect policy decisions. Clearly it would be folly to expect that Soviet policy could be predicted solely from an exegetic study of the Marxist-Leninist canon. Not only is it impossible for any group of practical politicians to base their decisions on an unvarying book of rules; there is any amount of historical evidence to show that the rules have been altered again and again to fit the practical decisions *ex post facto*. Moreover, there are vast parts of the Communist ideological structure, such as the scholastic refinements of 'dialectical materialism' or the labor theory of value, which in their nature are so remote from the practical matters to be decided that their interpretation cannot possibly affect policy decisions. They may be used in inner-party arguments to *justify* what has been decided on other grounds, but that is all.

How, then, are we to distinguish those elements of Soviet ideology which are truly operative politically from those which are merely traditional scholastic ballast, linked to the operative elements by the historical accident of the founding fathers' authorship? The answer is to be found by going back to the original Marxian meaning of the term ideology—conceived as a distorted reflection of social reality in the consciousness of men, used as an instrument of struggle. The fundamental, distinctive social reality in the Soviet Union is the rule of the bureaucracy of a single, centralized, and disciplined party, which wields a monopoly of political, economic, and spiritual power and permits no independent groupings of any kind. The writer proposes as a hypothesis that the operative parts of the ideology are those which are indispensable for maintaining and justifying this state of affairs : 'Marxism-Leninism' matters inasmuch as it expresses, in an ideologically distorted form, the logic of one-party rule.[1]

Totalitarian Parallels

There are a few interconnected ideological features which are common to all the totalitarian regimes of our century—whether of the nationalist-fascist or of the Communist variety. We may designate them as the elements of chiliasm, of collective paranoia, and of the representative fiction. Each totalitarian regime justifies its power and its crimes

---

[1] While this comes close to the position outlined in Mr. Carew Hunt's paper, I cannot follow him in his assumption that the totalitarian party monopoly is a by-product of the attempt to establish collectivist economic planning or to achieve the speedy industrialization of a backward country. This neo-Marxist view, held by such otherwise divergent authors as Professor Hayek and Milovan Djilas, is contradicted by the fact that the Bolshevik party monopoly, including the ban on inner-party factions, was fully established by Lenin at the time of the transition to the New Economic Policy (1921), when economic planning was reduced to a minimum and forced industrialization not yet envisaged. Independent of the concrete economic program, totalitarianism was implicit in the centralized, undemocratic structure of a party consciously created as an instrument for the conquest of power, and in the ideological characteristics resulting (to be discussed further in this article). Of course, totalitarian power, once established, favors total economic planning and the undertaking of revolutionary economic tasks by the state; but this is a consequence, not a cause. Marx never developed a concept of total planning, and even Lenin never imagined anything of the kind before 1918. But Marx in his youth at least equated the 'dictatorship of the proletariat' with the Jacobin model, and Lenin followed this model throughout.

by the avowed conviction, first, that its final victory will bring about the millennium—whether defined as the final triumph of communism or of the master race—and, second, that this state of grace can only be achieved by an irreconcilable struggle against a single, omnipresent, and multiform enemy—whether monopoly capitalism or world Jewry—whose forms include every particular opponent of the totalitarian power. Each also claims to represent the true will of the people—the *volonté générale*—independent of whether the people actually support it, and argues that any sacrifice may be demanded from the individual and the group for the good of the people and the defeat of its devilish enemies.

The Communist version of these basic beliefs is superior to the Nazi version in one vital respect. Because the appeal of racialism is in its nature restricted to a small minority of mankind, the Nazis' goal of world domination could not possibly have been attained without a series of wars, preferably surprise attacks launched against isolated opponents. Because the appeal of communism is directed to all mankind, it can be linked with the further doctrine of the inevitable victory of the rising forces of socialism over the imperialist enemy, which is disintegrating under the impact of its own internal contradictions. This central ideological difference, and not merely the psychological difference between Hitler and the Soviet leaders, explains why the latter are convinced that history is on their side and that they need not risk the survival of their own regime in any attempt to hasten its final triumph: they believe in violence, revolutionary and military, as one of the weapons of policy, but they do not believe in the inevitability of world war.

Awkward Aims and Claims

Yet the Communist version of totalitarian ideology also suffers from some weaknesses and contradictions from which the Nazi and Fascist versions are free. In the first place, its vision of the millennium has more markedly utopian features—the classless society, the end of exploitation of man by man, the withering away of the state—which make awkward yardsticks for the real achievements of Communist states. Secondly, in a world where nationalism remains a force of

tremendous strength, an internationalist doctrine is bound to come
into conflict with the interests of any major Communist power, or
with the desire of smaller Communist states for autonomy.

Thirdly, by rejecting the 'Führer principle' and claiming to be
'democratic,' Communist ideology makes the realities of party dictatorship and centralist discipline more difficult to justify; yet because
appeal to blind faith is not officially permitted, justification is needed
in 'rational' terms. It is precisely this continuous need for the pretense
of rational argument—the awkward heritage of communism's origin
from revolutionary Western democracy—which has led to the far
greater elaboration of its ideology compared to that of 'irrationalist'
right-wing totalitarianism, and which gives its constant interpretation
so much greater importance in preserving the cohesion of the party
regime. Due to the fictions of democracy and rationality, the morale
of party cadres has been made dependent on the appearance of ideological consistency.

The result of these inherent weaknesses of Communist ideology is
that the component doctrines—dealing with the 'dictatorship of the
proletariat,' the party's role as a 'vanguard' embodying the 'true'
class consciousness, 'democratic centralism,' 'proletarian internationalism,' and the 'leading role of the Soviet Union'—become focal points
of ideological crises and targets of 'revisionist' attacks whenever
events reveal the underlying contradictions in a particularly striking
way. Yet these are the very doctrines which the regime cannot renounce
because they are the basic rationalizations of its own desire for self-
preservation.

We can expect, then, that Communist ideology will have an effective
influence on the policy decisions of Soviet leaders when, and only
when, it expresses the needs of self-preservation of the party regime.
We can further expect that ideological changes and disputes within
the Communist 'camp' will offer clues to the conflicts and crises—the
'contradictions'—which are inseparable from the evolution of this,
as of any other, type of society. The fruitful approach, in this writer's
view, consists neither in ignoring Communist ideology as an irrelevant
disguise nor in accepting it at its face value and treating it as a subject
for exegesis, but in using it as an indicator of those specific drives and
problems which spring from the specific structure of Soviet society—

in regarding it as an enciphered, continuous self-disclosure, whose cipher can be broken by sociological analysis.

Two Camps—One Enemy

Let us now apply this approach to the doctrine of the 'two camps' in world affairs. The 'two-camp' concept was not, of course, a Stalinist invention, although this is sometimes supposed. The postwar situation with its alignment of the Communist and Western powers in two openly hostile politico-military blocs merely gave plausibility to a world image which was inherent in Leninism from the beginning but which attracted little attention in the period when the Communist 'camp' was just an isolated fortress with several outposts. Nor has the doctrine disappeared with the post-Stalin recognition of the importance of the uncommitted, ex-colonial nations and of the tactical value of incorporating them in a 'peace zone'; it remains one of the basic ideas of the Moscow twelve-party declaration of November 1957, and one of the fundamental subjects of ideological disagreement between the Soviets and the Yugoslav Communists.

The Yugoslavs can reject the 'two-camp' doctrine because they admit the possibility of 'roads to socialism' other than Communist party dictatorship—'reformist' roads for advanced industrial countries with parliamentary traditions, 'national revolutionary' roads for ex-colonial countries. It follows from this view that Communist states have no monopoly on progress, and that alliances have no ultimate ideological meaning.

The Soviets still assert that while there can be different roads to Communist power and minor differences in the use of power once gained, there is no way of achieving socialism except by the "dictatorship of the proletariat exercised by its vanguard." It follows that tactical agreements with semi-socialist neutrals are not different in kind from the wartime alliance with the Western 'imperialists,' or the prewar pact with Hitler—maneuvers which are useful in dividing the forces of the 'class enemy' but which remain subordinate to the fundamental division of the world into the Communists versus the Rest.

In other words, the 'two-camp' doctrine is the Communist version of what we have called the element of 'collective paranoia' in totalitarian

ideology—its need for a single, all-embracing enemy which is assumed
to pull the wires of every resistance to the party's power. The term
'paranoia' is used here not to infer that the phenomenon in question
is due to psychotic processes in either the leaders or the mass following
of totalitarian parties, but merely to describe, through a convenient
psychological analogy, the ideological mechanism of projection which
ascribes the regime's drive for unlimited power to an imagined all-
enemy. The essential point is that in the nature of totalitarianism,
any independent force, either inside or outside the state, is regarded
as ultimately hostile; the concept of 'two camps' and that of 'unlimited
aims' are two sides of the same phenomenon.

Moscow's Double-Indemnity Tactics

Now Professor Sharp is, of course, entirely right in asking where
this doctrine impinges on actual Soviet foreign policy—given the
undoubted facts that actual Soviet aims, and the risks incurred in
their pursuit, are limited at any given moment, that the Soviets are
perfectly capable of concluding 'temporary' alliances with 'bourgeois,' 'imperialist,' or even 'fascist' states, and that most other
alliances in this impermanent world are proving to be 'temporary'
as well, for quite non-ideological reasons. The present writer would
suggest to him that the difference has manifested itself in the peculiar
suspicion with which the Soviets treated their 'imperialist' allies
even at the height of the war, seeking in particular to isolate their
own population from contact, in the manner in which they sought
to create additional 'guarantees' for the reliability of those allies by
the use of local Communist parties wherever this was possible, and
above all, in the difference between the traditional and the Communist
concepts of 'spheres of influence' as illuminated by the different
interpretations of the Yalta agreements.

The peculiar forms taken by Moscow's suspicion of its wartime allies
are too well known to need elaboration here, but it is less generally
realized that such behavior was merely the reverse side of Soviet
efforts to 'strengthen' such temporary alliances where possible, by
the use of party ties. Existence of the party channel has not, of course,
been a *sine qua non* for Moscow's intergovernmental deals, as is shown

by the examples of Russo-Turkish cooperation after World War I, the Stalin-Hitler pact, and perhaps also present Soviet cooperation with Egypt. But wherever Communist parties were tolerated by the partner, Soviet foreign policy has assigned to them a vital role. Indeed the implication that Stalin never used the foreign Communists for any important purposes is perhaps the most astonishing aspect of Professor Sharp's article.

In the 1920s Stalin's Chinese policy was openly run in double harness; diplomatic support for the Nationalist advance to the north was supplemented by an agreement of affiliation between the Chinese Communist Party and the Kuomintang, enabling the Communists to occupy influential political and military positions—an attempt no less serious for its ultimate total failure in 1927. In the 1930s, a variant of the same 'dual policy' was evident when Moscow supported the League and 'collective security,' while Communist parties in France and Spain pursued 'popular front' policies which soft-pedaled economic and social demands for the sake of influencing governmental foreign policy. In the Spanish case the Communists, aided by the Republicans' dependence on Soviet supplies, ended up in virtual control of the Republic on the eve of its final collapse.

Again during World War II Communists in the resistance movements and in the free Western countries were ordered to pursue the same tactics of social moderation and occupation of key positions as were practiced in China in the 1920s and Spain in the 1930s. Wartime military and political cooperation between 'Soviet China' and Chiang Kai-shek was urged in the same spirit, with considerable success. All these are the foreign policy methods of a state *sui generis*—a one-party state enabled by its ideology to make use of a disciplined international movement organized for the struggle for power. To compare them—and the secondary opportunities for infiltration and espionage which they offer in addition to their main political objectives—to the use of vague cultural influences like 'Hispanidad' is to show a notable degree of innocence.

Yalta—a Historic 'Misunderstanding'

The crucial example to illustrate the role of ideology in Soviet foreign policy, however, remains the history of the postwar division of Europe.

The writer is not concerned here with the political controversy over whether this division, as first laid down in the wartime agreements at Teheran and Yalta, was inevitable in the light of the military situation as seen at the time or whether the Western statesmen committed an avoidable mistake of disastrous dimensions. What matters in the present context is the different meaning attached by the Western and Communist leaders, in concluding these agreements, to the concept of 'spheres of influence,' and the consequences of this 'misunderstanding.'

That great powers are in a position to exert a measure of influence over their smaller neighbors and that they use this influence in one way or another to increase as far as possible their security against attack by other great powers is an experience general in the politics of sovereign states and unlikely to be superseded by any amount of declamation about 'equality of rights'; hence, the fact that the wartime allies, in drawing a military line of demarcation from north to south across the center of Europe, should have tried to agree about their postwar spheres of influence is, by itself, proof of realistic foresight rather than of morally reprehensible cynicism.

To Mr. Roosevelt and Mr. Churchill, however, these spheres of influence meant what they had traditionally meant in the relations of sovereign states—a gradual shading over from the influence of one power or group of powers to that of the other, a shifting relationship which might be loosely described in terms of 'percentages of influence,' ranging from 50/50 to 90/10. To the Soviets, 'spheres of influence' meant something completely different in the framework of their ideology—the ideology of the single-party state. To them there could be no securely 'friendly' government except a government run by a Communist party under their discipline, no sphere of influence but a sphere of Communist rule, no satisfactory percentage short of 100. Hence the consistent Soviet efforts, which began even before the end of the European war, to impose total control by Communist parties in every country on their side of the demarcation line—an effort that was finally successful everywhere but in Finland and Eastern Austria; hence also the indignant protests of the Western powers that the Soviets had broken the agreements on free elections and democratic development, and the equally indignant Soviet retort that they were only installing 'friendly governments' as agreed, that theirs was the truly 'democratic' system, and that they had kept scrupulously to the essential agreement on the military demarcation line.

A large section of Western opinion has concluded from this experience that agreements with the Soviets are useless in principle, because 'you cannot trust them'; and Professor Sharp's insistence on national interest as the sole key to Soviet policy is probably at least in part a reaction against this emotional and moralizing approach. In fact, any interpretation of the postwar experience overlooking the fact that the Soviets have, for reasons of national self-interest, kept to the 'self-enforcing' agreement on the demarcation line, would be as seriously one-sided as one overlooking the fact that they have, for reasons of ideology or party interest, broken every agreement on 'percentages' and free elections.

There is no need, however, to base future policy on either of two one-sided views equally refuted by experience. Nobody in the Western world has argued more powerfully against the 'moralizing' approach to foreign policy, and for a return to the give-and-take of diplomacy based on real interests, than George Kennan; yet in his recent Reith lectures, as before, he insists that the specific ideological distortion in the Soviet leaders' image of the world, far from being magically cured by a return to diplomacy, has to be taken into account continuously in judging which kinds of agreements are possible and which are not. After all, the peoples of Eastern Europe are still paying for the illusion of the West that the Soviet Union was a state like any other, pursuing its power interests without regard to ideology.

The Soviet Dilemma in Eastern Europe

If we now turn to interstate and interparty relations within the Communist camp, we seem at first sight to have entered an area where ideology is adapted quite unceremoniously to the changing requirement of practical politics. Lenin, having barely seized power in Russia and looking forward to an early spreading of Communist revolution, could talk airily enough about the sovereign equality and fraternal solidarity of sovereign 'socialist' states. Stalin, having determined after the failure of short-term revolutionary hope to concentrate on 'socialism in a single country,' came to regard international communism as a mere tool of Soviet power and to believe that revolutionary victories without the backing of Soviet arms were neither possible nor desirable; he wanted no sovereign Communist allies, only satellites, and he got them in postwar Eastern Europe.

The independent victories of the Yugoslav Communists at the end of the war and of the Chinese Communists in 1949 nevertheless posed the problem he had sought to avoid, and thus required a revision of policy and ideology. But, so one argument goes, the stubborn old man had lost the flexibility to accept the situation; he precipitated a needless quarrel with the Yugoslavs and generally prevented the necessary adjustment while he lived. His heirs, however, hastened to correct his mistakes and to put inter-Communist relations back on a basis of sovereign equality and diplomatic give-and-take, not only with China and Yugoslavia but, after some trial and error, with all Communist states. Or did they?

In the above 'common sense' account, not only the facts of the final phase are wrong; by deliberately neglecting the ideological aspect, it loses sight of all the real difficulties and contradictions which remain inherent in the situation. Because the Soviet Union is both a great power and a single-party state tied to an international ideology, it cannot be content either to oppress and exploit other Communist states or to come to terms with them on a basis of expediency ; it must act in a way that will ensure the ideological unity of the Communist 'camp' and its own authority at the center.

Stalin's insistence on making the 'leading role of the Soviet Union' an article of the international creed expressed not just the idiosyncrasies of a power-mad tyrant but his perception of one side of the dilemma—the risk that a recognition of the sovereign equality of other Communist states might loosen the solidarity of the 'camp' in its dealings with the non-Communist world and weaken the ideological authority of the Soviet party leaders, with ultimate repercussions on their position in the Soviet Union itself. . . .

The Reassertion of Soviet Primacy

Even Khrushchev and his associates, however, never intended to grant effective sovereign equality to the other Communist satellite regimes of Eastern Europe, which in contrast to Yugoslavia and China had come into being exclusively through the pressure of Soviet power; they merely had planned to make the satellite regimes more viable by reducing Soviet economic exploitation and administrative interference, while maintaining full policy control. In the one case in which not full sovereignty, but at least effective internal autonomy, was in fact granted—the case of Poland—the Soviet leaders were forced to act against their will as a result of open local defiance in a critical international situation. To say that the other East European participants in the Moscow twelve-party meeting of November 1957, or for that matter the participants from Outer Mongolia and North Korea, represented 'governments of sovereign countries' is to mistake the fancies of Communist propaganda for political facts. Nor do the facts bear out Professor Sharp's interpretation that the outcome of the conference showed the Soviet leaders' willingness to rely in their future relations with these 'sovereign governments' on the give-and-take of diplomacy. Rather, they confirm Mr. Carew Hunt's view that the need for a single center of international authority is inherent in the Soviet Communist Party's conception of its own role and in its ideology.

The real purpose of that conference was to exploit the recent successes of the Soviet Union as a military and economic power in order to restore the indispensable but lately damaged ideological authority of its leaders in the international Communist movement. The principle of 'proletarian internationalism,' that is, unity in foreign policy, had been recognized by all participants, including for the first time in many years the Yugoslavs, before the conference started. Now Moscow was aiming at the further recognition both of its own leadership role and of the need for doctrinal unity, a joint struggle against 'revisionism' on the basis of common principles, abolishing once and for all the heresy of 'polycentrism,' that is, the concept of a plurality of truly autonomous Communist movements.

Moscow's partial failure, therefore, does not indicate that the Soviets will be content with less than they demanded, but that conflict continues. The Soviet press has already reactivated its campaign against Polish 'revisionist' ideologies, insisting to Mr. Gomulka that revisionism is the chief internal danger in *all* Communist movements, including that of Poland. Moreover, the proposition defending a Communist party's autonomy in deciding its policy—conceded in principle at the time of Khrushchev's Belgrade visit and at the Twentieth CPSU Congress—is now singled out as a 'revisionist' heresy; increasingly the example of Imre Nagy is invoked to show how a demand for autonomy led him down a 'road' of 'betrayal' and finally 'counter-revolution.' While the methods of Khrushchev remain conspicuously different from those of Stalin, the logic of the one-party regime, which requires insistence on Soviet authority as a precondition for unity both in foreign policy and in ideological principles, has forced the present first secretary to reassert some of the very doctrines he rashly threw overboard in 1955-56.

Ideology on the Home Front

Ultimately, the need to fight 'revisionism' in Eastern Europe, even at the price of renewed difficulties with both Yugoslavia and Poland, arises from the need to strengthen the ideological defenses of the party regime in Russia itself. To admit that in Hungary the workers rose against a Communist government would call into question the basic identification of the ruling party with the working class—the fiction of the 'dictatorship of the proletariat.' To let Yugoslav propaganda for 'workers' management' pass unchallenged would confirm the implication that Soviet factories, having no workers' councils with similar rights, are managed in the interest not of the workers but of the privileged bureaucracy. To keep silent when the Poles proudly report the improvement of their agricultural yields since the dissolution of most of their collective farms would encourage Soviet peasants to dream of similar reforms. To condone the increased, if still limited, freedom of artistic, literary, and philosophical discussion now permitted in Poland and Yugoslavia would strengthen the demands of Soviet writers and scholars for similar freedom.

The obvious and intended implication here is that Soviet reconciliation with Yugoslavia and the near-revolutionary changes in Poland merely aggravated pressures for change which *already* existed in Russia itself. Thus the present account would be incomplete without some attempt to indicate, however sketchily, how ideological changes can be used as aids in interpreting the Soviet domestic scene as well as Kremlin foreign policy and bloc relations.

Earlier in the paper, reference was made to some of the basic tenets which seem inseparably bound up with the preservation and justification of a Communist one-party regime. But within this unchanging framework, considerable variations in detail have taken place in the history of the Soviet Union. The appearance or disappearance of one of these 'ideological variables' may be a valuable indicator of the kind of pressures which are exerted on the regime by the growing society and of the manner in which the leaders try to maintain control, sometimes by partly yielding to such pressures and seeking to canalize them, other times by a sharp frontal counterattack.

The 'Permanent' Revolution

Among the most revealing of these variables are Soviet doctrines dealing with the economic role of the state and with the 'class struggle' within Soviet society. The underlying reality is that a revolutionary party dictatorship, once it has carried out its original program and by this contributed to the emergence of a new privileged class, is bound to disappear sooner or later—to fall victim to a 'Thermidor'—unless it prevents the new upper class from consolidating its position by periodically shaking up the social structure in a 'permanent revolution from above.' The ideological expression of this problem is the classical doctrine that the dictatorship of the proletariat should gradually 'wither away' after it has succeeded in destroying the old ruling classes; thus, if continued dictatorship is to be justified, new goals of social transformation must be set and new 'enemies' discovered.

In the early period of Stalin's rule, the new 'goal' was the forced collectivization of the Russian countryside; the prosperous peasants —the kulaks—took the place of the former landowners and capitalists as the 'enemy class' which had to be liquidated. Summing up the achievement in 1937, in the *Short Course* on party history, Stalin wrote—or authorized the statement—that collectivization had been a second revolution, but a revolution carried out from above, by state power 'with the help of the masses,' not just by the masses from below. The ideological groundwork was thus laid for assigning the state a function of continuous economic transformation from above, in addition to its terminable revolutionary task.

The second step, also taken by Stalin in 1937, at the height of the great blood purge, consisted in proclaiming the doctrine that the 'class struggle' in the Soviet Union was getting more acute as the 'construction of socialism' advanced, because the 'enemies' were getting more desperate. This was the ideological justification of the purge itself; at the same time, it was a veiled indication that another revolution from above was in effect taking place, though Stalin refrained this time from trying to define the 'enemies' in social terms. In fact, what Stalin accomplished was a mass liquidation of both the bearers of the party's older revolutionary tradition—considered unsuited to the tasks of a bureaucratic state party—and of the most confident and independent-minded elements of the new privileged bureaucracy; the end result was a transformation of the party's social and ideological composition through the mass incorporation of the surviving frightened bureaucrats.

Stalin's final ideological pronouncement was contained in his political testament, *Economic Problems of Socialism*, published in 1952. In this work he mapped out a program for the further revolutionary transformation of Soviet society, with the taking over of kolkhoz property by the state as its central element.

Khrushchev's Formula for Perpetual Rule

The first major renunciation of these Stalinist ideological innovations was made by Khrushchev in his 'secret speech' at the Twentieth Congress. Apart from his factual disclosures concerning Stalin's crimes, he denounced Stalin's doctrine of the sharpening class struggle with societal progress as dangerous nonsense, calculated to lead to the mutual slaughter of loyal Communists after the real class enemy had long been liquidated. This statement affords the master clue to the puzzle of why Khrushchev made the speech: it was a 'peace offering' to the leading strata of·the regime in the party machine, army, and managerial bureaucracy alike—a response to their pressure for greater personal security. But by his concession Khrushchev re-opened the problem which Stalin's doctrine and practice had been in-

tended to solve, that of preserving and justifying the party dictatorship by periodic major shake-ups of society.

By the spring and summer of 1957, Khrushchev showed his awareness
of the practical side of the problem: his dismantling of the economic
ministries, breaking up the central economic bureaucracy and strengthening the power of the regional party secretaries, was another such
revolutionary shake-up. By November, he responded to the ideological
side of the problem. First he repeated, in his solemn speech on the
fortieth anniversary of the Bolshevik seizure of power, his rejection
of Stalin's doctrine of ever-sharpening class struggle and ever-present
enemies, thus indicating his wish to avoid a return to Stalin's terrorist
methods even while following his social recipe of permanent revolution.
Then he proceeded to develop his own alternative justification for
maintaining the party dictatorship—a unique argument which identified the strengthening of party control with the 'withering away
of the state' predicted by Lenin.

Reviving this formula for the first time since it was buried by Stalin,
Khrushchev explained that the military and police apparatus of the
state would have to be maintained, as long as a hostile capitalist
world existed outside, but he added that the economic and administrative functions of the state bureaucracy would henceforth be steadily
reduced by decentralization and devolution, thus strengthening the
organs of regional self-government and of national autonomy within
the various republics. At the same time, he quietly took steps to
strengthen the control of the central party secretariat—his own seat
of power—over the republican and regional party organs, thus following
the old Leninist principle that the fiction of national autonomy must
be balanced by the fact of centralized discipline within the ruling
party.

In short, the same aim of maintaining the social dynamism of the
party dictatorship and justifying its necessity, which Stalin achieved
by exalting the economic role of the state, is pursued by Khrushchev
by means of the reverse device of claiming that the state's economic
functions have begun to 'wither away.' On the face of it, this doctrinal
manipulation seems to reduce the role of ideology to that of ingenious
trickery, obscuring rather than reflecting the underlying social realities.
Yet, in fact, the very need for a change in the ideological argument

reflects the change that is taking place in the underlying social situation—the resistance against a return to naked terrorism, the growing desire for a lessening of state pressure and a greater scope for local activity. Whether in industry or agriculture, in the control of literature, or in relations with the satellite states, the basic conditions which the regime needs for its self-perpetuation have remained the same—but they can no longer be assured in the same way. That, too, is reflected in the variables of the official ideology.

The Relations of Ideology and Foreign Policy

BARRINGTON MOORE, Jr.

The rapid adjustment to the ways of international politics executed by Lenin in 1918 has been continued by Stalin down to the present day. So far, however, there are few if any signs of the development in the Soviet Union of an overt tradition that recognizes the role played by the balance of power in Soviet foreign policy. For the most part, the major shifts in the international distribution of power have continued to find their explanation in the familiar Leninist categories, at least insofar as the public speeches and writings of prominent Soviet leaders are concerned. The enemy of the moment has always been showered with strong Marxist invective concerning the evils of monopoly capitalism and imperialism. First, the major recipients were the Anglo-French plutocracies. Later, Nazi Germany held the limelight, to be replaced after the war by the United States. Intertwined with these Marxist themes have been others of a more strictly nationalist nature, which came to the fore after about 1934 and were most prominent during the years of war against Germany. Even then, as has sometimes been asserted, the Soviet Union did not fight the war under strictly nationalist slogans. Stalin's major wartime speeches had strong Marxist overtones, as in his references to Hitler and Himmler as the 'chained dogs of the German bankers,'[1] his references to Nazi imperialism, and

Reprinted by permission of the publishers from Barrington Moore, Jr., *Soviet Politics: The Dilemma of Power* (Cambridge, Massachusetts: Harvard University Press). Copyright, 1950, by the President and Fellows of Harvard College.

Professor Moore, of the Harvard University Department of Social Relations, is also the author of *Terror and Progress: U.S.S.R.* and other studies of modern dictatorship.

[1] Speech of May 1, 1942, in Stalin, *O Velikoi otechestvennoi voine Sovetskogo Soiuza* (4th ed.; Moscow, 1944), p. 48.

his distinction, based on Lenin, between aggressive wars and wars of liberation.[2]

The Impact of Experience on Behavior and Doctrine

Perhaps the most striking modification of Communist doctrine concerning international relations is the sharp toning down of revolutionary optimism. It is necessary to go back to 1929 to find any statement by a top Soviet leader to the effect that the proletarian revolution would take place in the near future. In that year Stalin spoke of strengthening the Comintern to help the working class prepare 'for impending revolutionary battles,'[3] although the Third International had actually adopted a defensive policy by this time. Some five years later, in 1934, Stalin declared that, as a result of the economic tendencies of imperialism, war "for a new redivision of the world" was the order of the day, and drew the conclusion that the coming conflict was "sure to unleash revolution" and to "jeopardize the existence of capitalism."[4] But by this time the expression of revolutionary optimism was very much less. Stalin conceded that the "masses of the people have not yet reached the stage when they are ready to storm capitalism," though he did add, somewhat lamely perhaps, that "the idea of storming it is maturing in the minds of the masses—of that there can hardly be any doubt."[5]

From this time onward Stalin refrained from making revolutionary predictions. Only relatively minor figures continued on rare occasions to make such statements. In 1939, at a Party congress, L. Mekhlis, head of the Red Army's political indoctrination and control apparatus, spoke about the 'liquidation of capitalist encirclement' and remarked that, should "the second imperialist war turn its point against the first socialist state in the world," the Red Army would carry the war to the enemy and "fulfill its internationalist obligations and increase the number of Soviet republics."[6] Such remarks, moreover, were con-

[2] Speech of November 6, 1941, *ibid.*, pp. 25, 31.
[3] "The Right Deviation," in Stalin, *Problems of Leninism* (11th ed.; Moscow, 1941), p. 252.
[4] "Report to the Seventeenth Congress," *ibid.*, pp. 476, 478.
[5] *Ibid.*, p. 477.
[6] *XVIII S"ezd VKP (b): Stenograficheskii otchët* (Moscow, 1939), p. 273.

fined to Party circles, while the propaganda directed to the country at large adopted a more nationalist and patriotic tone.[7]

The mention of the Red Army as the chief instrument of revolution indicates that the Soviets had begun to doubt very seriously that 'spontaneous' proletarian revolutions, even if assisted by Moscow, would succeed in parts of the world over which the Soviets exercised no direct control. The experience of the years following the Second World War may have confirmed this viewpoint. In the course of acrid correspondence with Tito before the Soviet-Yugoslav break became public, the Central Committee of the Russian Party declared: "It is also necessary to emphasize that the services of the French and Italian CPs [Communist Parties] to the revolution were not less but greater than those of the CPY [Communist Party of Yugoslavia]. Even though the French and Italian CPs have so far achieved less success than the CPY, this is not due to any special qualities of the CPY, but mainly because . . . the Soviet Army came to the aid of the Yugoslav people. . . . Unfortunately the Soviet army did not and could not render such assistance to the French and Italian CPs."[8]

Historicus, the anonymous author of a widely publicized article, "Stalin on Revolution,"[9] has made an exhaustive study of Stalin's writings and cites no prediction of revolution made later than 1934. Nevertheless, as he points out, many of the earlier documents with their fire-eating passages are reprinted and circulated widely today with the cachet of authority. From this fact, however, the conclusion cannot be drawn that the older ideas are still accepted as the basis for policy since a number of Lenin's more equalitarian writings, which are no longer taken seriously as a basis for policy, also receive wide circulation. Nor is it necessarily correct to assume that the Soviet leaders believe in some kind of regular ebb and flood in the revolutionary situation, since the ebb of revolutionary optimism in Soviet statements is much more marked than the flood. Even the present Marxist revival fails to draw overt revolutionary conclusions. However, the continued circulation of the older revolutionary symbolism, even though it does not

---

[7] D. Fedotoff White, *The Growth of the Red Army* (Princeton, 1944), p. 414.

[8] *The Soviet-Yugoslav Dispute* (London and New York, 1948), p. 51.

[9] *Foreign Affairs*, XXVII, No. 2 (January 1949), 175-214.

appear in current statements, may well be an indication that this point of view remains a latent one, which could reappear in a modified form under favorable circumstances. Such a recurrence of latent and temporarily discarded ideas has taken place under favoring circumstances on other occasions, such as in the years of forced collectivization and industrialization following the relaxation of the NEP.

The evidence concerning changes in officially promulgated doctrine is abundant; that concerning the actual beliefs of Soviet policy-makers is highly fragmentary. Nevertheless, enough data are available to permit tentative inferences.

There are several indications that the Leninist theses concerning imperialism, war, and revolution underwent skeptical scrutiny in high Soviet quarters as a consequence of the experiences of World War II. Stalin on several occasions during the war expressed complete disenchantment with the German working class, formerly the apple of the Comintern's eye, and was particularly bitter about its support of the Nazi attack on the Soviet Union. It is worth noting that this represents a wartime shift in Stalin's expressed opinions, since at the outbreak of the conflict he had told the Soviet people that they could count on allies among the German people.[10]

Other evidence on this point is contradictory. The contradictions may be accounted for by two hypotheses: first, that the Soviet leaders themselves were not sure of their position; and, secondly, that they tried to maintain the appearance of consistency before outsiders and even moderately high officials in their own bureaucratic hierarchy. In other European Communist parties there was lively discussion during the war about whether or not capitalism was really aggressive and expansionist.[11] It is unlikely that the Soviets, despite their generally stricter controls, could avoid raising the question among themselves.

[10] Speech of November 6, 1941, in Stalin, *O Velikoi otechestvennoi voine*, p. 14 ; Robert E. Sherwood, *Roosevelt and Hopkins: An Intimate History* (New York, 1948), p. 782. In August 1942 Stalin told Churchill, according to Sherwood (*Roosevelt and Hopkins*, p. 617), that German homes as well as factories should be bombed. Churchill replied that, though civilian morale constituted a military objective, hits on workers' homes were merely by-products of misses on factories.

[11] See the report by the Yugoslav Edward Kardelj, in *Pravda*, December 5, 1947. Kardelj later became a supporter of Tito.

The American correspondent Edgar Snow reports that the late Alexander Shcherbakov, Vice-Commissar of Defense and an alternate member of the Politburo, agreed in private conversation that capitalist assistance to the USSR constituted a "profound deviation from the development of history as foreseen in Lenin's work *Imperialism*." Snow also reports that P. F. Iudin, a prominent Russian economist and head of the State Publishing House, told him, "It is proved that there is nothing in Marxism which need prevent progressive capitalist countries from cooperating closely with the Soviet Union in the economic and cultural spheres."[12] The report is significant in suggesting the possibility that the 'deviation of the economist,' for which Eugene Varga was to suffer at a later date, owes its origin to the experience of the war. Iudin's remark, if reported correctly, goes much further than any statement for which Varga was later attacked.

It is also worth noting that such 'subversive' ideas were the chief targets of attack in the closed wartime indoctrination meetings of Party bureaucrats, if Victor Kravchenko's account of such affairs may be accepted. Ironically enough, Iudin turns up in Kravchenko's report as one of the attackers. He is quoted by the Soviet exile as telling the assembled Party officials that the Soviet "war partnership with the capitalist nations must not breed illusions. . . . The two worlds of capitalism and communism cannot forever exist side by side. *Kto kogo ?*— who will conquer whom?—remains the great question now as always. It represents the chief problem of the future."[13]

Such reports need not be dismissed because they are superficially contradictory. They agree on the point that is significant: that 'illusions' concerning the possibilities of collaboration with capitalism existed. And it is also understandable that Iudin, in the light of his position, should be given the task of laying down the line to those at the lower levels of the Kremlin hierarchy.[14]

[12] Snow, *People on Our Side* (New York, 1944), p. 341.

[13] Kravchenko, *I Chose Freedom* (New York, 1946), p. 424.

[14] There is at least one report of disbelief in the official doctrine from more recent times. According to *The New York Times*, March 28, 1948, James Carey, the anti-Communist secretary of the Congress of Industrial Organizations, asked Vasilii Kuznetsov, the Soviet trade-union leader, whether or not the latter believed that the European Recovery Program was the creation of agents of reaction and sup-

Though there may have been a certain amount of questioning of accepted doctrines during the war, subsequent events have revealed that the top Soviet policy-makers, as early as 1944, became convinced of the necessity of making a strong effort to reimpose at least outward conformity to the Leninist theories of imperialism. The energy with which this has been done and the extent to which it has been carried might be a further reflection of the degree to which these doctrines were questioned during the war. After the war a process of ideological purification was carried out in the natural sciences, philosophy, economics, and the arts. The Leninist view of the world was repeated with much energy and little variety.

The polarization of world power into the two majors centers, Washington and Moscow, together with the resulting competition between the Soviet Union and the United States, has created a situation in which doctrinaires on both sides of the Iron Curtain can easily find justification for their views. It is highly likely that certain Soviet leaders who retained their suspicions of the West during the war, but whose influence was partly diminished by the necessities of cooperating against a common enemy, found their advice taken more seriously as the postwar tensions became more serious. One may even guess that Zhdanov may have been the spearhead of this anti-Western revival in private, as he was in public. Among other reasons for the postwar ideological purification may be fear on the part of the Soviet leaders that the events of the war, including widespread personal contact of Russian occupation forces with nonsocialist cultures, have undermined mass belief in official doctrines and hence threatened support of the Communist elite. Such fears might even be tinged with worries about the effectiveness of one of the chief competing doctrines, the American version of liberalism. Stalin in 1941 told Harry Hopkins that Roosevelt and the United States had more influence with the common people of the world than any other force.[15] Although it is unlikely that he considers President Truman an equally charismatic force, Stalin may retain traces of his original attitude.

porters of Wall Street. Kuznetsov's reply was—in Carey's words—that "he didn't believe the stuff and knew those charges to be untrue."

[15] Sherwood, *Roosevelt and Hopkins*, pp. 342-43.

While it is reasonably certain that doubts have continued to arise in Kremlin circles concerning the applicability of specific points of Marxist doctrine, just as they arose in the past during the days of open polemics, it is probable that the top leaders have not abandoned the Marxist-Leninist categories for the ordering of experience. Foreign affairs are in all likelihood still seen through the Marxist prism, even though the reddish hues may not take up so prominent a portion of the spectrum. On general grounds, it might be anticipated that one consequence of political responsibility would be to produce among the Soviet leaders a cynical and manipulative attitude toward their own public symbolism. In the history of Nazi-Soviet relations between 1939 and 1941 there are a number of striking illustrations of this attitude. It is worth noting, however, that this evidence gives no clear indication of a cynical attitude toward any of the central assumptions of Leninist doctrine.

One of the incidents concerns Soviet efforts to construct a communiqué justifying the Nazi-Soviet partition of Poland in 1939. According to the German records, both Molotov and Stalin concerned themselves personally with this apparently minor task, an indication of the serious attention given by the Politburo to the proper manipulation of words and symbols. At one point Molotov wished to give a presentable motive for Soviet actions by the argument (among others) that the Soviet Union "considered itself obligated to intervene to protect its Ukrainian and White Russian brothers and make it possible for these unfortunate people to work in peace." In discussions with the Germans, Molotov conceded that the projected argument contained a note jarring to German sensibilities, but asked that the Germans overlook this trifle in view of the difficult situation in which the Soviet government found itself. "The Soviet government," the report of Molotov's conversation continued, "unfortunately saw no possibility of any other motivation, since the Soviet Union had thus far not concerned itself about the plight of its minorities in Poland and had to justify abroad, in some way or other, its present intervention."[16] The

---

[16] U.S. Department of State, *Nazi-Soviet Relations, 1939-1941: Documents from the Archives of the German Foreign Office*, ed. Raymond J. Sontag and James S. Beddie (Washington, 1948), p. 95.

next day the German ambassador submitted a draft of the joint communiqué to Molotov for approval. Stalin, when called on the telephone
by Molotov, stated that he could not entirely agree to the German
text, "since it presented the facts all too frankly," and instead wrote
out a new draft in his own hand.[17]

Stalin's willingness to cast overboard old symbols and adopt new
ones as the occasion requires is shown by his reported remarks at the
meeting with Ribbentrop and Molotov on the night of August 23, 1939.
The German account reads: "In the course of the conversation Herr
Stalin spontaneously proposed a toast to the Führer, as follows: "I
know how much the German nation loves its Führer; I should therefore
like to drink to his health."[18] Few other Communists at home or
abroad were able to make the change with a lighthearted toast.

The Impact of Doctrine on Behavior

Even though the Soviet Union has been compelled by the structure
of international power relations to adopt a diplomacy closely resembling
that of any other modern state, there remain a number of individual
characteristics attributable to the Marxist-Leninist tradition. The
familiar comparison between the behavior of states under balance-
of-power conditions and the dance has been referred to elsewhere. It
might be added that the Marxist-Leninist tradition affects the way
in which the Russian bear hears the music, and hence the way it executes
the steps. It must be realized, of course, that we are dealing here with
groups rather than individuals, and that a group's composition, in the
widest sense of the word, including its specific ideology, affects the way
in which it responds to situations facing it. Though the similarities
are greater than the differences, the United States, England, and other
great powers exhibit their own special traits in their responses to the
ever-changing balance of power.

The role of Marxist-Leninist ideology can be observed in the Soviet
response to the danger presented by German National Socialism,
particularly in its beginning stages. As has been seen, this factor
helped to delay the Soviets in adopting a policy hostile to the Nazis.

[17] *Ibid.*, p. 99.   [18] *Ibid.*, p. 75.

Similar factors were at work in slowing up the Soviet response to Japanese expansionism in the early thirties. Marxist ideas also contributed to the series of mutual suspicions that broke up the first anti-Nazi coalition with the Western powers at Munich. They played a part in the difficulties and frictions connected with maintaining the wartime coalition of the Big Three, and contributed to its subsequent disintegration. Furthermore, an important part of Soviet diplomatic technique—the utilization of the Communist parties and the promotion of a specific type of economic and social transformation of society—is clearly derived from the Leninist tradition as modified by subsequent experience.

It is not possible to determine with mathematical precision, of course, the exact contribution of Marxist ideology to Soviet behavior in Russia's relations with other powers. The evidence seems to indicate that Marxist doctrine has not made the Soviet Union join any coalition or abandon any alliance that it would not have joined or abandoned on grounds of simple national self-interest. Yet there are clear indications that in some cases Marxist ideology retarded the shift, while in others it speeded up the change.

To Marxist ideology may also be attributed some portion of that dynamic expansionism that has been characteristic of Soviet policy since 1939. The important question, however, is how much?

Russian expansion can be explained very largely without reference to Marxist ideological factors. For the most part, each step in Soviet expansion can be considered a logical move to counter a specific actual or potential enemy. The absorption of part of Poland, the Baltic states, and the Rumanian portion of Bessarabia and the war against Finland were part of Soviet efforts to keep pace with Germany's growing power and were directed specifically against the German threat. In the Second World War the Soviets could scarcely have permitted their Anglo-American partners to extend Western influence into all sections of the power vacuum created by the Axis defeat. It is clear, of course, that the Russians never had any such intentions, and they did their best to emerge from the conflict in as strong a position as possible, a policy also followed by Great Britain and at a somewhat later date by the United States. American expansion in both Europe and Asia has often been hesitant and reluctant. Nevertheless, the war ended with an American general in Berlin and another in Tokyo. This the Soviets could hardly afford to neglect. They enlarged and consolidated their own sphere of influence by ways that are made familiar in the daily headlines. In rivalries of this type it is futile to argue which contestant has aggressive intentions and which has peaceable aims, since each move in the struggle calls out its countermove from the opponent.

What, then, is there left for the Marxist ideological factor to explain? This much at least—the Marxist-Leninist tradition has made it very difficult to reach a *modus vivendi* with the Soviets, which the Americans have been genuinely anxious to do. A belief in the inherently aggressive tendencies of modern capitalism obviously excludes any agreement except an armed truce of undetermined duration. Likewise, the acceptance of Leninist theory makes it almost impossible to believe in the friendly intentions of American leaders. Even though the Soviets may accept the personal honesty of individual American leaders, as seems to have been the case in Stalin's relations with Harry Hopkins, they are likely to feel that this is a matter of little consequence, since objective factors will push any capitalist state into warlike adventures. By heightening their suspicions, the Marxist-Leninist tradition makes the Soviets much more prone to take the protective steps just reviewed and hence to aggravate existing tensions.

The role of ideology in Soviet expansionism may also be examined from a slightly different standpoint. With the victory of Soviet arms there has been a sharp resurgence of statements about the superiority of the Soviet version of socialism as a way of life. Although such statements serve specific domestic purposes, it would be rash to disregard them as evidence of a continuing belief that the Soviet system represents the wave of the future. It is probably a belief only distantly related to immediate tactical problems of everyday diplomacy. When Soviet diplomacy was on the defensive, such ideas were relatively unimportant. Now that the situation has altered so tremendously in favor of the USSR, it is highly probable that such beliefs have been imbued with new life. While it is difficult to point to specific incidents and illustrations, this aspect of Marxist doctrine may account for the persistence with which the Soviets search for weak spots in the positions of their diplomatic opponents. At the very least, it has probably helped them to refuse to admit defeat when their fortunes are low, and to press every advantage home when their fortunes are high.

As was seen in connection with other aspects of Leninist doctrine, under the impact of political responsibility, goals and tactics, means and ends, have become jumbled up with one another and have often tended to change places. The familiar thesis that the Soviets have pursued a single aim through flexible tactics will not withstand the test of comparison with the historical record. Even though the proletarian revolution may still be a latent goal in Soviet policy, after the victory of November 1917 it was increasingly regarded as a technique, and only as one technique among many, for strengthening the socialist fortress. Soviet policy in the satellite states has been a very carefully modulated effort to effect a social and economic transformation of these countries in order to render them more amenable to Soviet interests. Isaac Deutscher, Stalin's recent biographer, has pointed out how the instruments of revolution, the secret police and the army, have in these areas assumed the leading role, and has contrasted the new movement with the original revolutionary impulse that created these instruments.[19] The contrast reveals in concrete and dramatic form the transformation of revolution from a goal into a technique. The change is, to be sure, not a complete one. Soviet leaders acquire Communist virtue by extending the influence of the Kremlin to foreign lands, no matter how this is done. If there is any central goal behind the policy of the Soviet leaders, it is the preservation and extension of their own power, by any means whatever, rather than the spread of a specific social system or the realization of a doctrinal blueprint.

Some Prospects

During the postwar years the hostilities and tensions between East and West have increased, with but few and transient interruptions. Each measure taken by one of the contestants to strengthen its position has been rapidly followed by countermeasures on the other side in a continuing vicious circle. For those who value peace the major question is an obvious one: Can the vicious circle be broken at any point? Is

[19] *Stalin: A Political Biography* (New York and London, 1949), pp. 534, 554.

there any possibility of achieving a reduction in tension or in stabilizing the present distribution of power?

Before this question can be answered, it is necessary to know the answers to certain others. For example, it is necessary to know whether the Soviets are impelled by the dynamism of the vicious circle alone, or whether there are important internal forces in Russian society that by themselves, and independent of the balance of power, work to produce expansionist tendencies. In other words, has Soviet expansion during the past decade been primarily defensive, and would it come to rest if external threats were removed? Or is the world now witnessing a special variety of expansionism—Communist imperialism? The same general series of questions would have to be answered about the United States, but the analysis of this study must necessarily be confined to the Russian side of the equation.

Four considerations enter into the conclusion advanced by many that the Soviet system contains a number of internal expansionist forces impelling it to seek one conquest after another. It is often said that, because the USSR is an authoritarian state, its rulers need a continuous series of triumphs in order to maintain their power. The rulers of a dictatorship, it is claimed, cannot afford to rest on their laurels. Occasionally this type of argument is supported by a neo-Freudian chain of reasoning. It is asserted that the frustrations imposed upon the individual in modern society, especially under a dictatorship, tend to produce socially destructive impulses that have to be channeled outward against an external enemy if the society is not to destroy itself. The second line of argument, at a different level of analysis, emphasizes the indications of a strong power drive in Stalin's personality. Parallels can be drawn on this basis between his urge for new worlds to conquer and the political aspirations of Napoleon, Hitler, and others. A third line of reasoning points to various indications in Soviet statements and actions of an old-fashioned interest in territorial expansion that shows strong resemblances to traditional tsarist policy. The latter argument draws its reasoning from the facts of geography and history, emphasizing traditional Russian interest in warm-water ports, the long drive to the south and east, and similar matters. Under the fourth type of argument, Marxist-Leninist ideology is selected as a separate expansionist force. Persons who hold this view point out the messianic qualities of Marxist doctrine and the continuous need for struggle and victory that it generates.

Each of these arguments and hypotheses represents some portion of the truth. It might even be possible to reduce them to a single theoretical scheme—a task, however, that lies outside the scope of the present work. And before such a task could be undertaken, it is necessary to break the arguments down even more and point to a number of additional considerations and factors that operate to prevent further Soviet expansion. This may be done by examining the validity of each of the four arguments presented above.

Concerning the first point, that authoritarian states tend to be expansionist ones, it is necessary to express reservations and doubts on both general and specific grounds. The connection between the internal organization of a society and its foreign policy is a complex question that cannot yet be answered on the basis of simple formulas. Athens engaged in foreign conquest perhaps more than did warlike Sparta, and the Japanese, despite the militaristic emphasis of their society, lived in isolation for centuries until the time of their forced contacts with the West. To show that the authoritarian structure of any state is a source of expansionist tendencies, one would have to show the way in which these pressures make themselves felt upon those responsible for foreign policy. At this point the argument often breaks down, though there are cases where it can be shown that the rulers have embarked on an adventurous policy to allay internal discontent. But those at the apex of the political pyramid in an authoritarian regime are frequently freer from the pressures of mass discontent than are the responsible policy-makers of a Western democracy. They can therefore afford to neglect much longer the dangers of internal hostilities. Furthermore, modern events reveal the weakness of the argument that a warlike policy is the result of hostilities toward outsiders among the individuals who make up the society. In the days of total war it is necessary to use all sorts of force and persuasion, from propaganda to conscription, to make men and women fight. To regard war as primarily the expression of the hostilities of rank-and-file citizens of various states toward one another is to fly in the face of these facts.

In the case of the Soviet Union, the Nazi-Soviet Pact of 1939 shows that the rulers of modern Russia had no difficulty in disregarding the hostilities to Nazism that had been built up during the preceding years, and that in this respect they enjoyed greater freedom for prompt adjustment of disputes than did other countries. Both totalitarian partners were able to keep mass hostility under control as long as it suited purposes and plans based on the configuration of international power relationships.

In addition, those who conclude that external expansion is necessary for the survival of the Soviet leaders overlook the fact that war places a severe strain on the Party's control over Russian society. War tends to raise the role of the military forces and to diminish by comparison the power of the Party. While no insoluble problems arose in this respect in the last war, these considerations have to be taken into account. The past war showed that Party doctrines had to give way, at least in part, to nationalist slogans and other viewpoints of a somewhat disruptive nature. To be sure, the situation would be different in a war in the near future, since the Soviets would not be troubled with capitalist allies and would undoubtedly pose as the victim of imperialist attack. Nevertheless, to win internal support unwanted concessions might have to be made.

An acceptable modification of the argument that the authoritarian nature of the present Soviet regime is a source of an aggressive and expansionist foreign policy may be found along the following lines. It is probable that a certain amount of hostility toward the outside world is an essential ingredient in the power of the present rulers of Russia. Without the real or imagined threat of potential attack, it would be much more difficult to drive the Russian masses through one set of Five-Year Plans after another. Yet it does not seem likely that this hostility is in turn a force that reacts on the makers of Russian foreign policy. Their power can be more easily maximized by the threat of war than by war itself—a precarious enough situation. Nor is there evidence that mass hostility is in any way cumulative or sufficient to force the Soviet leaders into an aggressive policy. There are a number of devices for draining off internally generated hostility into channels other than those of external expansion. Military and combative sentiments, aroused for specific purposes, can be and have been directed into the socially productive channels of promoting a conquest of the physical environment.

There are good grounds for concurring in the conclusion that a drive for power in Stalin's personal make-up has been and will remain a very significant element in Soviet policy as long as his leadership is maintained. Although biographical data on Stalin are scanty, it is probable that conclusions concerning this trait will stand the test of further impartial investigation. The way, however, in which this trait displays itself has important implications. It is difficult to accuse Stalin of being rash or foolhardy. One has but to contrast the bombastic speeches and writings of Hitler with the cold pedantic logic of Stalin, illuminated by rare flashes of heavy sarcasm, to get important clues to the differences in their personalities. Stalin has nearly always managed to keep his aggressive impulses and his drive for power under rigid control, for which he has been well rewarded in the defeat of his domestic and foreign enemies. He has arrived at his most important decisions cautiously and empirically, testing the political ground at each step of the way. The major decisions of collectivization and industrialization were reached only after numerous tentative trials. Once decisions have been reached by Stalin, he has not failed to display sufficient energy to carry them through. And like Lenin, though in a lesser degree, he has shown the ability to back out of an impossible situation without serious damage to his forces. Thus it is unlikely that Stalin would plunge the Soviet Union into war when the chances of victory were highly problematical.

Those who emphasize the continuity of the Russian historical tradition and the importance of Russia's geographical position in the determination of Soviet foreign policy are correct insofar as Russia's place on the globe and her past relations with her neighbors set certain limitations and provide certain readily definable opportunities for Russian foreign policy. In other words, an expansionist Soviet foreign policy can follow only certain well-defined lines of attack. It may have Persia, China, or Germany as its major object of infiltration, but Latin America and the Antarctic are much more remote objectives.

The reappearance of old-fashioned Russian territorial interests in various parts of the globe has been associated with the revival of Russian strength from the low ebb of revolution, intervention, and civil war. It may be suspected that the early idealist statements of the Bolshevik leaders about the abandonment of tsarist imperialism were inspired not only by Marxist doctrine but were also made on the grounds that they were the only possible tactics to follow in Russia's weak condition. Now that the proletarian revolution has a territorial base, it is understandable that attempts should be made to combine the interests of the two, and that some of the results should show marked similarities to tsarist policy. Furthermore, the possibility may readily be granted that the present rulers of Russia are somewhat influenced by the model of tsarist diplomacy. But the driving forces behind any contemporary Soviet expansionism must be found in a contemporary social situation. Historical and geographical factors may limit the expression of an expansionist drive. They cannot be expansionist forces in their own right.

Turning to the ideological factor, it has already been noted that the messianic energies of communism can be, and at times in the past have been, very largely directed toward tasks of internal construction. The creative myth of Leninism,' to use Sorel's suggestive term, involves the building of factories in desert wastes and the creation of a more abundant life for the inhabitants of the Soviet Union. One must agree, however, that a creative myth, if it is effective, is usually an article for export as well as for domestic consumption. Those who really believe in socialism usually believe it is necessary for the world as a whole, just as do the more emotional believers in the virtues of democracy and the four freedoms. There remains, however, another important aspect of Soviet doctrine which sets at least temporary limits to its expansionist qualities. It is a cardinal point in the Leninist-Stalinist doctrine that a retreat made in good order is not a disgrace. The Soviet creative myth does not have a 'victory or death' quality—there is no urge to seek a final dramatic showdown and a *Götterdämmerung* finale. When faced with superior strength, the Soviets have on numerous occasions shown the ability to withdraw with their forces intact. Although the withdrawal may be followed by a renewal of pressures elsewhere, it may be repeated once more if superior forces are again brought to bear.

The foregoing considerations are enough to suggest the complexity of the problem of interpreting the expansionist forces contained in the Soviet system. They should make us wary of dramatically pessimistic conclusions to the effect that the Soviet leaders, propelled by forces beyond their control, are marching to a world holocaust. But they give many more grounds for pessimism than for optimism concerning the probability of preventing a further increase in tension in the power relationships of Moscow and Washington. Even though Soviet expansionism of the past decade may be explained as primarily an adaptation to the changing balance of power, such an explanation by no means precludes the possibility, perhaps even the probability, that the series of adaptations and 'defensive' measures taken by the United States and the USSR may culminate in war.

The situation in which the two major powers stand at uneasy guard, carefully watching each other's activities and countering one another's strengthenings in all portions of the globe, contains internal forces of its own that could lead to a violent explosion. That it has not done so already is an indication that both sides are still making their political calculations largely in defensive terms, inasmuch as neither antagonist is committed by its own system of values to war for war's sake.

The resurgence of another major power, such as Germany or Japan, that constituted a threat to both the United States and the Soviet Union could bring about a drastic alteration in this situation. There is nothing in recent Russian actions to indicate that the Soviet Union would be unwilling to seek once more a common alliance with the West to ward off threatened danger. But the present polarization of power itself makes any such alliance an improbable eventuality. The struggle between Washington and Moscow has as one of its consequences the partition of Germany and American control of Japan. So long as this struggle continues, it is unlikely that either Germany or Japan can regain the semblance of an independent foreign policy. Nor is it likely, so long as modern warfare requires a powerful industrial base, that some other state will emerge in the near future to challenge the two giants of today. Should there be indications that some weak state might be developing a technology with which it would be possible to become a power in its own right, steps would probably be taken at once to gain control of this new resource by one or both of the existing great powers. In this manner the existing balance of power tends to inhibit any change in its structure or destructive potentialities.

If the prospects of fundamental improvement in American-Russian relations are dim indeed, they are not necessarily hopeless. One of the few warrants for hope is the Communist tradition that retreat from a situation that threatens the power of the leaders is no defeat. If, as seems most likely, neither side is yet actively seeking war, there is still room for the reduction of tension through the familiar devices of highly skilled diplomacy. To succeed, this diplomacy would have to part company with the parochial moralism that has characterized much American negotiation and free itself from the miasma of dogmatic suspicion likely to become chronic on the Russian side. Whether modern diplomats can escape from the pressures engendered by their own societies remains to be seen.

The Politburo and the West

NATHAN LEITES

The Politburo to which Mr. Leites refers is the present Presidium of the Communist Party of the Soviet Union. The term Politburo was abandoned at the Nineteenth Party Congress in 1952.

In reference to his "guesses about contemporary world politics" which are offered in the following study, Mr. Leites cautions the reader that almost every statement "should, if one wanted to be precise, contain a 'probably,' if not a 'possibly,' often also a 'largely' or 'mainly.' In order to simplify the exposition I shall omit words of this kind. The spurious air of certainty which this procedure will create seems preferable to the constant repetition of admissions of a partial ignorance which is obvious enough in view of the known secretiveness of the Soviet rulers."—A. D.

Politics Is a War

It is already difficult to recall how confidently the West expected the onset of an era of international calm at the end of the Second World War. To many it came as a shock that the Soviet government did not share this belief, but rather appeared to take it for granted that politics abhors a vacuum of strife. As some major conflicts of the preceding years had been 'liquidated' by the surrender of one side, other lines of cleavage would, naturally (to the Politburo), become more prominent. The new struggle had, of course, to be between the three great powers that were left, more specifically, between the 'Anglo-Americans' and the Politburo itself.

Published as Prologue to the author's book *A Study of Bolshevism* (Glencoe, Illinois, 1953).

Professor Leites, of Yale University, who is known for his studies of the Soviet Union as well as for his work on modern France, wrote *A Study of Bolshevism* while with the Social Science Division of the RAND Corporation.

All this seemed quite evident to the Soviet rulers in the context of their basic beliefs about politics. Once communism has achieved and consolidated victory 'on a world scale,' social life, they predict, will be harmonious. But before that time the opposite is true: for the present and the operationally relevant future, it is an illusion—which in effect serves the *status quo*—to believe that in domestic or in international relations there can, essentially, be anything between 'classes' and between states but utter incompatibility of interests and fierce conflict of wills. In some cases—for example, between various 'layers' of the 'bourgeoisie' and between various states of the bourgeois world—a conflict between two contestants need not be such that only one of them, in the long run, can survive. Conflicts may have more limited objectives: the issue of the two world wars (apart from the involvement of the Soviet Union) was the 'redistribution of the world' among various 'imperialist' powers, as their relative strength changed because of the 'uneven development' of world capitalism. However, in other cases conflicts are of a nature which is described by the question: "Who (will destroy) Whom?" This is the kind of conflict which prevails between the Party and the rest of the world.

It is a central Bolshevik belief that enemies strive not merely to contain the Party or to roll it back but rather to annihilate it. This belief was strong both in those early phases of Bolshevism and in those recent times (say, from 1944 to 1948) when many participants in, and·observers of, world politics took a less extreme view of the prevailing situation. On the other hand, if the Party acts on the belief that its enemies are annihilative, it is apt to render that belief less unrealistic by the very reactions which its conduct evokes. If imaginary enemies are treated as enemies, they are apt finally to become real enemies.

The dogma that the hostile arms of enemies are unlimited appears to Bolsheviks as so self-evident and as so fully confirmed by the course of events that they do not feel a need to re-examine it. (This is a characteristic Bolshevik attitude, the distinctive Bolshevik blend of empiricism and dogmatism.) Indeed, the belief we are discussing is so conceived that its factual re-examination by Bolsheviks would be most difficult: while enemies at all times strive to annihilate the Party, they proceed, on the whole, only as far in this direction as 'objective conditions' permit at any given moment. Also, they often use devious and hidden means. Hence, any manifest enemy behavior—extreme enmity, mild hostility, apparent neutrality, or an effective alliance with the Party—is felt as quite compatible with the enemy's destructive designs. Just like the Party, the enemy is capable of biding his time and of 'taking into account' the exigencies of the 'concrete' situation. Just like the Party, he knows how advantageous it often is to arrange a public façade which is quite at variance with one's true face.

As long as the question "Who-Whom?" has not been decided by the consolidation of world communism—and it cannot be decided short of that—the world is, basically, in a state of high tension. If the Party were to forget this, it would not reduce the tension but merely render certain its own annihilation in the further course of the conflict. To Bolsheviks, high tension is the normal state of politics. They do not experience it as something that just cannot go on, but rather as something that will necessarily persist. What Westerners call a 'real agreement' seems to Bolsheviks inconceivable. It is often predicted in the West that if particular issues—the Austrian treaty for instance—could be settled with the Politburo, an easing of the overall tension might ensue. For Bolsheviks, this does not follow. There might be less 'noise,' but the basic situation—the presence of two blocs attempting to annihilate each other—would be unchanged. The only 'real settlement' is that by which one of the contestants is utterly destroyed; before this end is reached all apparent 'solutions' (for example, an agreement on Germany in 1952) are but weapons in the continuing conflict. What a Western statesman called "local and limited settlements of outstanding issues" are usually possible and often required; but a 'general agreement to live and let live'—'toward' which this statesman proposed to 'work' by 'local and limited settlements'— is inconceivable. The Party is obliged to strive for the annihilation of its enemies, a necessary condition of the fulfillment of its mission. Were it prepared to be delinquent in this, it would merely lay itself open to annihilation by its enemies: they would not imitate the Party's delinquency but rather 'utilize' it to deprive of existence a party which had ceased to strive for victory. There are only two stable situations: being dead and being all-powerful. If one is less than fully determined to gain power over the world, one chooses annihilation, whether one knows it or not. Any 'four-power settlement' of the German 'problem,' for instance, will not eliminate the possibility, to put it mildly, of Germany's becoming part of an enemy bloc (unless such a 'settlement' were to transfer all of Germany to the Soviet sphere). But even if there were no such danger, an arrangement about Germany (or any other particular issue) would not eliminate the 'capitalist encirclement' of the Soviet domain. There is only one way to do this—to replace this 'encirclement' by the 'socialist encirclement' of the 'capitalist' world. Even when this has been achieved, the Party cannot relax its efforts on pain of risking annihilation. It must apply the principle of pursuit: destroy the beaten, but still existing, enemy in order to prevent a possible reversal in the relationship of forces.

Thus, whether the atmosphere of international relations seems to become calmer and more harmonious or more agitated and tense, the basic structure of the relations between the Soviet domain and the rest of the world remains at all times indicated by the question, Who will destroy Whom? Bolshevik leaders must be oriented on this unchanging core—which it is their privilege to perceive clearly— rather than on the changing surfaces which absorb the attention of 'vulgar' and ephemeral politicians. They must yield neither to panic in what seems to be a crisis nor to complacency in what seems to be a condition of stability. In particular, they must not permit themselves to be 'lulled to sleep' by the appearance of calm with which an enemy may camouflage his preparations for an attack. Bolsheviks perceive the situation at all times as acutely tense. Whenever there is no 'hot' war between the Party and the world, there is always a cold war, in which it may or may not be practicable and useful to distract attention from the fact that it is only by the political death of one of the contestants that the situation can really be changed.

However, in the Bolshevik view, one cannot predict what particular forms this basic conflict will assume. On the one hand, Bolshevik leaders despise those who do not perceive the underlying tension in all politics (particularly in all politics involving the Party—and which kind of politics does not, in the mid-twentieth century?). On the other hand, they have contempt for those romantics who assume that a conflict which is basically about life and death is therefore bound to lead to a third world war in the near future. The Party must be utterly flexible in the choice of its strategy and tactics, and must keep an entirely open mind about the shapes which the basic conflict of the century may yet assume. Prepared to use quite undramatic and slow procedures, it must envisage the possibility of a protracted era of apparent stability ('coexistence') in international affairs. In this case the Party, as well as its enemies, would of course continuously calculate whether they should use drastic means against each other, that is, start a total war. However, in view of the prevailing relationships of strength, they would again and again decide against such a change of method. Still, some day—any day—a change in estimated relative strength might lead either one of the two parties to make the calculated decision to proceed to all-out attack. In any case, the cold war will not 'automatically' lead to a hot war; it will not 'erupt' into an irrepressible large-scale use of weapons, as Western observers often assume. To the Politburo there is a perfectly normal *modus vivendi* between itself and the West now; there is always a *modus vivendi* between two parties engaged in a life-and-death struggle until one has been annihilated by the other.

Push to the Limit

At the end of the Second World War the power commanded by the Politburo was very much greater than it had been before that war broke out or before the Soviet Union became involved in it. Hence there were many in the West who expected the Soviet government to concentrate its energies for a number of years on reconstruction and consolidation in the expanded Soviet area, and to accept *status quo* elsewhere. Instead, the Politburo initiated without delay a variety of policies designed to expand its power yet further. In the years following the end of the Second World War the Politburo established a very high degree of control over almost all of the areas occupied by the Soviet Army in 1944-45 (the exceptions were Finland, Eastern Austria, and—involuntarily— Yugoslavia); and the Politburo or its agents undertook various kinds of offensives—with varying degrees of success—against West Berlin, northern Greece, northern Iran, Burma, Malaya, Indochina, the Philippines, China, Tibet, South Korea. At

various times agents of the Politburo in France and Italy—the leader-
ships of the local Communist parties—seemed to approach the seizure
of power or at least to occupy positions from which they could inhibit
vital activities of the existing governments; and they often threatened
to do just that. After the break between Moscow and Belgrade the
Politburo and its Hungarian, Bulgarian, Rumanian, and Albanian agents
committed many acts—verbal and others—which seemed to presage
an attack on Yugoslavia.

Why were those Western observers proved wrong who in 1945
predicted a *status quo* policy on the part of the Soviet government?
What were the motivations behind its expansionist policy?

Western interpretations of the conduct of the Politburo in foreign
affairs sometimes stress the limited nature of its objectives (is there
not, one asks, a continuity between tsarist and Soviet policy?), and
sometimes an unlimited goal: the world. There are those who believe
that its motivation is essentially offensive—to achieve the expansion
of Politburo power all over the world—and those who maintain that
the Soviet government is chiefly concerned with the defense of its
domain against annihilative enemies. There is, I believe, a part of
truth in every one of these interpretations. Where they may be incorrect is in opposing each other as incompatible, while the operational
code of the Politburo actually involves a blend of all these seemingly
contrasting tendencies.

The Politburo does aim at the world-wide expansion of its own
power, as the necessary condition of the world-wide establishment of
'communism.' Bolsheviks deny that a conflict between power and
ideology is conceivable: the salvation of mankind by communism
presupposes the search for maximum power by the Party at any
moment before the complete realization of communism (when all
power vanishes); Bolshevik doctrine 'arms' the Party with principles
guiding its search for more power. What Westerners may regard as
the substantive merits of a particular policy are to Bolsheviks irrelevant; a policy is only, and fully, justified by the increment of power
which it procures for the Party.

However, the Politburo also believes that its very life—the very
life of the great instrument for the realization of communism—remains
acutely threatened as long as major enemies exist. Their utter defeat

is a sheer necessity of survival. Also, while the Politburo views itself as the agent of 'gigantic' changes, it feels obliged to achieve the next practicable step at any given moment; and this step may be quite small, or may coincide with a traditional objective of pre-Soviet policy. Thus Politburo policies are both offensive and defensive, limited and unlimited in objective.

An advance has a defensive rationale for Bolsheviks not only because the politically dead enemy is the only safe enemy, but also because it improves one's defensive position in relation to the enemy's next onslaught. By advancing as far as possible one denies to the enemy as many assets as possible; the enemy will occupy any temporary no man's land unless one anticipates him. By doing so one also increases the resources with which one will have to withstand his next assault. One procures for oneself—for example, by the acquisition of more 'glacis' areas—additional leeway to engage in retreat, if that should become necessary. As Bolsheviks must look far ahead and remain aware of the recurrence of 'ebbs and flows' in history, a present advance may be thought of, in part, as an aid in mastering future setbacks by retreats. It is thus both on behalf of survival and of victory that the Party must always mobilize its entire energy to transform into a 'reality' each existing 'opportunity' for advance.

It has often been observed that there is a strong 'determinist' streak in the Bolshevik view of history: the course of events is held to be determined by the factors discovered in 'Marxism-Leninism.' This belief, however, is balanced by strong 'indeterminist' conceptions, which reinforce the Party's ever-present sense of obligation to push as far ahead as possible. According to Bolshevik doctrine, in fact, the direction and end of a major historical development (the transition from capitalism to communism, for instance) are predictable, but the rate of development and its particular paths are not. At many junctures more than one outcome is 'objectively possible.' 'Objective conditions' create certain 'opportunities' for the Party; it cannot be predicted whether the Party will succeed in 'utilizing' them, transforming them into 'realities.' But the Party is obliged to attempt to do just that, and thereby not only to improve its chances of survival but also to shorten the road to total victory. Bolsheviks should be equanimous in the face of the prospect of a very long path to the goal; but this is required only because it is taken for granted that the Party will use all its energy to shorten that path. 'History' is infinitely more powerful than men who can take part in its power by actively discovering and pursuing its necessities (while they will expose, and suffer for, their impotence if they oppose these necessities). But History chooses, as it were, not to exercise its power in 'details.' Hence men can, within fairly wide limits, determine the cost and duration of an 'inevitable' social change, such as the transition to communism.

After the outcome of a situation which permits of a variety of 'solutions' has been decided, it becomes possible to explain that outcome by the 'relationship of forces' which brought it about. But this relationship of forces can become known only in the very process of a 'struggle' which is carried out 'to the end.' Action begins with an incomplete knowledge about the outcome; it is action itself that will increase knowledge. In initiating an action the Party must be concerned only with making sure that the aims it chooses are 'objectively possible.' It should then exercise maximum energy to attain them rather than make the impossible and unnecessary attempt to predict when and to what degree they will be reached. The Party should remain aware both of the possibility that certain objectives will be fully achieved within a certain time-span, and that they will not. Once it is clear that the aims chosen are 'objectively possible,' they should not be 'pared down' even if they prove difficult to attain.

It is thus only by 'struggle' that any advance can be achieved. Gains must be conquered in fierce conflict with those who hitherto possessed the desired objects.

In insisting on this, Bolsheviks oppose the temptation to expect outside groups—enemies—to bestow favors on one from good feelings, 'just for the sake of one's beautiful eyes.' As there is usually no ground of common interest between the Party and outside groups, the enemy's ostensible favors to the Party are apt to be based on intents to damage it in covert and indirect ways. The Party must never permit itself to fall into such a trap—an attitude which must have played an important role in the Politburo's reaction to the Marshall Plan in 1947.

In requiring that the Party always push to the limit of its strength, Bolsheviks also combat the disposition to rest, as it were, on one's power potential: every ounce of available power must be immediately utilized to expand the Party's domain. Bolsheviks seem obscurely afraid of falling into the trap of believing that there are superior interests to which those of the Party might have to be sacrificed; they affirm that such a situation is inconceivable. They seem equally apprehensive of the danger of being weak—from fear or passivity or complacency—in pursuing one's interests, and require a total, unceasing effort to this end. The Party must not yield to the temptation of relaxing its pressure once it has made an advance. On the contrary, it must view any concession made by the enemy—even a trivial one—as an indication that more, and perhaps more important, advantages can be gained by unrelenting exertions. The probable penalty for violating the principle of pursuit is, as usually in the Bolshevik view of the world, annihilation.

These strong motives for always pushing to the limit tend to make Bolsheviks underestimate the undesired consequences of such conduct. One might argue that if the Politburo had been able to tolerate the existence of a power vacuum in South Korea in 1950, the 'relationship of forces' between the Soviet and the American 'blocs' (to think in Bolshevik terms) in 1952 would have been more favorable to the Soviet Union than it actually was: without the Politburo's insistence on transforming all 'opportunities' into 'realities' of expansion, the military strength and the cohesion of its enemies would have been much lower. The impact of the Politburo on its enemies was thus such as to decrease the divergence between what they actually were and what the Politburo believed them to be. As the Politburo, having gained in power, refused to gain in realism about its environment, it became to some extent capable of remaking that environment in the image of its dogma.

It is very difficult for the Politburo to perceive the processes which I have just described. It does recognize the possibility of 'provoking' the enemy to all-out attack. But it cannot believe that what it regards as a normal mode of political conduct—advancing until you come up against prohibitive obstacles—will affect the broad policy lines of the 'Anglo-American' enemy. How could, they must ask themselves, the elevation of an already dominant Czechoslovak Communist Party to full power in 1948 change the policies of Washington, which had agreed to the presence of the Soviet Army in Czechoslovakia in 1945? Washington, after all, could hardly imagine that Moscow would indefinitely tolerate the presence of enemies—non-Communist parties—within its domain! Similarly, why should Washington greatly change its rate of armament because of the entry of forces controlled by the Politburo into South Korea, an area which the United States had evacuated, physically and in public delimitations of its sphere of vital concern?

The Politburo is thus not given to advances which would be expedient only if one succeeded in exercising an indirect influence on the enemy's actions. Viewing their big enemies to a large extent in their own image and having a deep horror of being manipulated as well as a fierce determination that this catastrophe shall never happen, Bolsheviks are reluctant to base their conduct on the assumption that they can make their major enemies succumb to this terrible danger. To proceed on such an assumption is reckless. Hence it is, for instance, improbable that the invasion of South Korea was undertaken mainly as a device to induce Washington to divert large parts of the American armed forces to a theater unimportant in itself. Probably it was, as I suggested above, simply a case of moving into a power vacuum.

In doing this—generally, in accomplishing a feasible advance—there must be neither procrastination nor precipitation. On the one hand the Party must be able to bide its time indefinitely. On the other hand it must act as soon as a certain move becomes possible. It is forbidden to defer an advance which is feasible now (though difficult) in the necessarily uncertain expectation that it might become easier later. One must never rely on the continued availability of present opportunities, but rather 'utilize' each as soon as it presents itself. When in 1951 the military strength of NATO increased, some Western observers believed that the Politburo might decide to invade western Europe, as it saw its ability to do so slipping away. But if in the Soviet view such an ability existed before the rearmament of the NATO countries, the Politburo would have moved against western Europe between 1945 and 1950—even if it had then believed that a delay might reduce the cost of incorporating that area. The Politburo's question for any major operation is whether it is required or impermissible (for the Bolshevik mind there is little in between) rather than whether it is tough or easy.

It Pays To Be Rude

In the spring of 1952 the Politburo made various moves which Western observers viewed as parts of a 'peace offensive.' Stalin used vaguely conciliatory words to a group of American editors and to the Indian ambassador; offers to increase Soviet foreign trade were proferred at a conference which was kept rather free of attacks on the world outside the Soviet domain; such attacks decreased slightly in Soviet communications at large (but the campaign charging the United States with the use of bacteriological weapons in the Korean War continued). The dominant Western reaction was skeptical. Some voices were hopeful; they predicted 'real' Soviet concessions, in Korea and Austria, for instance. Others were fearful; they viewed the partial change in the public tone of the Politburo as a danger to the rate of Western rearmament and the degree of Western cohesion. But most spokesmen of political groups near to the Western governments refused to take the pleasing nuances in the public Soviet attitude at their face value. The long record of Soviet rudeness had increasingly limited the impact of the interludes of partial moderation which the Politburo introduced from time to time (it is difficult to say in what particular circumstances).

During the critical years of the Soviet-German war, 1941-43, the Politburo had, it is true, instituted what came near to being a taboo on public attacks against its allies. This was an expedient policy: that the Soviet government seemed to have become less unfriendly toward the West reinforced the willingness of the Western peoples and governments to comply with Soviet demands as to how the war should be conducted and concluded. Nevertheless, when Soviet defeat seemed averted and victory increasingly probable, a hostile note toward the outside world began to appear in the public behavior of the Soviet government. Very early in 1944 the Soviet press and radio alleged on one occasion that the British were attempting to secure a negotiated peace with Germany. In the winter of 1945 Stalin sent personal communications to Roosevelt in which he charged the Western Allies with an attempt to deceive and damage the Soviet Union in negotiating the surrender of enemy forces in Italy. One year later the Politburo initiated a prominent campaign of words against the outer world, and particularly its 'Anglo-American' center. True, the distinctive revolutionary terminology of Bolshevism, which had been toned down in public statements since the middle thirties, did not reappear. But the non-Stalinist world was now violently attacked in the name of conventional symbols such as 'peace.' And now the Soviet government, which had on the whole exercised great verbal restraint in international affairs between 1921 and 1941, took direct responsibility for these attacks. Hostile propaganda was accompanied by a variety of damaging acts, ranging from restrictive measures against Western diplomats through the imprisonment of citizens of Western countries to the siege of West Berlin and the invasion of South Korea. Though there were between 1946 and 1952 some partial and brief reductions in the level of attack against the West—as I mentioned at the beginning of this discussion—that level rose to heights quite unprecedented for 'peace.'

The publicly expressed hostility of the Soviet government influenced the policies of other powers toward the Politburo. It became easier for Western policy-makers who wanted to carry out a policy of 'containment' to secure public consent for the resulting burdens (and for what often appeared to be the implied risks) than it would have been had the Politburo continued the soft tone of the first half of the war period. In this fashion the Politburo unwittingly restricted its opportunities for further expansion.

Actually, the Soviet government was during these years mainly engaged in the consolidation of the domain which, it felt, it had acquired by the advance of the Soviet Army and the agreements of Yalta and Potsdam. Besides, it was trying rather cautiously to advance further so that it could determine the point at which the enemy would impose prohibitive obstacles. However, the tone of its words and symbolic acts (for example, the trials of Western nationals) greatly reinforced the emerging Western belief that the policy of the Politburo was recklessly offensive. Suppose the Soviet government had enhanced, rather than discontinued, the (very) relative friendliness toward the West which it had shown in 1941-43; suppose it had abstained from such blatant offensives as those against northern Iran, West Berlin, and South Korea, but that it had executed its other policies which, as a whole, were of much greater importance than these particular sallies (the restoration and development of Soviet economic and military strength; the consolidation of control over the newly acquired areas in central and eastern Europe; advances by proxy in Greece, Burma, Malaya, Indochina, China; non-cooperation—which might have been accompanied by politeness rather than by vituperation—in the United Nations, in Germany and Japan, and in European undertakings such as the Marshall Plan). It seems likely that under these conditions Western public opinion and Western policy-makers would have become much more deeply divided in their estimates of Soviet foreign policy than was actually the case. In 1945-46 the Soviet Union appeared to many in the West as the common enemy's noble victim and heroic conqueror for whose exertions one was grateful and about whose larger sacrifices one felt guilty. In the early 1950s a similarly predominant opinion in the West had come to view the Politburo as a menace of the magnitude of Hitler. The question had largely become what methods would be adequate to deter the Soviet government, not whether this was an enemy requiring determent. That the apparent rise of Western 'Bevanism' in the spring of 1952 was felt to be a novel event implied that in the West (of course, outside the sphere of influence of Communist parties) a high degree of agreement had been reached about the identity of the major potential enemy—an undesirable situation (from the Politburo's point of view) which the Nazis had never allowed to develop to this extent among their future targets.

Why, then, had the Soviet rulers not continued to simulate a measure of friendliness toward the outer world, despite the excellent results of this approach during the war years? To recall one of numerous incidents, why did they send Shostakovich to the United States to make what was largely viewed as a hostile speech, rather than have him present his music? Imagine that the Politburo had arranged for a continuous flow to the United States, for instance, of what would appear to be ideal members of Soviet society (with suitable hostages left behind)—champion snipers, 'people's artists,' model collective farmers, eminent mathematicians, advanced Uzbeks—and so forth, and so on. Imagine that they had been given directives similar to those which must have been issued for the economic conference in

Moscow in the spring of 1952: no criticism of the West, an emphasis on Soviet achievement and on possibilities of collaboration between East and West, and, mainly, a 'nonpolitical' exhibition of the talents and personalities of these representatives of the Soviet order. If this had been done, it is very unlikely that Americans, on all levels of influence, would have become as hostile to the Soviet Union as they in fact have, with the help of publicly expressed Soviet hostility. There is also little doubt that such a divergent development of attitudes would have been accompanied by different sizes of arms budgets and different degrees of commitments abroad. Similar considerations could be made for other Western countries and other aspects of the public conduct of the Soviet government. I believe that the Politburo's mistake was due to certain basic Bolshevik views of politics; views that are supported by such strong (and usually obscure) emotions that Bolshevik leaders are not capable of testing these views with a really open mind, much as they pride themselves on being attentive to facts.

According to Bolshevik belief, the major enemies of the Party strive to annihilate it. However, a realism similar to that of the Party leadership enables these enemies to keep their hostile moves, on the whole, within the limits of what is feasible at any given time. If, on the other hand, certain major obstacles to an intensified attack on the Soviet Union disappear, the attack will occur, unless the Party itself is able to deter the enemy more powerfully. One of the ways in which it can attempt to do so is by taking up a generally offensive posture. By reinforcing its verbal attack on the threatening enemy, the Party heightens the enemy's estimate of its strength and determination, and weakens the enemy's own 'mass basis.' This device may also serve an offensive purpose: it may induce a retreating enemy to relinquish positions which he had not quite decided to give up.

At the end of the Second World War both reasons for intensifying public hostility against the West seemed to apply. The loss of great-power status by Germany, Japan, Italy, and France and the weakening of Great Britain confronted the Politburo for the first time in its career with a situation which Bolsheviks had always dreaded: the enemy world seemed unified around one ruling group—that of 'Wall Street'— which dwarfed its partners. Although, in the view of the Politburo, 'contradictions' within the enemy camp remained and had to be 'utilized' and 'sharpened,' it seemed much less probable that a great anti-Soviet coalition would be prevented by, or would dissolve into, internecine conflicts between the enemies. True, in 1952 it seemed to the Politburo to be more possible and profitable than, say, in 1949 to utilize and sharpen contradictions between the United States and various other parts of the non-Soviet world. But the aim of this line was to weaken the total strength of the global enemy rather than to facilitate a war between the United States and other powers. After the First World War, on the other hand, the Soviet government expected—and believed it would be able to foster—a war between America and Japan, or between Britain and France, or between Britain and America.

At the same time that enemies had attained an unprecedented degree of unity by the appearance of the American 'hegemon,' that chief enemy had acquired a temporary superiority in the new nuclear weapons; the Strategic Air Command of the United States Air Force emerged as a belated embodiment of the old Bolshevik fantasy of the annihilative enemy.

A radically changed situation which to the politically naïve (so much despised by the Bolsheviks) seemed favorable to the Soviet Union thus appeared, on analysis, to be potentially most dangerous. Once again the Bolshevik presumption seemed confirmed that the political essence of a situation is very different from its façade, and that what looks like a reduction in tension is but a condition of latent crisis which carries with it the additional danger of succumbing to comfortable illusions. Thus the Politburo believed after the end of the Second World War that a new crisis was beginning to develop: in some form or other the unified enemy would at some future date take the offensive against the Soviet Union. There was not much that the Politburo felt it could do to modify this course of events. But at least the Party leadership—transforming passivity into activity, as it likes to do—could conduct a preventive counteroffensive in the sphere of words and other symbols against the enemy, who was as yet merely preparing his more devastating attacks and who had perhaps not yet decided on their timing and details. By appearing brazen when it was deeply apprehensive, the Politburo could attempt to impress upon the enemy that it expected these attacks and was ready to meet them. From the Politburo's verbal aggressiveness the enemy was supposed to conclude—as the Party would, in the inverse case—that if he proceeded to war, he would encounter full and effective resistance. Having been induced to overestimate Soviet strength (did the Politburo not have to be strong to be as aggressive as it was?), he might be deterred from undertaking an all-out attack at a moment when it would lead, the Politburo feared, to its retreat or collapse. If the Politburo was not certain that these favorable effects would occur, it was confident that it had little to lose on adopting the posture which I have described.

This conscious rationale for verbal hostility toward feared potential attackers covered less conscious defenses—defenses against inner rather than outer dangers. Bolsheviks are obscurely afraid of the disposition to reveal to the enemy one's weaknesses—the wounds which he has inflicted on one—so as to make him desist from further aggression (out of pity, for instance). In contrast to such belief Bolsheviks are convinced that, if the enemy learns of one's weakness, he redoubles his blows and proceeds as far as practicable toward annihilation: the major enemies of the Party accept the principle of pursuit as much as does the leadership of the Party. The defiant attitude which hides one's inferiority from enemy eyes also protects one from panic, and from the fear of 'yielding' to the enemy under the influence of panic. Bolsheviks intensely fear their own disposition to fear. Brazenly attacking in the medium of words combats the fear that one may be annihilated by bombs; but the fear that is warded off invades the defense in the apprehension that one may be provoking the enemy.

In a related and yet less conscious motivation, the expression of strong hostility toward the major power centers outside the Party's domain enables Bolshevik leaders to prove to themselves that they are not succumbing to two fatal temptations: that of entertaining any kind or degree of good feelings toward enemies, and that of imputing such feelings to them. Both vices, they believe, lead to the same catastrophe of being 'used,' controlled, and then destroyed by enemies who are in reality annihilative. In answering an ostensibly friendly outside group in a hostile fashion, one shows that its attempt at deception has failed. One is proving oneself worthy of the 'serious' enemy by reacting to his 'true face' only. Similarly, any moderation of tone toward a potential attacker (one whose attack is, however, not already fully prepared and impending) tends to appear to Bolsheviks as an act of 'yielding': one would be vainly trying to induce the enemy to abstain from attack on the basis of harmlessness and weakness rather than deterring him through strength.

However, a major mode of Bolshevik conduct is apt to have both an offensive and a defensive rationale. Similarly, after the end of the Second World War the Politburo viewed the outer enemy not only as preparing a future assault, but also as actually engaged in a retreat from the areas peripheral to the Soviet Union. How far this retreat would go could not, in Bolshevik calculation, be determined beforehand, and was held to depend in part on the degree of pressure which the advancing Party exercised on the withdrawing enemy in such areas as Berlin, Trieste, northern Greece, northern Iran, Malaya, Indochina, China, Korea. Among the devices of such pressure, public expressions of hostility came to figure prominently. It is inconceivable to Bolsheviks that one might predispose an outside group to further concessions by expressing good feelings about those which have already been granted; only more pressure can bring new gains.

But what of the enemy's reactions to this device? Could the Politburo not have predicted that its display of hostility would anger him, convince him that the Politburo was an implacable enemy, make him establish an anti-Soviet alliance, arm, and envisage a war for which he otherwise might have been as little prepared as the Western powers prior to 1938 were for Hitler's war (a war which had been preceded by years of ostensible Nazi moderation toward the West)? Is it possible that a ruling group so given to ruthless realism and the single-minded pursuit of expedience can have overlooked this undesirable impact of its conduct—conduct not required by other overmastering considerations and which worked its damage slowly yet visibly?

We may be able to approach the solution of this puzzle if we recall that the Bolshevik devotion to 'facts' is, in part, one to certain laws of 'Marxism-Leninism' which Bolsheviks regard as so self-evident or so completely proved that it is unnecessary to check up in every new instance whether or not doubt has been thrown upon them. Regardless of such appearances—appearances which are often enemy camouflage— these laws must serve as bases for Bolshevik action. One of them tells that the leadership of the 'big bourgeoisie'—though not that of the 'petty bourgeoisie'—on the whole accepts, and conforms to, standards of political conduct similar to those of the Party: the standards of 'serious'—that is, big—political operators. According to these standards one must take it for granted that the essential relationship between the Party and the centers of 'capitalism' is indicated by the single question: Who (will destroy) Whom? As 'Wall Street' and 'the City' know for certain that the Politburo strives to annihilate them (as they strive to annihilate it), their estimate of basic Politburo intentions will not be changed whether it simulates friendliness or hostility. (Western negotiators have often reported a strong impression that their Soviet counterparts are spontaneously friendly in non-official contacts and deliberately affect a tone of intense hostility in official ones.) Nor will the ruling groups which dominate the 'capitalist' world be in any way emotionally aroused by violent expressions of intensely hostile feelings toward them: a 'serious' statesman is one who cannot be influenced by a babying of his sensitivities, who is impermeable to the assaults of hate or love, flattery or contempt (as a Bolshevik believes he himself is, and as at least earlier generations of Bolshevik leaders found it very difficult to be). If a leader is not impassive, he has indeed grounds for self-contempt, and an obligation to leave a profession for which he is unsuited; and in the opinion of a still respectful Politburo the 'ruling circles' of Britain and the United States are on the whole well qualified for their jobs. It is true that, as the decline and fall of capitalism proceeds, individuals in these ruling groups are increasingly prone to lose emotional control; and the Politburo attempts to 'utilize' this, as any other, 'opportunity,' by evoking rage in them. But it does not count on a large-scale success in this subsidiary enterprise, though it welcomes windfalls here as elsewhere. It is only public opinion, as distinct from the 'ruling circles,' which permits itself to be 'carried away' by feelings. In directing symbolic attacks against foreign governments, the Party hopes to arouse the potentially revolutionary feelings of their 'masses' against them. But the Politburo does not seem to perceive that its technique of rudeness materially enhances the capacity of other elites to execute anti-Soviet policies. In any case, the Politburo has increasingly tended to assume that foreign public opinion is under the adequate control of foreign ruling groups, as it knows Soviet public opinion to be under its own control. (One might ask whether the policy of public hostility toward the West was not adopted in order to justify the sacrifices which the Soviet population had to make for the sake of military strength. But it is unlikely that the Politburo would have adopted this particular way of stimulating morale had it perceived the unfavorable impact abroad. At the very least it would then have attempted to differentiate its line sharply in addressing domestic and foreign publics, but this was not done.)

If Bolsheviks, thus, do not believe that 'serious' enemies will be emotionally aroused by expressions of strong hostility toward them, it is in the Bolshevik view even less conceivable that a major ruling group should derive policies from feelings rather than from a sober calculation of the 'relationship of forces.' If one did this, one would have let oneself be 'provoked' by the enemy; that is, one would have submitted to the enemy's control, becoming his 'tail' or 'appendage.' This is most unlikely to happen to the 'experienced' ruling groups in the centers of the capitalist word. (If 'provocation' does happen, disaster will ensue, either to the one who has been 'provoked' or to the one who has engaged in 'provocation'—this is stressed in warning the Party against 'provoking' a powerful enemy when it is expedient to delay the showdown and when the enemy happens to be inclined toward such a delay himself.) On the whole, the enemy is already doing as much as he believes he can to damage the Party. Hence the Party's display of hostility toward him is not apt to make him more dangerous (except in the special case of 'provocation' which I just mentioned), while it may well restrain him to some extent in the fashion which I discussed above. Publicly expressed hostility, as I already noted, is thus one of the weapons by which the Party may 'force' an enemy to modify his conduct in a way favorable to it. Short of certain special situations in which the Party and an enemy have particular interests in common (for example, the defeat of a third party in a war), such a change can only be a 'forced' one, as the enemy unceasingly aims at the most unfavorable outcome for the Party, its annihilation.

The Bolshevik beliefs which I have sketched are so strong that facts which appear to refute them suggest to Bolshevik leaders complicated interpretations rather than factual re-examinations. When the Korean war induced a very sharp increase in actual and projected Western arms budgets, the Politburo was apt to assume that the enemy elites were using the war as a pretext to introduce a change in the rate of militarization which they had decided upon in advance and on general grounds. To assume that the Korean 'episode' itself was a major causal factor behind the change in armament policies which began in the summer of 1950, would, to the Politburo, mean to impute to the respected leadership of the 'big bourgeoisie' the contemptible stupidity of the 'petty bourgeoisie' and its willingness to let itself be dominated by events. On the contrary, in arriving at its estimates of the 'Anglo-American' bloc, the Politburo is acutely conscious of the extreme penalty for underestimating an enemy of one's own (or an even larger) size.

Similarly, if the enemy seems to manifest increasing hostility toward the Party after the Party has intensified its verbal attack on him, this is not because rage evokes rage. Rather, this means that the enemy—with a lucidity equaling that of the Party leadership—has accurately perceived the correctness of the Party's policy (of which the intensified verbal assault on the enemy is a crucial component); this is what dismays him. Hence the enemy's rage is a favorable sign. Indeed, on a less conscious level the Bolshevik is content with evoking his enemy's rage, as he fears his enemy's friendliness by which he might be seduced, or which seems to indicate that he has already been seduced unwittingly: the friendly enemy expresses satisfaction with the conduct of a Party which has become his 'tail.' Hence a Bolshevik must not yield to the fear of the rage he may evoke in the enemy. Nonetheless it is this fear that breaks through in the Bolshevik apprehension of 'provoking' the enemy.

By such beliefs the Bolsheviks manage to overlook the disadvantages of antagonizing those whom they have decided to make into, or to perpetuate as, their enemies.

The Controlled Neighbor Policy

The decisions of the conferences of Yalta and Potsdam and the peace treaties of 1946 envisaged democracy and independence for the liberated areas of Eastern Europe as well as for Germany's former satellites in that region. But a few years later whatever very modest degrees of real sovereignty and freedom had come into existence after the war in the areas entered by the Soviet Army had been obliterated. Full power had in each of these areas passed into the hands of the local Party leadership, which in its turn deferred to Moscow.

When the Politburo became aware of the expressions of shock and anger which multiplied in the West as standard Soviet practices were applied to the newly acquired Eastern territories, it must have found it difficult to believe in the sincerity of the Western reaction. Why should the West ever have assumed that the Politburo would give 'democratic' terms applied to, say, Poland, a meaning different from that which they have in the Soviet Constitution of 1936? The Politburo rather took it for granted that in consenting to the occupation of various East European areas by the Soviet Army, the Western leaders had also consented to the establishment of full Politburo control in these areas, at the Politburo's convenience: "Who says A, says B." Hence Western protests were construed by the Politburo as the beginning of an attempt to induce a 'rollback' of Soviet power, an attempt which had to be resisted at once—among other means by accelerating the political assimilation of the new territories, including eastern Germany. In those areas where in 1944-46 the Politburo held only certain 'commanding heights' (for instance, the ministries of the interior and of the armed forces), it proceeded yet more speedily to the liquidation of all actual or potential dissent.

This line of conduct was enjoined upon the Politburo by all the considerations which we have discussed in analyzing the Bolshevik requirements of pushing to the limit. Bolsheviks attach great importance to a rule which corresponds to what in military language is called the principle of pursuit. It follows from the belief in "Who will destroy Whom?" that, when the Party has made an advance against an enemy, it must attempt to utilize it to secure further gains, proceeding as far as possible toward the enemy's full liquidation, without a 'remnant' or a 'trace' remaining. If the Party violates the principle of pursuit, its victory is apt to be followed by defeat. The weakened, but not exterminated, enemy is likely to reverse the situation: though reduced to a mere remnant, he may grow back to full strength. Hence the

Party must not permit itself to yield to the temptation of delaying, of not persevering, of becoming complacent after a merely partial victory (one which leaves the enemy in existence). It must avoid such mistakes all the more as the extermination of enemy remnants is not only extremely important but also exceedingly difficult. However, it must be performed. As long as, say, a genuine Eastern European peasant party is permitted to survive, an enemy of the Politburo is tolerated, when it might be eliminated by the utter destruction of its source. Those who tolerate the continued existence of enemies whom it is within their power to destroy deserve indeed to be thrown in history's 'ash heap.'

There Are No Neutrals

In the Bolshevik view of almost any political situation, there are two opposed positions which can be taken up toward it (one imputed to the 'bourgeoisie,' the other to the 'proletariat'), but there is no 'third path,' as 'petty bourgeois' elements like to believe. What appears to be a third position (and may be a consciously adopted camouflage behind which the 'bourgeois' enemy hides) is always a view which is logically inconsistent and empirically false, which has an actual impact similar to that of the 'bourgeois' position, and which will, in time, 'slide down' to become manifestly identical with it. Every view which is not strictly identical with the Party's views (however similar it may appear to the naïve) and which is not utterly favorable to the Party (however friendly it may seem to the naïve) is actually or potentially, consciously or without awareness, an enemy view. Every group which is not quite controlled by the Party is, or will become, an enemy, unless it is brought under complete Party control.

It is in this context that the Politburo views the pretension of a group outside its domain to be 'neutral' in the conflict between the Soviet Union and its avowed adversaries. The Politburo is apt to assume that such a claim is a maneuver of deception. It believes that small states tend to be controlled by the biggest centers of power. Hence the 'Anglo-Americans' virtually dominate all areas which are not controlled by the Politburo, whether the ostensible rulers of small

.states are aware of their subjection to Washington or not. (In this instance again, the Politburo perceives the world at large in the image of its relations to such subordinate agencies as the Polish government.) The division of the world into two blocs, each dominated by one center of power, has often appeared to Western observers as the fatal end result of a dangerous trend which might be stopped; to the Politburo it represents itself as an almost accomplished fact. In the international conferences during and after the Second World War, and in the United Nations, the Soviet government has rather consistently tried to reduce the role of weak states. It has advocated procedures which would overtly express what the Politburo believes to be a basic fact, namely, the dominance of the big few over the many small.

To be sure, a few areas may at times reduce their dependence on one or the other world centers. But such emancipations are apt to be ephemeral and should never be 'relied upon' by the Politburo: the Party must plan for the normal (or even the worst) course of events, ready to utilize windfalls when and as long as they occur. If an area becomes a no man's land between the two world blocs, the Politburo should proceed on the assumption that the enemy will incorporate it unless it does so first.

Short of gaining control over such an area, there is one main method by which the Politburo can attempt to sustain the relative detachment of the area from the enemy center: by charging that the local ruling group is, or is about to become, an Anglo-American satellite, and by exercising various kinds of pressure on it. Western observers have repeatedly noted how often the effect of such Politburo procedures was to make the estimates of the Politburo more true than they had initially been: a government which is treated like an enemy by the Politburo becomes its enemy.

Thus, if Western Europe were to proclaim itself 'neutral' and if the United States were to guarantee it against a Soviet attack, the Politburo would find it difficult to believe that Western Europe would or could refuse an American demand to participate in an attack on the Soviet Union. Western Europe would in this case continue to owe its immunity from Soviet domination to the United States; but, in the view of the Politburo, neither Washington nor any other 'serious' political force will grant such benefits without requesting and receiving

services in return. The pretended neutral can thus easily be recognized
as a covert satellite of the enemy.

To make a yet more improbable assumption for the sake of clarifying
the Politburo modes of calculation : if war between the United States
and the Soviet Union were to break out and if Western Europe were
at first to be neutral, the Politburo would again be apt to view this
as a measure of deception designed to catch it off guard by a sudden
attack once the Soviet Union was engaged elsewhere, or as the expression of a temporary recalcitrance of a satellite, presently to be
overcome by the master's pressure or force. In any case, the Politburo
would hardly consider the claim of neutrality as a major factor in
deciding if, when, and how, to subdue Western Europe. If that claim
had led to a reduction of European military strength below what it
would otherwise have been, the net effect of 'neutrality' would be
to make a Soviet attack more probable.

Revolution by Army

Some Western analysts of contemporary politics maintain that,
however much the Politburo may be interested in expanding its domain,
it relies primarily on nonmilitary means. It counts, they say, on local
seizures of power by Communist parties, whether by classical 'revolution' or by infiltration into the existing state apparatus.

This is a hypothesis which had some validity when applied to the
early twenties, but which is at considerable variance with the mind
of the Politburo in the early fifties. In the intervening decades Bolshevik leaders have steadily reduced their reliance on the 'collapse'
of capitalism and the seizure of power by nonmilitarized Communist
parties abroad, and steadily increased their estimate of the role of
the Soviet Army as an agent of the expansion of Politburo power.
(During the same period Bolshevik leaders preceded the Nazis in discovering the high potency of total violence, both against small elites
and larger. classes.)

The present attitude was already prefigured in 1920 : after the Red
Army had repelled the Polish thrust into the Soviet Union, the Politburo had to decide whether to undertake an offensive into Poland in
order to seize power there and to stimulate revolution in Germany.

A minority within the Politburo warned that this course would fail as it would arouse anti-Soviet attitudes in Poland. They advised that one should rely on the 'revolutionary situation' which defeat by the Red Army would create in an uninvaded Poland. However, even at this early date the military course was chosen. It is true that it failed; but so did all attempts of Communist parties between the two world wars (except in China) to expand the sector of the world ruled by affiliates of the Comintern.

With the passage of time and failures, the Moscow leadership developed what came near to being contempt for the Comintern. The events of the Second World War seemed to justify this attitude. On the one hand, the German party—which traditionally had been viewed as the second most important in the world—was neither able to influence Hitler's policies before his attack on the Soviet Union nor to weaken the force of that attack to a significant extent. On the other hand, the advances of the Soviet Army in 1944-45 led to an expansion of Communist power into all those areas which that army had entered (with the exception of Finland and eastern Austria, where the Politburo exercised an unusual self-restraint, and with that of northern Iran, where it had to retreat). The other areas gained during and after the Second World War—the territories which came to be held by the Chinese, Indochinese, Malayan, and Burmese parties, and those conquered by the Yugoslav and Albanian partisans—all had one thing in common: they were located in 'backward' areas difficult of access, where the Party employed a technique which could not even be envisaged in western and central Europe. The Party, in these instances, seceded from an existing state by withdrawing into the interior. There it built up a military force of its own, with which it later attempted to overcome the internal enemy in a guerrilla or even in a regular war. In these cases too, then, the expansion of the Communist domain was brought about by the action of armed forces, though not of the Soviet Army; while the Soviet Union, among other forms of support, furnished instruction and material and diverted the enemy's energies elsewhere.

In the highly developed areas of the world, however, there is no substitute for the Soviet Army. It has become an established Politburo belief that expansion into such areas requires direct military intervention. The local party is expected to facilitate this intervention and to exploit it. But the local party will be put into power by the pressure or the advance of the Soviet Army (or its satellites), as happened in the Baltic states, Poland, Czechoslovakia, Hungary, Rumania, Bulgaria, North Korea, and temporarily in parts of South Korea.

Do Not Yield to Provocation

During the last few years there has been much discussion in the West as to whether certain policies—the bombing of Manchurian air bases, or the rearmament of Western Germany—would not 'provoke' the Politburo to general war. Whatever the merits of the various positions which have been taken on such issues, there is no doubt that the Politburo is much concerned with 'provocation.' Bolsheviks always suspect the occurrence of provocation in politics and always attempt to conform to the rules which should govern Bolshevik conduct toward this important and dangerous phenomenon. Specifically, when a Bolshevik hears the noun *provokatsiia* .or the verb *provotsirovat'*, he thinks of two rules: first, never provoke an enemy; second, never be provoked by him. We have already discussed the first point and shall now consider the second.

There is a virtue which to a Bolshevik leader is as central as his dedication to the Party, and which he calls *soznatel'nost'*, usually translated as 'consciousness.' To act from Bolshevik consciousness means to act after protracted and arduous calculations undertaken in a sternly sober mood. Thus the Bolshevik leader obtains what he believes to be precise, comprehensive, and realistic estimates of the 'relationship of forces' which prevails and impends and whose shape determines expedient conduct.

One must never lapse from full consciousness: not only does consciousness maximize one's effectiveness in action, but it is also one of the major safeguards against the ever-threatening catastrophe. At the height of a 'revolutionary crisis' the Party must be as exacting in its calculations as during a temporary 'stabilization' of the enemy's position. It must maintain meticulous realism both against the danger of complacency in victory and against that of despair in defeat. Otherwise it will 'break its neck.'

'Consciousness' brings a feeling of mastery, even if the decision at which one arrives is, for instance, that of accepting the enemy's ultimatum. For if one is 'conscious,' one's conduct is entirely determined by two factors: the goal to which one is dedicated (to maximize the power of the Party) and the correctly and completely understood reality which has to be transformed. A lack of consciousness implies, on the other hand, that one is being controlled—whether one knows it or not—by alien and hostile forces; one's feelings are aroused by events or one's enemies who try to distort the Party's estimates of the situation, and to reduce the Party into giving in to the emotions which they attempt to evoke in it. If the Party 'yields' to 'provocation' of any of these varieties, its very existence is imperiled: it will have adopted an incorrect line—that is, a line threatening annihilation. In those cases in which yielding to provocation does not lead directly to being shattered by a frontal attack, the one who has permitted himself to be provoked is being 'used' by the one who provoked him and who now has him where he wants him. But when one is being 'used,' one 'manures the soil' for the user; having been used, one is 'thrown away like a dirty rag.'

Insisting that the Party preserve its freedom—that is, its orientation on the supreme goal and on relevant facts only—Bolshevik doctrine thus requires that the Party never permit an enemy to predetermine the Party's acts by his own. For example, the Party must not feel that immediate and full retaliation is the only appropriate response to a hostile act against it; if it did accept this view, the enemy could control its behavior by making an appropriate move. He would then have 'provoked' the Party, that is, deflected it from a self-set course in favor of a course set by him. If this happens, the Party becomes the enemy's 'appendage' or 'tool,' though it may not know it. It is not the person who lets himself be 'provoked' to a duel by his enemy (an occasion at which he may be killed) who is in a position of mastery, but the one who—without becoming a slave of his enemy's actions—calculates how best to kill that enemy. The upshot of such a calculation may be to withhold any retaliation against the enemy's aggressions for the time being. Thus yielding to provocation (and the provocation may consist in the enemy interpreting as weakness one's refusal to retaliate directly against his aggressions) threatens self-destruction: full consciousness is a necessary condition for destroying the enemy.

The Party must ascertain at all times whether the moment for a showdown with an enemy has come or not—whether such a showdown is here and now required or prohibited. In the first case, the Party must proceed to an all-out offensive without waiting until the enemy furnishes a pretext for it. (If a pretext is necessary, the Party must produce it.) In the second case—when an all-out struggle is to be deferred—the Party must not let itself be provoked by any incidents arranged by the enemy, by any local actions to which he may proceed, or by misinformation which he may attempt to plant. In 1950 and 1951 high American officials often clearly implied in their public statements that these were the last years during which the Politburo could strike against western Europe, that the Atlantic powers should speed up the rate of rearmament to shorten the period during which the Politburo was still in a position to overrun the continent. If a minority in the Politburo was during this time in favor of immediate general war, I should surmise that they were bitterly asked by spokesmen of the majority: So you propose that the Political Bureau of the Central Committee of the All-Union Communist Party (Bolsheviks) should yield to the provocation of the representative of Morgan in Washington, Charles Wilson?

Avoid Adventures

The enemies of the Party never 'lay down their arms.' In the intervals between all-out assaults, they incessantly calculate whether it is possible to heighten the level of attack. Another total onslaught may come at any time; the situation is usually so precariously balanced that even an ostensibly minor change may upset it.

The incessant danger of attack carries with it a continuing likelihood of actual annihilation. Until the moment when 'socialist encirclement' of the rest of the world has been substituted for the 'capitalist encirclement' of the Soviet Union, the Party will be weaker than its enemies. Neither the gains it has made nor its very existence are ever secure—a stark fact which the Bolshevik should not forget even as the Party's power rises.

The Party's increase in power affects the enemy in opposite ways. On the one hand, his insight, energy, and skill tend to decrease as he approaches his doom. On the other hand, he intensifies his efforts to annihilate the Party; he does not resign himself to his demise; he does not become harmless. On the contrary, as his previous devices become less effective, he resorts to ever more extreme ones, with greater risk of failure, but also with greater impact in case of success. He behaves like a mortally wounded beast: he tries to make up for his reduced strength by enhanced recklessness and ferocity. Unable to prevent his own death at the hand of the Party, he may yet make a serious attempt to kill it even in his last minutes.

But if catastrophe always remains possible, it is never inevitable. Bolsheviks oppose the disposition to feel, in a crisis, that all is lost, and hence that passivity toward the impending disaster is permissible. There is always a way out—it is for the Party to discover and to take it. In doing so, it must be able to bear the anguish of protracted danger and never yield to the inclination for desperate action with a possible horrible end as an alternative to horrors without end.

If it seems expedient to defer a showdown with an enemy until a later date but if the enemy seems to be intent upon producing a crisis in the near future, the Party must do all it can to deter him. Under these conditions the Politburo will allow itself to consider a preventive war only if it is absolutely certain that the enemy has definitely decided on an imminent attack. The Politburo will not allow the enemy to make it abandon its resolve to avoid war for the time being merely because he appears to be developing yet greater strength than the Politburo had estimated when it determined to avoid war, or merely because he seems to be considering—without having come to a decision yet—an earlier attack on the Soviet Union than he had previously envisaged. Thus the Politburo did not initiate a preventive war against Western rearmament during the last few years. Though it may have been increasingly apprehensive of Western intentions to attack the Soviet Union, the Politburo did not believe that such an attack was so imminent as to justify the abandonment of a resolve which had governed its policies since 1920: to do all it could to defer a total collision with a major enemy.

In any situation falling short of extreme crisis, history offers the

Party a 'respite' which it must use to prepare itself for coming conflicts by adding to its power as much and as quickly as possible. The
ceaseless search for more power must be conducted with unremitting
vigilance. The briefest and slightest reduction in watchfulness may
be fatal; it is for such a lapse that the enemy may be waiting in order
to strike.

More generally, there is in every situation just one 'correct line';
all other policies—even those which to the politically unsophisticated
seem only slightly different—tend to lead—directly or indirectly, now
or later—to 'ruin,' that is, to the collapse of Party and regime. Mistakes are rarely harmless or anything less than acutely dangerous.
The consequences of merely exaggerating a correct line, or of erring
in the opposite direction, are as dangerous as the effects of a thoroughly
erroneous orientation. Hence 'every smallest step' has to be 'weighed.'

It is in such a context that we should view the Bolshevik apprehension
of unwittingly committing suicide by rash offensive acts. Bolshevik
doctrine emphatically opposes the disposition to engage oneself in
forward operations with an uncertain chance of success and a big
risk of severe loss or annihilation in case of failure. The Party must
neither gamble nor complacently overestimate its strength, nor cease
to calculate. It must exercise 'caution' and never be 'adventurist'
in its attempts to advance. It must never risk already conquered
major positions, or even existence, for the sake of uncertain future
gains. It must undertake only those offensive operations for which
its resources are fully adequate. It must be able to bide its time indefinitely. The Party knows that intermissions between advances are
necessary. Ostensibly standing still, the Party is accumulating forces
which will render possible and successful a subsequent expansion.
The Party also knows that in this epoch of the decline and fall of the
existing order, time is working in its favor, that painful and protracted
delays turn out to be, essentially, minor and irrelevant when they
are viewed against the magnitude of the historical change which the
Party is accomplishing.

Consider in the light of these views the self-restraint of the Politburo
after the end of the Second World War—a behavior as pronounced
as that of pushing to the limit which we discussed before. The Soviet
Army could easily have seized northern Iran and West Berlin; with

or without Soviet help, satellite forces could have advanced in Greece and Yugoslavia; and a full offensive of the Soviet Army would have led to the occupation of most or all of Europe. From the late forties on, moves of this kind were avoided by the Politburo because of the atomic striking power which was by then in possession of the Strategic Air Command of the United States Air Force. But if we assume that the Politburo knew the limited size of the American stockpile in the first postwar years and of the limited capacity to deliver it, we must also assume that what then deterred the Politburo from incorporating western Europe into its domain was the vivid awareness of not the first but the last round of the war which a move against the West would have brought on—a last round in which the United States would be able to employ a greatly increased atomic and conventional arsenal. The Politburo required of itself a 'serious' calculation taking account of the entire range of the relevant future. The Party must never let itself be dominated by a favorable appearance of the moment. Its actions should be based on long-run forecasts, and on the assumption that the worst is going to happen.

The length to which the Politburo goes in attempting to avoid 'adventurist' policies is apparent in its conduct in France after the end of the late war. It might be argued that when the Anglo-American armies left France in 1945-46, the positions of strength enjoyed by the French Communist Party in the armed forces, the administration, and the working class were sufficient to enable it to seize power in important areas and to conduct a civil war with a good prospect of conquering the rest of France. However, at no time did the French Party aim at the seizure of power. Presumably the Politburo took it for granted that the 'Anglo-American ruling circles' were determined not to allow defections from their domain and were ready to intervene with forces adequate to crush the cadres of the French Party if it were to attempt the seizure of power. The preservation of these cadres—to weaken the French war effort in a future conflict and to facilitate as well as to exploit the entrance of the Soviet Army into France—became the main objective of the Politburo policy in internal French affairs. Eschewing 'adventurism,' Moscow exercised 'maximal caution.'

Or take the Politburo moderation—characteristically accompanied by extreme vehemence in words—toward the Tito regime. The break

of the Yugoslav leadership with Moscow must have presented itself
to the Politburo as another instance of a haunting Bolshevik fatality:
the Party leadership, though highly suspicious and requiring of itself
to expect the worst from anybody, decides to extend its confidence
to a very few persons, but even some of these will in time turn out
to be unreliable, or worse. The Yugoslav leadership was the only group
of Communists in Europe which had been allowed by the Politburo to
build a powerful state apparatus of its own which would be difficult
to subdue in case of defection. Had the Politburo not been absolutely
confident of the loyalty of the Yugoslav leaders, it could have
secured their replacement or instituted more stringent controls over
them when the Soviet Army dominated the Balkans in 1944-45. It
was the confidence then extended to him by the Politburo which enabled
Tito in 1948 to destroy an important Bolshevik record, that of ensuring
that an opposition to the Party leadership is rather powerless when
its break with the Party comes. In view of the great importance
which the Politburo attaches to the prevention and destruction of
Communist oppositions to it, the defection and continued existence
of the Tito regime were defeats of a high order. When the devices
of subversion on which the Politburo at first relied to annihilate the
new regime proved ineffective, it refused nevertheless to take a course
which it must have often debated—to proceed to the military annihilation of the Yugoslav schism by satellite and, if necessary, Soviet
forces. Given the significance of this goal to the Politburo, it cannot
have been deterred by considerations of the direct cost of the operation
itself. It must have feared the possibility of 'provoking' a general
war. That this possibility should have prevented the Politburo from
undertaking so vital an operation as the destruction of Tito again
indicates the high degree of caution which the Politburo requires
of itself. For one may argue that a Soviet assault on Tito in, say,
1949 would by no means have led to an all-out American intervention—just as little as did the invasion of South Korea in 1950. However, presumably the Politburo followed its habit of assuming the
worst: a chain of events which would lead from an invasion of Yugoslavia to 'strikes' of the Strategic Air Command of the United States
Air Force against the Soviet Union. The Politburo must in any case
have been puzzled by the fact that Washington did not attempt to

use its atomic superiority for offensive purposes, that is, that the United States made no effort to secure by atomic threats a Soviet withdrawal from certain areas of central and eastern Europe. The Politburo must have constantly dreaded the possibility that this American inactivity would cease, and this dread reinforced its determination to avoid any decisive action which might facilitate the operations of the Washington 'war party,' while continuing tentative offensives, such as that against Berlin.

On the other hand, when Washington in 1950 seemed to have indicated conclusively that it had retreated from South Korea, the Politburo acted on a maxim which complements the requirement of cautiously abstaining from rash offensives, the maxim of utilizing all opportunities—of pushing to the limit. Once engaged by proxy in this forward operation, which had seemed so safe before the surprising American decision to intervene after all (Did we fall into an American trap? Bolshevik leaders must have asked themselves, if not each other), the Politburo was prepared for two possibilities. Either Washington would conduct a limited war in Korea, in which case the Politburo might increase its military commitments in that theater with a variety of particular purposes in mind, but always within the framework of a limited war. Or Washington might decide to enforce a Soviet retreat by the threat of total war, in which case the Politburo would consider whether to accept the American ultimatum when it came. Presumably the Politburo did not believe that the probability of Washington's unconditionally deciding on all-out war (as Hitler had in 1941, when the Politburo waited for an ultimatum in vain) would be materially affected by events in one sector of the Asian border between the two blocs. In other words, while the offensive against South Korea would probably not have been undertaken if American intervention had been predicted, the Politburo, once engaged, did not believe that there was any considerable risk of 'provoking' Washington by intensifying and prolonging the limited war in Korea. (For once, the Politburo's estimate of America was realistic.)

I would interpret the Soviet offensive against West Berlin in 1948-49 in a similar manner. The Politburo was prepared both for an ultimatum asking it to retreat or to face general war, and for a local military offensive of the enemy. In the first case it was, I surmise, pre-

pared to retreat. In the second case, the Politburo would consider
the expediency of limited war as it later did in the case of Korea—only
that it was much less confident of a war in central Europe remaining
circumscribed, and hence much more disposed to retreat if its enemies
were to show their unmistakable willingness to use adequate force.
In northern Iran and northern Greece the Politburo did, in effect,
retreat in similar circumstances.

During its entire career the Politburo initiated sizable military
operations, directly or by proxy, three times: against eastern Poland
and Finland in 1939 and against South Korea in 1950. The Soviet
Army crossed the Polish frontier when the Polish Army had already
been routed by the Germans; in Finland and South Korea the Politburo
thought it had an overwhelming military superiority over the forces
it took to be its immediate opponents. If the Politburo aims at world
dominance, it is also determined to play it safe.

Know When To Stop

In a conversation with Eden in December 1941—at one of the most
critical moments in the career of Bolshevism—Stalin compared himself
with his chief enemy of the moment : "Hitler is a very able man, but
he does not know when to stop. I do." As I indicated in the preceding
section, the ability to know when to stop, and to stop accordingly,
is as necessary for Bolshevik self-esteem as the incessant utilization
of all possibilities of going forward. To be 'carried away' by the
impetus—the dynamism,' as some put it in the West—of one's advance beyond the ultimate point which 'consciousness' requires one
to attain at the present moment is to lose control. One allows oneself
to fall into subjection to a force which is not less alien and hostile for
being internal, namely, 'spontaneity.' As we know, being controlled
—by whatever agency—is the prelude to being annihilated : 'running
ahead,' the Party 'breaks its neck.' It is, however, just as devastating
to Bolshevik self-esteem to feel that one might not be able to prevent
oneself from falling into the abyss as it is to be unable to advance to
its very brink for fear of falling. The Bolshevik position is to stand
securely at the brink.

Some Western observers have felt in recent years, for instance, that the prospect of a divided Germany with two armed forces, each patrolling its own end of the Elbe bridges within rifle shot of the other, is frightening. Is not the first rule for avoiding the lesser explosions which detonate war to keep enemies apart from one another? To the Politburo, however, the situation which I just described seems normal—it only shows clearly the essence of all politics; it is not less safe than politics in general. If the forces facing each other are controlled by 'serious' ruling groups, there will be no automatic or accidental progression from cold to hot war.

I have already, by implication, indicated in the previous chapters how far Bolshevik consciousness requires one to go: only when, and always when, protracted attempts or conclusive analysis have fully proved a certain advance to be impossible or inexpedient must the attempt to secure it be temporarily abandoned. That is, the Party must temporarily discontinue an offensive as soon as the enemy position it attacks has become a 'fact' which cannot, for the time being, be modified. But up to this very moment, however, attempts to go forward must be stubbornly continued. The siege of West Berlin illustrates both the Bolshevik perseverance in trying to overcome an obstacle on one's road and the Bolshevik acceptance of failure in such an attempt. Many negotiations between the Soviet Union and the West in the first years after the Second World War also furnish examples of this pattern.

Determined, prolonged, and fruitless insistence is thus usually for Bolsheviks both a necessary and a sufficient condition of final sudden withdrawal. As Bolsheviks regard recurrent setbacks as inevitable and stress the slow maturation of major historical changes, they do not expect quick successes; they are prepared both for success and failure as the solution to protracted deadlock. If Bolsheviks are for the time being to abandon a certain offensive, their enemies must clearly show them that it would be fruitless and wasteful—or dangerous—to continue to press for the objective at stake. One might ask why the Politburo undertook in 1948-49 an offensive against West Berlin which went beyond words, but restricted itself to words in its public operations against the Tito regime. One of the factors making for this difference was the following. The Politburo felt free to stop or withdraw any time or to any extent in its attempt to seize West

Berlin, as it actually did stop and finally withdraw. But it would not have felt equally free in an overt attempt against Belgrade. To undertake a military effort to capture at least the centers of the Tito regime, whether by proxy or directly by the Soviet Army, and then to be forced to halt this effort or to call it off in order to comply with a possible American ultimatum—this must have seemed a forbidding prospect to the Politburo, which presumably envisaged with equanimity such a sequence of events in the case of Berlin. The very existence of the Belgrade schismatics and heretics (the two are inseparable in Stalinism) was to the Politburo a defeat of an unprecedented kind—a defeat which would only have been compounded by the failure of an overt attempt to undo it.

If the Party at a given moment discontinues its attempts to make a certain advance, it is with the intent of utilizing the ensuing 'respite' for an accumulation of forces, which will enable it to resume its offensive with more success. The Party must therefore combat any tendencies to relax its efforts during an ostensibly calm period.

One may contrast this attitude with one often expressed by Western spokesmen during those brief periods when the Soviet government seemed to conduct a 'peace offensive': they would declare themselves dissatisfied with mere words and demand acts—for example, in the spring of 1952, a settlement in Korea and Austria. The implication seemed to be that if the Politburo were to abandon its offensives, or were even to retreat, in certain spheres, its antagonists would indeed be prepared to relax their defensive efforts—that is to succumb to what Bolsheviks regard as the specific danger of a period of a 'respite.'

Ward off Penetration

One of the aspects of Soviet policy which most impressed the West in the years following the Second World War was its determination to isolate the Party's domain from the rest of the world. In those border areas for which the West had envisaged a degree of common rule by the victors, the Politburo tended to create, and make inaccessible, a domain of its own: eastern Germany, northern Korea. It severely restricted the use of the conventional ways by which foreigners might enter as tourists, correspondents, researchers, and so forth, and it refused to agree to novel modes of contact involved in, for instance, the Marshall Plan or the plan accepted by the majority of the United Nations Atomic Energy Commission. Whatever verbal concessions the Politburo might from time to time make, as in the matter of 'inspection' of atomic installations, Western observers and negotiators increasingly sensed that a Bolshevik aversion to contact with enemies largely determined the 'iron curtain' policy. This policy was often, and correctly, related to the totalitarian character of the Soviet regime. In addition, however, some distinctive Bolshevik feelings were involved in it.

Bolsheviks feel that on pain of incurring the gravest risks all lines of demarcation between the domain of the Party and the essentially hostile rest of the world must be made and kept perfectly clear, and quite impassable except at the Party's will. (There are also vital lines of demarcation within the sphere controlled by the Party, and within the Party itself, but with these I am not concerned here.) Bolsheviks fear and oppose the disposition to permit the borders between oneself and the enemy to be fuzzy: there must be no 'jumbling,' 'merging,' or 'mingling' between them. If this rule is violated, the Party is threatened by 'dissolution' into its hostile environment. Establishing 'clear demarcations,' 'precise divisions,' 'solid walls' between the world and oneself is a necessary condition of survival (though not a sufficient one—but, then, in the Bolshevik view survival is never certain). This is particularly the case when conditions require the Party to ally itself with outside groups—groups which have been and will again become overt enemies. The Party must be aware of the dangers of such proximity and counteract the disposition to permit a fatal 'merging' by a strict (and not necessarily public) insistence on its separateness—its 'sovereignty,' in the public language of the Soviet Union.

Apart from the danger of the Party 'dissolving' into its hostile environment, there is that of its being 'penetrated' by that environment, with equally fatal effects. Alien 'elements' always tend to seep into the Party, and foreign 'intelligence services' constantly attempt to send agents into it (and to 'recruit' Party members). All these enemies unceasingly try to 'crawl' into the Party's 'fortress,' using 'the smallest crack.' And even a very small noxious object gains immense destructive power if it succeeds in introducing itself into one's vital interior.

However, if the Party just 'surrenders to spontaneity,' it will be penetrated and destroyed. It is only by incessant and intense counter-action that it can enhance its chances of survival: the Party must make itself into an impenetrable fortress, and keep itself in that shape. The 'iron curtain' practices, which so much surprised the West, appear as essential measures of self-preservation, once the beliefs I have sketched are accepted as self-evident, as they are by Bolsheviks.

The enemy agent operating in the Soviet interior is, to Bolsheviks, a member of a 'conspiracy' which 'organizes' 'terrorism' and 'wreck-ing.' He is also a 'spy' in the more conventional sense of the word who obtains secret information, as a prelude to destructive action. Against the intense endeavor of enemies to look at the true face of the Party and its works, the Party must make that face invisible. It must succeed in knowing more about the enemy than it permits the enemy to know about the Party. On realistic grounds the Politburo may be well satisfied by the fact that data bearing on nuclear weapons are more easily accessible in the United States than in the Soviet domain. But beyond this Bolsheviks are apt to be profoundly reassured by any situation which seems to fulfill the wish for being invisible to an enemy whom one has well within one's sights: being inviolable to an enemy in whom one can already perceive his corpse. We come here upon the deep roots, in the Bolshevik mind, of a characteristic attitude taken by the Soviet delegate in the United Nations Disarma-ment Commission when it discussed, in the spring of 1952, a proposed global census of military strength. This, he said, was a proposal for an 'international intelligence service' to procure data for the British Intelligence Service and the Pentagon.

Resist from the Start

Western officials have often commented on the posture of resistance which Soviet negotiators habitually assume. Even when Western proposals are not really controversial, Soviet delegates are apt to begin with a negative reaction and then to introduce motions for modifications which on analysis turn out to be rather irrelevant. In top-level contacts one could observe a Soviet disinclination to accept the hour which the Western side would suggest for the next session; the request would be made to meet half an hour earlier or later. To Bolsheviks the complete acceptance of the proposal of an enemy (any non-Communist) tends to signifiy 'yielding' to that enemy, regardless of how harmless the proposal may appear or how much it may seem to correspond to a common interest of the Party and its partners—but then it is a Bolshevik assumption that any harmless façade is apt to hide a noxious core, and that the transitory common interests which may emerge between the Party and other groups (for instance, in a war of coalition) are apt to be outweighed by the unceasing basic enmity between them.

Bolsheviks are intensely and obscurely apprehensive of the danger that they will permit themselves to 'yield' to enemies (who will thereupon proceed to their annihilation). They are afraid of the temptation just to suffer an attack, without resisting or counterattacking in feeling or act. To ward off this temptation, they maintain that the Party can survive and be victorious only if it opposes a most intense and all-sided resistance (preferably by counterattack) to all encroachments of the enemy on its domain, an attitude symbolized by Soviet and satellite reactions to minor violations of their air space by foreign planes in the years after the Second World War.

The Party must thus rigorously apply the rule of *principiis obsta*: it must attempt to undo hostile events in their earliest manifestations. Bolshevik doctrine emphatically opposes the tendency to interfere with undesired developments too little and too late, rather than 'cutting them off at their roots.' If intervention is delayed or insufficient, the initially small bad development is apt to grow at an accelerating rate, inducing catastrophe. An enemy may have decided to execute a campaign against the Party in mounting installments; to make him desist, his plan has to be foiled as early as possible.

A small unfavorable event may also appear as highly dangerous in itself: instead of a sequence of increasing evils a sudden transition from 'scratch' to 'gangrene' will then be feared. Thus the enemy may lay a trap: an ostensibly small concession to somebody who is on the surface not an enemy at all may lead to one's being utterly dominated by the other who then reveals his 'true face.'

In recent years the Politburo has applied the rule of *principiis obsta* in certain characteristic ways in its foreign relations. In institutions in which the Party and its enemies temporarily coexist—for example, in international conferences and in the United Nations—the Soviet representatives have usually insisted on stringent rules of procedure. Their aim was often to prevent certain undesirable decisions not only from being taken but even from being considered—either by excluding the issues involved or by excluding potential participants who might bring them up. Underlying this is a fear that once an undesirable decision is being considered, a pressure toward adopting it is set up which is best counteracted at the very source. In a related vein, Soviet representatives may attempt to secure a falsification of records, expunging undesirable statements from them.

There is a similar motivation behind the extreme touchiness which Soviet officials seem to show in the face of what they regard as prestige slights toward the Soviet Union (and they are apt to view in this light many events which seem harmless to Westerners). It is true that Bolshevik doctrine opposes the propensity really to take offense and to act on feelings of offense. The Bolshevik leader must view politics as a sphere in which one cannot offend and in which one must never be offended. Still less should one permit oneself to be disastrously carried away in action by feelings of offense which one should not have experienced in the first place. Being offended by an enemy implies, after all, that one does not really feel one's relation to him to be summarized in the question, Who will destroy Whom? Bolsheviks have, however, with the passage of time, increased their regard for prestige as a political instrument. They have come to insist on the rule of *principiis obsta* in countering even ostensibly mild slights to their prestige. It is by such slights that an enemy may begin a campaign which in its further course would inflict severe damage. Not reacting to them means to encourage the enemy. As we shall see below, once a severe enemy attack has materialized, or is about to do so, the Party must be able to disregard considerations of prestige. But in situations falling short of severe crisis one must often release, or simulate, feelings of offense against enemies to counter the beginnings of their encroachments on one's domain. In such situations the trivial is the first line of defense on which to meet the enemy assaults which always aim at the crucial.

Retreat before Superior Force

If Bolsheviks must never 'yield' to an enemy, they must sometimes —and on very important occasions indeed—'retreat' before him; for example, accept a precise ultimatum of his, which reduces, but does not liquidate, the Party's possessions.

Retreat is required when standing fast threatens annihilation in view of the enemy's superior force. As long as the Party and its state power are preserved (even in a reduced area and to a reduced degree), the chances of ultimate victory are good. From the remote bases to which it will have retreated in order to preserve its existence, the Party will in time launch a successful counteroffensive. During the 'respite' procured by retreat, it will have accumulated forces; and those of the historically doomed enemy may have declined. On the other hand, Bolsheviks are deeply apprehensive about how quickly resurrection would follow annihilation, and (on a less conscious level) whether it would follow at all. Hence the most precious good, existence itself, must never be risked, even if securing some measure of existence involves retreating to a much reduced state. Skill in retreating is just as indispensable for both survival and victory as skill in attacking.

Not only is any degree of retreat preferable to risking the Party's and the regime's annihilation, but very large degrees of retreat are in fact compatible with the survival which makes a future counteroffensive possible. While Bolsheviks are intensely reluctant to abandon even the smallest position unless they see overwhelming reasons for doing so, they can with equanimity envisage very far-reaching withdrawals if the threat to survival seems sufficiently acute. That is, as the enemy's pressure mounts, he achieves no results before a very high degree of pressure is reached; from that moment on, the results may become substantial. It is only *in extremis* that Bolsheviks can permit themselves to consider retreats, but then they are required to perform them.

Bolsheviks expect a 'serious' enemy clearly to indicate a *casus belli*—more specifically, to issue an ultimatum—before he strikes, unless he aims at the Party's immediate and full annihilation. However, if his momentary objective is limited, he will want to gain it economically, by the threat rather than by the use of force. In order to achieve this purpose, he must make his threat very clear—as Bolsheviks do in the corresponding situation. Thus the Politburo was explicit in its threats toward Finland in 1939, and vague in its protest against West German rearmament in 1950-1952, when it did not intend to go to war to prevent it.

Retreating is thus for Bolshevik leaders a conduct which is as legitimate—that is, as much required in certain conditions—as advancing. Any required retreat is forced in the sense that it is chosen in view of the enemy's power; but it is chosen as the most expedient means to preserve the Party and to prepare its victory, that is, the annihilation of the enemy before whom one is retreating. In retreating when 'consciousness' bids them to do so, Bolsheviks maintain the sense of control so essential to them.

Feelings of distress about retreating and conceptions of what is 'revolutionary' or compatible with dignity must never keep the Party from executing an expedient retreat. If one allows oneself to be dominated by feelings in one's political conduct, one ensures one's futility or disaster. One also shows one's lack of dedication: instead of being guided entirely by the standard of efficiency (in maximizing the Party's power and thus in bringing about communism), one is selfishly concerned with the little displeasures of one's conventional conscience. If one allows conceptions of honor to intrude into one's political calculations, one surrenders to the enemy's control. A code of honor requires specific reactions to certain acts of others, and thereby allows an enemy to predetermine one's behavior. The enemy can then, in effect, force the Party to commit suicide. Real Bolsheviks never permit themselves to 'put political questions on a sentimental basis'; they are capable of executing any expedient policy, however repugnant it may be to those who maintain a 'sentimental' point of view. They know that it is of the very essence of politics that the useful and the agreeable frequently diverge. Thus the Party must in any given situation consider only expediency to decide whether it can, and must, assume a posture which would be manifestly 'revolutionary' (the

Party is always revolutionary, in reality, when it pursues a correct line). The emotional urge to take up what seems to be a 'revolutionary' position must not influence the Party's conduct. It is the pseudorevolutionary who wants to exhibit his present acts; the really revolutionary Party will, when the time comes, exhibit its completed product, a new world.

The Party's insight into the nature of history prepares it for retreats. Bolsheviks know that even if the line of the Party is correct, recurrent setbacks are to be expected. History moves in ebbs and flows. In order to reduce unfavorable developments, one must face them fully. In a situation in which one has to retreat, one must clearly realize the full measure of the losses and threats which render a retreat necessary, and also the damage which the retreat itself involves. But one must not permit oneself to be overcome by despair, fear, or rage: Bolsheviks are convinced of the fatal consequences of yielding to passion, to sensitivity, excitement, and emotional incontinence. All energy must be channeled into the analysis by which the Party 'takes account' of the unfavorable situation, and into the resulting actions by which the Party reverses it.

But, as we have already seen, retreat is permissible (and then, required) only under duress; it will usually have been preceded by the fierce and prolonged resistance by which one acquires the right (and convinces oneself of the duty) to retreat. It has sometimes been proposed in the West that the Politburo be induced by means short of war or threat of war to relinquish control over some or all of the eastern European areas which fell under its domination in 1944-45. (We should in this context not forget that the Soviet Army could evacuate some or all of these areas, and yet the Politburo retain control over them.) The Western powers might, it has been suggested, attempt to heighten disaffection in these parts of the Soviet domain and thereby increase the cost to the Politburo of holding them as well as reduce the profit accruing from them (by the impact of low morale on production, for instance). If developments of both kinds were to occur on a large scale, the Politburo, it is predicted, would find it expedient to withdraw. Enslavement, it has been said, can be made so unprofitable that the master will let go his grip. I would rather make another prediction: if the situation, say, in East Germany were to become sufficiently difficult for the present regime, the Politburo might proceed to mass deportations of the population of this area to the interior of the Soviet Union; but it could never even consider a withdrawal under these circumstances without feeling that it had 'degenerated' into envisaging an act of 'yielding' to the enemy. Such an act carries with itself, for a Bolshevik, the immediate penalty of devastating guilt and shame, and also an imminent penalty of further setbacks leading to annihilation. It is only by force or threat of force that the Politburo could conceivably be induced to withdraw from an area it now controls.

It has also often been suggested in the West that the Politburo might withdraw from an outlying area of its domain in order to set into motion a chain of events which would eventually lead to gains greater than the loss by which they would have been obtained. These gains might include the territory one had voluntarily surrendered, or they might consist of other advantages more important to the Politburo than what it had given up. Thus it was often surmised in the spring of 1952 that the Politburo was willing to abandon control over East Germany. The Politburo predicted, according to many Western observers, that the ensuing unification of Germany would in various ways greatly weaken the power of the Western bloc on the continent of Europe and create the possibility of a Soviet alliance with a powerful Germany. Again, I believe that such calculations are extremely uncongenial to the Politburo. Bolsheviks may well believe that, if they actually surrender a certain position (without duress), events may follow which will in the end bring them a benefit far surpassing the loss they initially assumed. The difficulty for Bolsheviks to act on such a forecast lies in the word 'may.' How will such a course of policy look if the worst will turn out to be the real, rather than the favorable variant of the future which alone would make the operation profitable? In the instance which I was just discussing, what if a reconstituted powerful Germany were really to become what the Politburo had dreaded from 1936 to 1944 it might become, the battering ram of the West against the Soviet Union? Then a great Bolshevik fear would have come true, the fear of being actually 'used' by the enemy while believing that one 'uses' him; specifically, in this case, the fear of being taken in by a deceptive maneuver of enemies who pretend to be in conflict while they have already concluded a secret agreement at the Party's expense. By forgetting to orient its policy on the worst possible future—by succumbing to 'adventurism'— the Politburo would have inflicted on itself a series of losses, starting with the one which it voluntarily assumed, in this case the surrender of East Germany. The disaster would have begun with the crime of actually surrendering a tenable position in the mere hope of superior returns.

War by Negotiation

In certain circumstances any kind of agreement, with any kind of enemy, may be just as much required as all-out violence against an enemy is in others. The aim of both methods is the same, to decrease the chances of the Party being annihilated, to increase the chances of its annihilating its enemies. Revulsion against being allied with an outside group must affect Bolshevik conduct as little as the pleasure Bolsheviks might experience in inflicting heavy damage on it. The aim is, of course, to liquidate that group, but it must be left entirely to the calculation of power relations to ascertain whether this aim is at present best served by, for instance, alliance or by, for instance, war. When, at the end of the period of civil war and intervention, Lenin was in favor of offering economic 'concessions' on Soviet soil, he said that foreign entrepreneurs coming to the Soviet Union under such arrangements would come in a 'new war'; the very existence of these entrepreneurs was already, he added, 'war' against the Soviet regime—which, we may add in turn, feels its very existence to be war against the part of the world which it does not yet control.

When the Party and a certain enemy have failed in their attempts to advance against each other, the conditions for an effective agreement between them have come into existence. An agreement is then the result of overt conflict pursued up to the very last moment. It is by maximizing one's success in that conflict—by maximizing the damage one inflicts on the enemy—that one maximizes the enemy's incentives to substitute, for the time being, a struggle by negotiation for the preceding type of war, whether hot or cold. The struggle by negotiation, in its turn, proceeds in the same fashion: the exertion of pressure on each other by both sides—including the threat to break off negotiations and actual rupture—is apt to foster the conclusion of an agreement. The more pressure one has exercised not only before but also during the negotiations, the more favorable will the final agreement be. At any point it is the 'sharpening' of conflict which is likely to increase the chance of a favorable settlement. If the issue is important—and which is not, directly or indirectly?—the conflict is likely to be protracted.

Bolsheviks do not share the belief of many Western negotiators and observers that it is usually appropriate to be friendly during the working hours of a negotiation (though Bolshevik negotiators make it a point to be at least perfectly correct after hours—no feelings should interfere with the observance of protocol). Bolsheviks tend to apply to negotiation the techniques which I have already discussed: they strive to push to the limits of their strength, using verbal assault as one of their means and trying hard and long for all their objectives, whether big or small. They fiercely resist anything which seems to be a concession unless a condition of duress requires them to retreat—then, perhaps, quite substantially.

Westerners have often commented that there is, in negotiating with the Soviet Union, no common search for a solution to common problems, no discussion in the Western sense of the term. The Soviet delegates elaborate or change their position in strict isolation and then present it in dogmatic fashion. They rarely take account of the views and objections of the other side, and frequently affirm and repeat points which the other side (they know) as well as they themselves regard as grossly false, without bothering to furnish evidence. Again, what seems at first sight to be unintelligible oddities turn out to be closely related to central feelings and thoughts of Bolsheviks. They are indeed intensely afraid—whether obscurely or quite consciously— that they might permit themselves to be influenced by voices outside the Party, and thus fall under the control of enemies. To ward off this danger, Bolsheviks attempt to make themselves impervious to 'alien' opinions. They try to extract intelligence from them but forbid themselves a spontaneous consideration of the possibility that they might contain truth. To be openminded on the spot toward what enemies may have to say is to surrender to their control. True, to 'utilize' an enemy fully, as Bolsheviks must, may imply learning from him. But this must be done in strict isolation and secrecy, and with the most exacting vigilance; one must always assume that the points made by the enemy are solely to his advantage. The discussions in the United Nations Atomic Energy Commission illustrate this attitude.

Bolsheviks also react against the temptation to believe that enemies can be persuaded by appeals to their morality or their real interests, and their enmity thus reduced. On the contrary, Bolsheviks insist, the major enemies of the Party are just as impervious to outside persuasion as the Party itself ought to be; their total enmity against the Party corresponds entirely to their interests. Bolsheviks and their enemies—all non-Bolsheviks—have essentially nothing in common; there is no shared standard of value between and above them.

The enemy selects the statements he makes in talking to the Party without any regard for their truth and only with a view to their damaging impact on the Party. The Party must act likewise toward the enemy. Thus neither the Party nor the enemy is (or should be) open to persuasion, and neither the Party nor the enemy shows (or should show) any regard for the truth in their dealings with each other. On all these grounds a real discussion between the Party and the outside world is impossible and undesirable.

So is a consideration of political issues on their merits, to use a Western term. The Party must not forgo even the smallest amount of power in order to reduce the distance of the existing world from the principles of communism. First, the Party must achieve predominance in the world at any cost; then it will complete the radical transformation of life. The Party must never consider a current issue on any merit other than that of the power which may be won by manipulating it in a certain way. Hence the Party may use a certain sphere of activity to retaliate against what enemies have done in a quite different sphere. For instance, in the years after the Second World War the Soviet attitude on 'technical' questions involving refugees might depend on 'political' developments concerning Greece and Turkey; in the Bolshevik view both issues are equally political. Or a Soviet concession in one matter might be offered to obtain an advantage in another matter which, from a conventional point of view, seems wholly unrelated to the first. In acting thus, the Party prevents itself from becoming absorbed in the irrelevant details of affairs, focusing at all times on the goal: more power. Concessions may be made only under duress or as parts of a profitable bargain. It is inconceivable to Bolsheviks to offer unilateral concessions to groups viewed as actual or potential enemies in the expectation that this will 'pay off' later by inducing more favorable attitudes in these enemies. They rather expect the enemy to behave according to their own requirements of themselves: having been granted an advantage, he will reinforce his push for more.

As the Party applies its general techniques to negotiations as well as to any other kind of political war, it prevents itself from succumbing to 'petty bourgeois' illusions about the peculiar difficulty and efficacy of negotiation. Western observers often attribute a particular potency to top-level meetings, and at the same time feel that they are very difficult to arrange and especially fragile—great forces for good or evil. The Politburo, on the other hand, feels that if 'serious' ruling groups have decided to conclude a major arrangement, they will not need intermediaries and will easily find suitable channels for negotiation and decision, whichever they may be—if necessary, anything will do. If the 'ruling circles' involved really mean business, questions of prestige will be quickly discarded: one or the other side will make an interesting offer. If the need is felt to conclude an agreement quickly, the offer will be quite specific from the outset. There will then be no necessity to have a prolonged conference in order to clarify the meaning of ambiguous terms. On the other hand, highly ambiguous terms may be deliberately used in less pressing circumstances—or when there is no wish to reach any agreement at all.

To mention a similar point, Western observers of conferences with the Soviet Union have often stressed how the public character of some of the proceedings made agreement more difficult; but Bolsheviks, while mindful of the frequent expediency of secrecy, would locate the major causes of an impasse in the substance rather than in the technique of the negotiation.

Being oriented on what they consider as the substance of politics —the power relations between major groups in the world—Bolsheviks may view it as a secondary matter whether these groups conclude a formal agreement, or whether they fail to do so and break off their attempts in this direction. In the years following the Second World War the Politburo engaged in negotiations with its previous allies in order to advance further beyond the positions secured at Yalta and Potsdam. But it knew, on the one hand, that it could not improve its position much by diplomacy and, on the other hand, that failure in these negotiations would hardly affect the existing situation. Negotiating with the West thus appeared much less important than, for instance, consolidating the power of the Politburo in its newly acquired eastern and central European domains. Specifically, Western observers in the first years after the Second World War seemed to regard it as almost inconceivable that there should be no German peace treaty; they seemed to assume that this would imply a chronic state of some kind of extreme uncertainty. But the Politburo knew that it was creating a new order in eastern Germany from the very first day of occupation on, and that it would continue to do so, with or without a peace treaty. Similarly, I would surmise that the creation of the North Atlantic Treaty Organization did not radically change the Politburo's estimate of the situation at its western borders. The Soviet Army had abstained from crossing them since 1945 because the Politburo believed that this might be a *casus belli* for the Anglo-Americans.

Ever since the beginning of overt tension between the Soviet Union and the West in the fall of 1945, there have been Western observers who have felt that at least some relief from that tension would be achieved by negotiation—now or later, when 'positions of strength' had been acquired. They usually did not indicate what they could offer the Politburo and what they would ask in return, or what pressures they would apply to the Politburo to make it retreat from certain vital positions, and how the result would justify a sharp reduction of armament levels in the West. One often had the impression that these attitudes were based on a belief in the sheer power of 'negotiation' to reduce 'tension'—a belief which is not held by the Politburo, and which is false when one applies it to dealings with the Politburo.

Stalin on Revolution

HISTORICUS

The stress laid by Stalin on the importance of theory is so foreign to American habits of mind that we are prone to underestimate the influence which theory plays in determining his action. Any such tendency would lead us into especially grave error when we come to estimating the importance of his theoretical conception of the nature of revolution, for on this he has been amazingly consistent.

In a preface to the first volume of his collected works, Stalin takes the trouble to point out deficiencies in certain views expressed in his youthful writings, years before the October Revolution.[1] Since then eight volumes of the collected works have appeared, but they contain no more prefaces by Stalin; the inference is that he considers the rest doctrinally correct. Stalin exhibits the same meticulous care about doctrine in a letter to members of the Politburo in which he opposes

Reprinted by special permission from *Foreign Affairs* (January 1949). Copyright by Council on Foreign Relations, Inc., New York.

Historicus has been identified as George A. Morgan, of the U. S. Department of State, who wrote this paper at the Russian Institute of Columbia University.

Note: Where the period of republication of particular items for mass consumption is relevant to the discussion, this information is supplied in parentheses in the footnotes. Thus '(1925-39)' means 'originally published in 1925, republished until 1939,' and '(1925 to present)' means 'originally published in 1925, republished up to the present time.'

[1] *Sochineniia*, I (1946), xi. The author of the present study found only one other instance in which Stalin in his mature years modified an earlier statement. "K voprosam Leninizma" (1926) quotes the original version of one paragraph in "Ob osnovakh Leninizma" (1924), relating to the victory of socialism in one country, and points out its inadequacy; and subsequent versions of "Ob osnovakh Leninizma" contain a revised wording of the passage. See *Voprosy Leninizma* (11th ed., 1945), pp. 25, 137. [The abbreviation *Voprosy* hereafter used for this title refers to the 11th ed., 1945 printing, unless otherwise noted.]

the republication of an obscure article of Engels' in *Bol'shevik* unless the errors in its conception of imperialism are pointed out. Publication of an article in "our fighting magazine," he holds, means that it is to be taken "as directive or at least deeply informative for our Party workers."[2] Back of such pains about detail on the part of so busy a man lies a conviction that correctness of theory is vitally important. Stalin denies that "Leninism is the primacy of practice over theory." On the contrary, "the tendency of practical workers to brush theory aside contradicts the whole spirit of Leninism and is pregnant with great dangers for the cause." And again : "None other than Lenin said and repeated tens of times the well-known thesis that '*Without revolutionary theory there can be no revolutionary movement.*'"[3]

The present study summarizes the body of ideas on revolution which has presumably played a part in Stalin's thought and action, as revealed in his published writings and statements. Except for two reports of interviews with Stalin published in the United States but apparently not in the Soviet Union, it makes use of Russian sources only. The author believes that he has discovered and examined for relevant material nearly everything by Stalin originally published between January 1, 1929, and March 28, 1948; and, in addition, he has read all of Stalin's writings likely to be of central importance as far back as February 1919. Much of the material was republished on a large scale during the periods investigated. The general character of Communist thought makes it extremely unlikely that this would have happened if the statements were considered out of date or in any way inconsistent with current ideology, and, above all, if the outmoded features were not at the same time pointed out clearly. The sacredness in which the faithful hold every word of Stalin's makes it doubly improbable that anything of his which was obsolete would be republished without proper correction. *Voprosy Leninizma* [Problems of Leninism], the basic collection of Stalin's writing (hereafter referred to in this study as *Voprosy*) has gone through 11 editions to date and has been reprinted in many millions of copies; the 1947 printing of the eleventh edition (first published in 1939) states, on the last page, that it amounts to 4,000,000 copies. Stalin's *Istoriia Vsesoiuznoi Kommunisticheskoi partii* [His-

---

[2] *Bol'shevik* (May 1941), p. 1.
[3] "Ob osnovakh Leninizma" (1924 to present), in *Voprosy*, p. 14.

tory of the All-Union Communist Party] (hereafter referred to in this study as *Istoriia*), first published in 1938, is still being reprinted; in 1946 *Pravda* stated that the total number of copies exceeded 31,000,000.[4] The fundamental role played by these two volumes in the indoctrination of Party workers and in the compulsory courses in Marxism-Leninism justifies us in attributing high value to their testimony on matters of current orthodoxy according to Stalin.

The few instances where passages in republished works are (or at first sight appear to be) inconsistent with passages in new publications will be discussed on their merits when occasion arises. In view of the acknowledged Communist practice of pursuing long-range strategy by means of highly variable tactical lines, the presumption is by no means necessarily in favor of the new statements. The burden of proof must rather fall on whoever maintains that the new statement represents a permanent change in doctrine and not a mere temporary shift in the 'line.'

The cornerstones of *Voprosy* are found in two works by Stalin published in 1924, "Ob osnovakh Leninizma" and "Oktiabr'skaia revoliutsiia i taktika russkikh kommunistov." They contain the essence of his revolutionary theory, which he attributes to Lenin. This theory has been clarified or supplemented from time to time with respect to particular points. Thus it received more explicit Marxist-Leninist philosophical setting in the *Istoriia*. But it has never been abandoned or altered in fundamentals.

Americans, though of course admitting the role of science in engineering, industry, and similar fields, will be surprised by Stalin's conviction that in Leninist Marxism he has a science of human society and its development in history which makes possible the prediction—and, within limits, the engineering—of the course of history. Thus he writes in

---

[4] *Pravda*, October 2, 1946, p. 2. [The *Istoriia Vsesoiuznoi Kommunisticheskoi partii* was ascribed to Stalin until Khrushchev, in his secret report of February 24-25, 1956, at the Twentieth Party Congress disclosed the falsity of Stalin's claim to authorship and stated that the work had been written by a commission of the Party Central Committee. This perplexity of authorship, however, in no way vitiates Historicus' argument. Whether Stalin himself wrote a substantial part of the book or not a single line, the work was unquestionably done under his dictate and close supervision. See *The Anti-Stalin Campaign: A Selection of Documents*, edited by the Russian Institute, Columbia University (revised edition, New York, 1956), pp. 72-73. — A.D.]

his history of the Party: "Marxist-Leninist theory is science of the development of society, science of the workers' movement, science of proletarian revolution, science of the construction of Communist society." And again: "The strength of Marxist-Leninist theory consists in the fact that it enables the Party to orient itself in a situation, to grasp the internal connection of surrounding events, to foresee the course of events and to discern not only how and in what direction events are developing in the present but also how and in what direction they must develop in the future."[5]

Only such a view could explain the strong language Stalin uses on the ideological training of Party cadres:

One can say with confidence that, if we could prepare our cadres in all branches of work ideologically and temper them politically to such a degree that they could easily orient themselves in the domestic and international situation, if we could make them fully mature Marxist-Leninists, able to solve the problems of running the country without serious errors—then we would have reason to consider nine-tenths of all our problems already solved. And we are absolutely able to accomplish this task.[6]

The Science of Revolution

In outlining Stalin's revolutionary theory, we shall first consider his views on those determinants of revolution which he calls 'objective,' that is, those historical forces which, though modified by the action of conscious human wills, determine the basic pattern of history regardless of human will.

Stalin calls the philosophical framework of his theory "dialectical and historical materialism." It is, in effect, revolution writ large into the cosmos; its basic postulates are so many reasons why 'the bourgeoisie' are on the way down and 'the proletariat' on the way up, why 'capitalism' must inevitably give way to 'socialism' everywhere, and why this must occur by violent revolution. It is sufficient for our present purposes to state briefly those postulates which are most important for Stalin's theory of revolution.

[5] *Istoriia* (1938 to present), p. 339.
[6] "Otchëtnyi doklad t. Stalina na XVIII s"ezde partii o rabote TsK VKP (b)" (1939 to present), in *XVIII s"ezd: Stenograficheskii otchët* (Moscow, 1939), p. 31.

Relativity. Nature is a "connected, single whole," in which "phenomena are organically related to each other, depend on each other, and condition each other." Applied to human society, this means "that every social system and every social movement in history must be evaluated not from the point of view of 'eternal justice' . . . but from the point of view of the conditions which gave birth to that system and that social movement and with which they are connected." Thus a slave-owning economy, which would be absurd for modern conditions, was once a 'step forward' in comparison with the primitive communal system; and 'a bourgeois-democratic republic,' though it would have represented a 'step forward' for Russia in 1905, would be a 'step backward' for the USSR today.

Change. Nature is constantly changing; "there is always something arising and evolving, something declining and living out its time." This means that "the dying off of what is old and the growth of something new is the law of evolution," hence that there are no "'stable' social orders" or "'eternal principles' of private property." It means further that "only that which is rising and developing is invincible, that is, that a rising class, though yet relatively weak, is a better bet politically than one which has had its rise and, though still relatively powerful, is beginning to decline. Hence, according to Stalin, the Marxists were right in basing their policy on the proletariat even in Russia in the 1880s, because it was evolving as a class, while the peasantry, though in the enormous majority, was declining as a class.

Sudden Qualitative Change. The process of evolution is not simply one of quantitative growth; 'insignificant and hidden quantitative changes' repeatedly accumulate to a point at which radical and 'open' 'qualitative changes' suddenly occur. For human society this means that "revolutionary overturns, produced by oppressed classes, are a perfectly natural and inevitable phenomenon." In contemporary terms "it means that the transition from capitalism to socialism . . . can be accomplished not by means of slow change, not by means of reform, but only by means of qualitative change of the capitalist system, by means of revolution."

Progress. The previous postulate, according to Stalin, implies that evolution is progress, that is, that nature moves not in a circle but in an upward direction, from "the simple to the complex, from the lower to the higher.'"[7] We state this here as a separate postulate, because on it depends the claim that revolution is not merely inevitable but right, since it leads to a 'qualitative change for the better.' Stalin does not go into this, preferring, as Marxists generally do, to stress the 'scientific' rather than the ethical aspects of his theory. But that he has deep convictions on the matter is evident from the general tone of his writings. When in an interview with Stalin, Emil Ludwig compares him to Peter the Great, Stalin replies: "The task to which I am dedicating my life consists in elevating ... the working class. That task is not the strengthening of any national state but the strengthening of a socialist, and that means international, state."[8]

Contradiction and Struggle. "The process of evolution from the lower to the higher takes place not as a harmonious unfolding of phenomena but as a disclosure of the contradictions inherent in things and phenomena, as a 'struggle' of opposite tendencies which operate on the basis of these contradictions," "in order to overcome these contradictions." This means that "the class struggle of the proletariat is a perfectly natural and inevitable phenomenon," that "we must not cover up the contradictions of the capitalist system but uncover and draw them out, not extinguish the class struggle but carry it to its conclusion." Here, and in the theory of sudden qualitative change, is Stalin's philosophical ground for his position that a basic policy (as distinguished from temporary tactics) of compromise and reform is a mistake.

Materialism. Objective reality is material; consciousness is a 'reflection' of matter and a product of it. From this Stalin infers that "the material life of society ... is primary, and its spiritual life secondary, derivative"; that is, "one must look for the source of social ideas, social theories, political views, and political institutions ... in the conditions of the material life of society," of which the ideas and institutions are a 'reflection.'

The Means of Production. Of the various factors composing 'the material life of society,' the one which determines "the character of the social system and the evolution of society from one system to

[7] This quotation and the quotations used in the preceding three paragraphs are from *Istoriia* (1938 to present), pp. 101, 102, 104, 105.

[8] "I. Stalin, Beseda s nemetskim pisatelem Emilem Liudvigom," *Bol'shevik* (April 30, 1932), p. 33.

another" is "the means of production of material goods." This in turn consists of 'productive forces'—the instruments of production and the people who operate them—and 'productive relations,' that is, the relations between people in the productive process, such as master-slave, capitalist-laborer. "Changes in the means of production inevitably evoke change of the whole social system," including political institutions.

The Primary Contradiction of Capitalism. The prime mover of social progress is change in the productive forces, especially tools: as new types of tools develop they enter into 'contradiction' or 'nonconformity' with the increasingly outmoded productive relations, until the latter are demolished and new ones created to correspond with the requirements of the productive forces. With this 'sudden, qualitative' change comes a change in the whole social system. Such is the inmost dynamic of revolution. Capitalism, for example, develops large-scale industrial plants as productive forces; but "by gathering millions of workers together in enormous factories and plants, capitalism gives a social character to the process of production and thereby undermines its own basis," namely, the productive relations that center around private ownership of industry. Thus the primary contradiction that develops inside capitalism as it evolves is that between actual private ownership and the new productive forces which require social ownership for their full expansion. This maladjustment expresses itself in the periodic crises of overproduction familiar to capitalism, and finally in revolution which resolves the contradiction by socializing the means of production.[9]

The foregoing is not a complete summary of Stalin's dialectical and historical materialism, but it gives the basis of his claim to know with 'scientific' certainty that socialist revolution must come sooner or later in capitalist countries. It should be stressed that for Stalin the decisive issue is the substitution of socialist ownership and operation for private ownership and operation of the means of production; all other differences in modern social systems are of subordinate importance. This is the basis of his insistence to H. G. Wells, in 1934, that the New Deal reforms in the United States cannot affect the

[9] The quotations in this paragraph and the preceding three paragraphs are from *Istoriia* (1938 to present), pp. 104, 106, 110, 114-15, 121.

ultimate necessity for revolution, and to Harold E. Stassen, in 1947, that the United States and Nazi Germany had the same kind of economic systems.[10]

The next step in our inquiry is to analyze in greater detail Stalin's conception of the social forces, apart from conscious leadership, which contribute to the build-up and final achievement of revolution. These forces are formed around four secondary contradictions, which are aggravated by the primary contradiction between productive forces and productive relations.

The Class Struggle. Antagonism between classes is not peculiar to capitalism, in Stalin's view. It is inherent in slave-owning and feudal social systems as well — in short, wherever one class monopolizes ownership of the means of production and thereby 'exploits' the rest. Under capitalism the chief protagonists of class struggle are the 'capitalists' and those who must sell their labor to the capitalists in order to live—the 'proletariat.' The rest of society—petty bourgeois, peasants, intelligentsia—form a comparatively amorphous and fluctuating mass, gravitating now to one side, now to the other.[11]

Hence the proletariat is the inevitable vehicle for the socialist revolution. In contrast to the peasantry, it is connected with the most advanced form of economy and therefore has 'more future.' Further, "the proletariat as a class is growing year by year, is developing politically, is easily accessible to organization by reason of its work in large-scale production, and is most revolutionary because of its proletarian position, as it has nothing to lose by revolution except its chains."[12] In contrast to the intelligentsia, on the other hand, the proletariat has the mass necessary for revolutionary power: "for that, a large class is needed, which would replace the class of capitalists and become just as sovereign a master as it is."[13] Thus arises the central Leninist doctrine that socialist revolution can occur only through substitution of the dictatorship of the proletariat for the

[10] "Beseda t. Stalina s angliiskim pisatelem G. D. Uellsom" (1934-39), *Bol'shevik*, September 15, 1934, p. 8; "Zapis' besedy tov. I. V. Stalina s deiatelem respublikanskoi partii SShA Garol'dom Stassenom," *Pravda*, May 8, 1947, p. 1.

[11] *Istoriia* (1938 to present), pp. 15, 120; "Ob osnovakh Leninizma" (1924 to present), pp. 54, 60, 74.

[12] *Istoriia* (1938 to present), pp. 14-15.

[13] "Beseda t. Stalina s angliiskim pisatelem G. D. Uellsom" (1934-39), p. 13.

dictatorship of the bourgeoisie (which, in Stalin's view, is the essence of all capitalist states).[14]

It is ultimately from the growing contradiction between social productive forces and private property productive relations that the class struggle receives the dynamism, the increasing tension, which impels it toward revolution.[15] Just how this occurs is not fully clear from Stalin's writings. The earlier Marxist doctrine of 'increasing misery' of the proletariat was modified by Lenin and others in view of the observable fact that workers were not getting poorer. Stalin does not discuss this topic, but possibly he, too, as a disciple of Lenin, does not hold the earlier view. What certainly does increase, according to Stalin, is tension between the two classes—the bourgeoisie puts more and more 'pressure' on the proletariat, which the proletariat meets with growing resistance and resentment. The 'pressure' or 'oppression' by the bourgeoisie takes various forms. One is the effort to reduce wages or hold them down, which becomes ever more powerful as capitalism enters its monopoly stage. Another is the actual misery caused by falling wages and unemployment in times of economic crisis—the recurrent crises being due to the fact that the capitalists do not allow wages to rise in proportion to production, thus curtailing purchasing power and bringing about 'overproduction' as a result. Another form of pressure by the bourgeoisie is Fascism, which deprives workers of important means of resistance—labor unions, parliaments, the freedom to form labor or Communist parties.[16]

As will be explained later, the tension between bourgeoisie and proletariat does not increase uniformly but in a wave-like ebb and flow. While tension mounts, the social system nears the flashpoint of revolution: there is "aggravation of the revolutionary crisis inside the capitalist countries, accumulation of explosive elements on the internal, proletarian front."[17]

[14] "Ob osnovakh Leninizma" (1924 to present), p. 26; *Istoriia* (1938 to present), p. 11.

[15] *Istoriia* (1938 to present), pp. 117, 121.

[16] "Ob osnovakh Leninizma" (1924 to present), pp. 3, 17; "XVI s"ezd" (1930-39), *Pravda*, June 29, 1930, p. 1; "XVII s"ezd" (1934 to present), *ibid.*, January 28, 1934, p. 1; *Istoriia* (1938 to present), pp. 117, 121, 288.

[17] "Ob osnovakh Leninizma" (1924 to present), pp. 17, 55.

The Imperialist Stage of Capitalism. Stalin, following Lenin, holds that capitalism in its last stage, when it becomes ripe for revolution, turns monopolist and imperialist. The scene is dominated by giant trusts and combinations of international finance which rival each other for control of world markets, raw materials, and opportunities for investment of surplus capital. This means that there is no longer an assortment of capitalist systems, one for each country, but one world capitalist system. Revolution accordingly occurs in particular countries as a result of the total interplay of forces within the world system and not, as earlier Marxists expected, simply as the result of local conditions.

Formerly it was usual to speak of the presence or absence of objective conditions for proletarian revolution . . . in one or another well developed country. . . . Now we must speak of the presence of objective conditions of revolution in the entire system of world imperialist economy as an integral whole; the existence within this system of some countries that are not sufficiently developed industrially cannot serve as an insurmountable obstacle to revolution . . . *because* the system as a whole is already ripe for revolution.[18]

From this it follows that revolution need not occur first in the countries that are most advanced industrially, as Marx's historical materialism seemed once to imply. Revolution occurs rather as a break in the world 'front' of the capitalist system, and therefore at the point where the chain has its weakest link. So in 1917 it came first in Russia, an admittedly backward country, and in 1924 Stalin said it might occur next in Germany or in India—in any case, again at the weakest point in the world system. In a later comment Stalin points out that the weakest point in the world system of capitalism is not the point where industry is *least* developed, else revolution would have begun somewhere in central Africa. A 'certain minimum' of industrial development and of culture is prerequisite for revolution.[19]

The direct effect of the rise of monopoly capitalism on the contradiction between bourgeoisie and proletariat has been mentioned. In addition, two further contradictions are now generated within the capitalist system.

[18] *Ibid.,* p. 18.
[19] *Pravda,* December 18, 1929, p. 3.

One of these is the international counterpart of the class struggle: the great monopolies seek to exploit the foreign as well as the domestic field, which leads to a few powerful capitalist countries dividing up the world as colonial possessions and spheres of influence. Thus arises a contradiction within the capitalist world economy between the exploiting imperialists and the exploited colonies. As tension rises, a revolutionary crisis develops in the exploited countries, taking the form primarily of movements for national liberation from imperialism.[20]

The other contradiction develops between rival capitalist countries. Since some evolve more rapidly than others, they come to demand a larger share of colonies and spheres of influence than the one allotted on the basis of their former power. Since no country will voluntarily hand over part of its present share, tension mounts until imperialist war—for example, the First and Second World Wars—inevitably breaks out as the sole means of redividing the world and restoring equilibrium.[21] In Stalin's thinking, the importance of war as a midwife of revolution can scarcely be exaggerated.

The Contradiction between Capitalist and Socialist Systems. According to Stalin, the contradictions above described created the 'objective' basis for the October Revolution of 1917, but in so doing they helped to generate yet another contradiction, that between the capitalist and socialist systems. For henceforth the system of world capitalism has lost its monopoly of the world and its claim to be the latest work in progress. Beside it grows a socialist system which "by the very fact of its existence demonstrates the rottenness of capitalism and shakes loose its foundations."[22] This predicament, together with the loss both of economic equilibrium and of authority in colonial areas occasioned by the war of 1914, constitutes what Stalin calls the 'general crisis of capitalism,' a condition of permanently impaired health. The capitalist system will never recover its pre-1914 stability and self-assurance.

Increasing tension grows from both sides of this contradiction between the social systems. It is an axiom with Stalin that capitalists are filled with envy and hatred and that, whenever they can and dare,

[20] "Ob osnovakh Leninizma" (1924 to present), pp. 3, 17.

[21] *Ibid.*; *Pravda*, February 10, 1946, p. 1.

[22] "XVI s"ezd" (1930-39), p. 1.

they will seek to intervene in the socialist country and restore capitalism. This danger he dramatizes as 'capitalist encirclement,' declaring that socialism cannot be considered finally achieved as long as this danger of intervention and restoration persists.[23] From the other side of the contradiction, every triumph of the Soviet socialist system is considered by Stalin to have a profoundly revolutionizing effect on capitalist countries. In 1933 he states : "The successes of the Five-Year Plan are mobilizing the revolutionary forces of the working class of all countries against capitalism."[24] In addition, there are various kinds of deliberate aid on the part of the socialist system for revolutionary movements inside the capitalist system. These are, properly speaking, not part of the 'objective' determinants of revolution.

The primary and secondary contradictions of capitalist society, which we have just described, interact upon one another to produce revolution. There are three chief types of interaction.

Productive Forces vs. *Productive Relations: Economic Crises.* The effects which the fundamental capitalist contradiction and economic crises have on the class struggle were briefly discussed above. The most striking feature of Stalin's treatment of the contradiction between productive forces and productive relations under capitalism is how little he has to say about it. He does not formulate it expressly until 1938, in his exposition of historical materialism. We have found only one brief earlier allusion to it, as the cause of economic crises.[25]

It would nevertheless be unsafe, as in other cases, to infer from Stalin's comparative silence on this subject that he considers it of minor importance or that he only half believes in it. On the contrary, this doctrine is an integral part of the bedrock of Marxist 'scientific' certainty about the future course of history on which Stalin evidently

[23] "Ob osnovakh Leninizma" (1924 to present), pp. 25, 32; "K voprosam Leninizma" (1926 to present) in *Voprosy*, p. 140; "O nedostatkakh partiinoi raboty i merakh likvidatsii trotskistskikh i inykh dvurushnikov," *Pravda*, March 29, 1938, p. 2; "Otvet t-shchu IVANOVU Ivanu Filippovichu," *ibid.*, February 14, 1938, p. 3; "Otchëtnyi doklad" (1939 to present), p. 32; *Istoriia* (1938 to present), p. 261.

[24] "Itogi pervoi piatiletki" (1933 to present), *Pravda*, January 10, 1933, p. 1. The example of the Stalin Constitution is likewise expected to exert such a revolutionizing force; see *ibid.*, November 26, 1936, p. 3.

[25] "XVI s"ezd" (1930-39), p. 1.

bases his entire life work. It is his cardinal reason for holding that no matter what happens, in the long run all the contradictions of capitalism will get worse and worse until revolution cures the source of trouble by substituting socialism. Indeed, the chief function which this central contradiction of capitalism performs in Stalin's thinking may be to impart certainty to the doctrinal framework. If so, that would explain the brevity of its role in his published writings.

If, however, the idea also operates directly in Stalin's concrete estimates of the pattern of forces in the capitalist world system, this should find expression as some definite relationship between the increasing disparity between productive forces and productive relations —the ultimate mainspring of the trend to revolution—and resultant increases of tension in the derivative contradictions of capitalism. The sole clue of this kind discovered during the present investigation is Stalin's explanation of economic crises. Noting that they have occurred in capitalist countries every eight to twelve years for a century, he claims that they are "an example of the noncorrespondence of productive relations to productive forces," in other words, of the contradiction between "the social character of production and the capitalist form of appropriating the results of production." As capitalism evolves, productive forces (that is, productive capacity) are dynamically expanded, but wages are kept as low as possible in order to make more profits. The result is a 'relative curtailment of purchasing power.' Goods accumulate for which there is no market, and a crisis of overproduction is precipitated. Finished goods and even productive forces are destroyed, factories are closed, and millions suffer unemployment and hunger not because goods are scarce but because they are plentiful. Stalin stresses the destruction of productive forces as conspicuous evidence of the way in which their development is hampered by capitalist productive relations. His account in 1930 concludes : "If capitalism could adapt production not to getting maximum profit but to the systematic improvement of the material conditions of the masses of the people ... then there would not be any crises. But then also capitalism would not be capitalism."[26]

[26] *Ibid.; Istoriia* (1938 to present), pp. 117, 121; "Beseda t. Stalina s angliiskim pisatelem G. D. Uellsom" (1934-39), p. 9.

The role of economic crises in Stalin's writings must be stated carefully. He pays almost no attention to them until after 1929 and, as his writings show, probably did not expect the world depression. The emphasis given to economic crises after 1929—notably in the reports to the Party congresses in 1930, 1934, and 1939—suggests that the lesson of 1929 actually produced an important change in Stalin's thinking about the capitalist world. However, that change appears to have been a modification not in fundamental theory but on an intermediate level between it and concrete data. The doctrine of the contradictions of capitalism remains the basic framework. Within it, after 1929, economic crises play a very prominent role as *symptoms* of the progressive decay of capitalism at its roots—namely, of the increasing contradiction between productive forces and relations—and as added *causes* of greater tension in the four secondary contradictions. In 1930 Stalin sums up his first analysis of the world economic crisis by saying:"The most important results of the world economic crisis are to uncover and aggravate the contradictions inherent in world capitalism."[27]

The fact that Stalin depicts the crisis of 1929 as the worst so far in capitalist history, and that of 1937 as worse still,[28] together with his general picture of capitalism as now in its decadent phase, suggests that such crises do in fact play an important diagnostic role in Stalin's estimates of the degree of deterioration reached at a given time by the capitalist system, and also that he would expect each future crisis—at the customary interval of eight to twelve years—to be worse than the last. The principal indices used in his discussions of particular crises are statistics of production and of unemployment. These are further possible clues to his method of diagnosis.[29]

[27] "XVI s"ezd" (1930-39), p. 1. See also "XVII s"ezd" (1934 to present), p. 1; "Otchëtnyi doklad" (1939 to present), p. 11.

[28] "XVI s"ezd" (1930-39), p. 1; "Otchëtnyi doklad" (1939 to present), p. 9.

[29] Stalin mentions, but does not give statistics on, bankruptcies, ruin of peasants, falling prices, maintenance of monopoly prices at the expense of restricting production, bank failures, trade wars, dumping, currency wars. In 1939 he gives statistics on gold reserves as evidence that the avoidance of economic crisis in Fascist countries is only temporary. See "XVI s"ezd" (1930-39), p. 1; "XVII s"ezd" (1934 to present), p. 1 ; "Otchëtnyi doklad" (1939 to present), p. 10.

The 'Objective' Conditions for Revolution: War. We have seen that, for Stalin, capitalism in its imperialist stage has become a single world system in which the total interplay of forces determines the ripeness of conditions for revolution in particular countries, revolutions actually occurring where the world front of capitalism is weakest in relation to the forces of revolution. The foregoing discussion of capitalist contradictions has provided a ground plan of the lines along which the revolutionary forces are organized. The next step is to consider the criteria for judging the ripeness of the revolutionary situation. Stalin writes that "the proletarian revolution must be regarded primarily as the result of the development of the contradictions within the world system of imperialism, as the result of the snapping of the chain of the imperialist world front in one country or another."[30] How does Stalin estimate when and where the chain is ready to break?

Pointing out that there are "several absolutely necessary conditions, in the absence of which seizure of power by the proletariat is not to be thought of," Stalin quotes Lenin's formulation of them:

The fundamental law of revolution . . . consists in this: For revolution it is not enough that the exploited and oppressed masses should feel the impossibility of living in the old way and demand change; for revolution it is necessary that the exploiters should not be able to live and rule in the old way. Only when the *'lower classes'* do not want the old way and when the *'upper classes'* cannot carry on in the old way—only then can revolution conquer. This truth may be expressed otherwise in the words: *Revolution is impossible without a nation-wide crisis (affecting both the exploited and the exploiters).*[31]

'Revolutionary crisis' is accordingly Stalin's usual name for the total complex of forces constituting the 'objective' conditions necessary for revolution.[32]

[30] "Ob osnovakh Leninizma" (1924 to present), p. 19.

[31] *Ibid.,* p. 25.

[32] Stalin uses the term 'crisis' in so many ways that we must not jump to conclusions from a particular statement. Besides 'revolutionary crisis' he speaks of 'economic crisis,' 'general crisis of capitalism,' 'crisis of world capitalism,' and so forth. So 'crisis' does not necessarily mean 'revolutionary crisis.' Moreover, 'revolutionary crisis' does not necessarily mean revolution, for leadership may fail to take advantage of the situation. Again, 'revolutionary crisis' sometimes

Two features stand out in the above quotation: the power of the bourgeoisie is shaken; the proletariat is aroused. More detail is supplied by a sketch written in 1921 but first published in 1947:

How define the arrival of the moment for revolutionary outbreaks? . . . When the revolutionary mood of the masses . . . brims over and our slogans for action and directives lag behind the movement of the masses . . . when uncertainty and confusion, disintegration and dissolution in the adversary's camp have reached the highest point . . . when the so-called neutral elements, all that mass of many millions of city and village petty bourgeoisie, begin definitely to turn away from the adversary . . . and seek alliance with the proletariat.[33]

This introduces a third feature of the 'objective' conditions for revolution: the masses (other than the proletariat) swing away from the bourgeoisie and toward the proletariat, thus isolating the former and becoming allies or 'reserves,' as Stalin's military phraseology often puts it, of the proletariat. The above quotation mentions petty bourgeoisie, but in other passages Stalin stresses even more the role of the peasantry as ally of the proletariat.[34] In the present context only the general point is important: the bourgeoisie proper must be bereft of mass popular support and the proletariat must have it.

Support is not confined to the boundaries of one country: the local bourgeoisie must to a considerable degree be isolated internationally, while the proletariat receives direct or indirect support from the proletariat of other capitalist countries and from the proletarian state already in existence—the USSR. Hence a further condition for successful revolution is that the balance of potential outside aid for revolution as against potential outside aid for counterrevolution must be sufficiently favorable.[35]

means the full ripeness of the objective conditions for revolution, sometimes the long period of rising tensions which in some cases culminates in ripeness, for which Stalin sometimes employs a special term, 'the immediate revolutionary situation.' On the latter see *Pravda*, February 10, 1930, p. 2.

[33] *Sochineniia*, V, 73.

[34] "Ob osnovakh Leninizma" (1924 to present), pp. 23, 56, 60 ; *Istoriia* (1938 to present), p. 65.

[35] Stalin does not formulate this condition definitely, but it is a clear implication of: (1) his thesis that capitalism is now a world system and revolution the product of forces throughout the system; (2) his emphasis on the international ties of the

To sum up, Stalin's necessary 'objective' conditions for revolution are: bourgeoisie isolated and disorganized, proletariat aroused to revolt and supported by the masses, and a favorable balance of proletarian as against bourgeois aid from outside the country. With these as a frame of reference, we are now able to indicate how, according to Stalin, the contradictions of capitalism interact to produce revolutionary crises. Only certain main lines of influence will be described; details vary endlessly with the concrete configuration of forces.

The primary contradiction, both chronically and in its acute manifestation as economic crisis, impels the bourgeoisie to increase pressure against the proletariat, against colonial peoples, against each other (in rivalry for spheres of influence), and against the Soviet Union. The culmination of these trends is war of one kind or another: the colonies fight for liberation, the capitalist nations who demand greater spheres of influence fight to get them, or capitalist countries attack the Soviet Union as the major threat to their whole system and also as another big area to be exploited. Preparation for war on the part of the bourgeoisie further arouses the proletariat and the other masses who desire peace and resent having to die for their masters, and who also resent the added economic and political pressures—including Fascism, in some cases—which are imposed in order to prepare for war. When the war is to be directed against the Socialist Fatherland, this fact of course greatly adds to the resentment of the proletariat, whose deeper sympathies are on the side of the Soviet Union. Bourgeois preparation for war likewise leads to increased pressure on colonies, with a correspondingly greater tendency of colonies to rebel.[36]

Actual war, however, is the crux of the matter. Stalin writes of the relation of the First World War to the contradictions of capitalism

bourgeoisie and the constant threat of intervention from that quarter (for example, "Ob osnovakh Leninizma," p. 26) ; (3) his statement that the proletariats of capitalist states, and the state in which socialism has already won, will assist the proletariats in other countries to achieve revolution. See "Oktiabr'skaia revoliutsiia i taktika russkikh kommunistov" (1924 to present), in *Voprosy*, p. 104. The topic of outside aid for revolution includes conscious leadership and will be dealt with later in this study.

[36] "Politicheskii otchët TsK" (1927), in *XV s"ezd: Stenograficheskii otchët*, p. 44; "Ob itogakh iiul'skogo plenuma TsK VKP (b)" (1928), in *Voprosy* (9th ed., 1932), p. 336; "XVI s"ezd" (1930-39), p. 1; "XVII s"ezd" (1934 to present), p. 1.

that "the imperialist war . . . gathered all these contradictions into
one bundle and threw them onto the scales, thereby accelerating and
facilitating the revolutionary battles of the proletariat."[37] War between
capitalist countries further intensifies the resentment of the masses
and at the same time both exhausts the strength of the bourgeoisie at
home and makes it difficult for them to intervene against revolution
abroad. Again writing in 1924 of the First World War, Stalin speaks of

the enormous significance of the fact of mortal war between the chief
groups of imperialists in the period of the October Revolution, when
the imperialists, occupied with war among themselves, lacked the ability
to concentrate forces against the young Soviet power, and the proletariat
just for that reason was able to get down to the work of . . . consolidating
its power. . . . It must be presumed that now, when the contradictions
among the imperialist groups are becoming more and more profound,
and when a new war among them is becoming inevitable, reserves of
this description will assume even greater importance for the proletariat.[38]

Thus for the past quarter century, according to the overwhelming
testimony of his writings, Stalin has expected the next crop of revolutions to come during, or in the immediate aftermath of, the Second
World War. To the Seventeenth Party Congress in 1934 he stated
that a new imperialist war "will surely turn loose revolution and place
in jeopardy the very existence of capitalism in a number of countries,
as happened in the course of the first imperialist war."[39] His history
of the Party makes explicit the connection between war and the development of a 'weak link' in the chain of world imperialism : "Lenin
showed that precisely in consequence of this unevenness in the development of capitalism imperialist wars occur, which weaken the forces
of imperialism and make possible a breakthrough in the front of imperialism at the point where it proves to be weakest."[40]

[37] "Ob osnovakh Leninizma" (1924 to present), p. 4.
[38] Ibid., p. 56. Stalin here used the term 'reserves' to include all favorable factors,
not merely men.
[39] "XVII s"ezd" (1934 to present), p. 1. The inevitability of war is the central
theme of the foreign affairs section of each of Stalin's reports to the Party congresses from 1925 through the one in 1939; the direct connection with revolution is
obvious in each case, and made explicit in most.
[40] Istoriia (1938 to present), p. 162.

Imperialism, he maintains, is the fundamental antagonist of the Soviet Union, and Fascism only its worst reactionary form. "Hitler, Goebbels, Ribbentrop, Himmler, and the other administrators of present-day Germany are the chained dogs of the German bankers."[41] The capitalist, not the Nazi, is the ultimate enemy. The theoretical framework is made fully explicit in Stalin's election speech of February 1946 : "It would be incorrect to think that the Second World War arose accidentally or as a result of the mistakes of some statesmen or other.... The war in fact arose as the inevitable result of the development of world economic and political forces on the basis of contemporary monopolistic capitalism."[42]

The case of a war against the Soviet Union, according to Stalin, presents an additional factor favorable to revolution. To the Seventeenth Party Congress in 1934 he declares : "It can hardly be doubted that this war will be the most dangerous for the bourgeoisie. ... The numerous friends in Europe and Asia of the working class of the USSR will endeavor to strike from the rear their oppressors who have started criminal war against the Fatherland of the working class of all countries."[43] Though Stalin hopes for proletarian revolutions in certain colonial areas, he values all local movements for national liberation, whether proletarian or not: in any case, each step they take toward emancipation is 'a steam-hammer blow against imperialism' and thus has 'objective' revolutionary significance, that is, weakens the bourgeoisie of imperialist countries by depriving them of markets and raw materials.[44] Hence a colonial war would become an added factor promoting a revolutionary crisis in the metropolitan country.

The Law of Ebb and Flow. According to Stalin, the October Revolution of 1917 ushered in "a new era in the history of humanity—the era of proletarian revolutions," in fact, "the epoch of world revolution."[45] This means, in terms of his theory, that the contradictions in

[41] *Pravda*, May 1, 1942.

[42] *Ibid.*, February 10, 1946, p. 1.

[43] "XVII s"ezd" (1934 to present), p. 1.

[44] "Ob osnovakh Leninizma" (1924 to present), pp. 3, 17, 48, 54; *XIV s"ezd: Stenograficheskii otchët*, p. 12; *XV s"ezd: Stenograficheskii otchët*, p. 44; *Sochineniia*, IV, 166, 238, 378.

[45] *Istoriia* (1938 to present), pp. 214, 338; "Ob osnovakh Leninizma" (1924 to present), p. 4.

the world system of capitalism have evolved to the point where revolutions are generally in order. Actual revolution, however, occurred first in only one country, and Stalin expects further revolutions usually to occur in one country at a time, as state after state breaks away from the capitalist system and joins the socialist one.[46]

But the course of the revolutionary movement is not expected to be uniform. Stalin notes that it has always moved in a wavelike rhythm of ebb and flow, rise and fall. For example, one wave reached its crest in the 1905 revolution and subsided in the Stolypin reaction. Another rise occurred in the years 1912-14. Under the stress of the First World War a major crest came with the two revolutions of 1917—though in the short interval between them there were also rapid changes of ebb and flow—and the wave spread out to Europe in the years immediately following. In 1925 Stalin announces that another decline has set in, corresponding to a "partial and temporary stabilization of capitalism," but he now generalizes the alternation of ebb and flow in a prediction of the future : "The epoch of world revolution . . . is a whole strategic period, embracing a whole series of years and, I dare say, even a number of decades. In the course of this period there can and must be ebbings and flowings."

Though an ebb tide has set in, Stalin goes on to say, the contradictions of capitalism will inevitably bring on a new flood tide in due time. With the flood tide new victories may be won for the revolution; if they do not complete world revolution, there will follow another ebb, and so on until revolution has spanned the globe.[47] In 1927 Stalin announces that the 'stabilization of capitalism' is drawing to a close, a new 'crisis of world capitalism' is gathering, and with it is beginning another revolutionary rise. In 1930 and 1934 successive reports to Party congresses continue the same line of thought: the contradictions of capitalism, accentuated by the world economic crisis of 1929, are converging inevitably on another imperialist war. Therefore "a rev-

[46] "Oktiabr'skaia revoliutsiia i taktika russkikh kommunistov" (1924 to present), p. 102.

[47] "K itogam rabot XIV konferentsii RKP (b)" (1925-34), in *Voprosy* (9th ed., 1932), pp. 109, 111; "Ob osnovakh Leninizma" (1924 to present), p. 55; "Beseda s inostrannymi rabochimi delegatsiiami," in *Voprosy* (9th ed., 1932), p. 301; *XV s"ezd: Stenograficheskii otchët*, p. 44; *Istoriia* (1938 to present), pp. 27, 80, 84, 127, 138, 140, 221, 258.

olutionary crisis is ripening and will continue to ripen."[48] In his report to the Party congress in 1939 he announces that the imperialist war has already begun and is gradually becoming a world war.[49]

Up to March 1948 Stalin has published nothing to indicate that the revolutionary wave—so long expected in connection with World War II —has passed its crest, though his doctrine of ebb and flow suggests that he must expect another ebb within a few years unless capitalism collapses completely in the meantime. Thus the entire period from 1929 to March 1948 moves before Stalin's eyes on a rising tide of revolutionary opportunities.

The Art of Revolution

Having outlined Stalin's conception of the 'objective' determinants of revolution, our inquiry now turns to the 'subjective' side: the role of conscious organization.

Communist Leadership. Notwithstanding the remorseless and unavoidable evolution of the contradictions of capitalism, making socialist revolution sooner or later inevitable, Stalin holds that actual revolution can occur only through conscious human efforts. In this he is a disciple of Lenin, and his history of the Party records with sympathy Lenin's battles against 'reformist' Marxists, compromisers, opportunists, gradualists—any and all who held that the 'objective' factors would automatically bring about the change to socialism, or that anything short of the most resolute and uncompromising revolutionary policy should be adopted.[50]

Stalin's ultimate reason for this position lies in his dialectical and historical materialism. As has been noted, one postulate of this theory is that objective reality is material, and consciousness only a 'reflection' of it. This view now requires further elaboration. Stalin does not mean that consciousness plays no causal role, but only that its role is secondary. The direction of history, its movement from one mode of production to another, with consequent changes in class structure,

[48] "XVII s"ezd" (1934 to present), p. 1; "Politicheskii otchët TsK" (1927), pp. 38, 44; "XVI s"ezd" (1930-39), p. 1.

[49] "Otchëtnyi doklad" (1939 to present), p. 11.

[50] For references in this and the following two paragraphs, see *Istoriia* (1938 to present), especially pp. 11, 16, 36, 45, 105, 110, 111, 337, 339, 343.

social institutions, and ideas, is indeed determined by the evolution of the means of production, and no conscious human effort can change this direction. But consciousness does have a positive and important function: it affects not the pattern of history but its pace. It can accelerate or retard the coming of the inevitable. Social theories which accelerate historical evolution do so because they "reflect the needs of the development of the material life of society" and by mobilizing the masses lead them in the direction of revolutionary change. Social theories arise "because they are necessary for society, because without their organizing, mobilizing, and transforming work the solution of the problems which have come to a head in the evolution of society is *impossible.*"

This is Stalin's ground for holding that conscious leadership is necessary for revolution. The primary contradiction in capitalism gets worse and worse, and increasing strain works out from it through the secondary contradictions, causing suffering, war, and destruction, but conscious effort, following correct theory, is necessary to help these blind forces produce the readjustment which alone can bring relief. Hence arises the necessity for the Communist Party. Stalin writes that "socialist ideology arises not from the spontaneous [working-class] movement but from science." The Party is that vanguard of the working class which, because it is guided by 'scientific' insight into the ills of capitalism and the sole means of cure, can and must organize the proletariat and lead it to revolutionary victory: "The Marxist Party is a part of the working class. . . . The Party differs from other detachments of the working class primarily in that it is . . . the *leading* detachment, the *class-conscious* detachment . . . armed with knowledge of social life, knowledge of the laws of the class struggle, and for this reason able to lead the working class and to direct its struggle."

Stalin's conception of Marxist theory is likewise his justification for the character and organization of the Bolshevik Party as opposed to Marxist parties of the Western type. Because the Party is the embodiment of 'scientific' truth, and because that truth is uncompromisingly revolutionary—teaching that class war must be fought to a finish—the Party must be 'monolithic,' a centrally controlled army under strict military discipline, tolerating no other parties except for

temporary reasons of expediency, hunting down and destroying compromisers—all who are disposed to take the edge off the revolutionary
drive, to let things move more gradually—both in society at large
and within its own ranks. The same claim to infallible 'science' lies
at the base of Stalin's theory of the Party purge, so strange to Western
modes of thought: "The Party strengthens itself by purging itself
of opportunist elements." A procedure that to Western minds is a
sign and a further cause of weakness is for Stalin a means to strength
because strength derives ultimately not from numbers but from 'knowledge' which harnesses revolution to the laws of history: the purge
eliminates those whose allegiance to this 'knowledge,' and the program based on it, is dubious.[51]

From Stalin's point of view 'democratic liberties' have always been
compatible with strict Communist Party control. In his report on the
Draft Constitution, he claims that the Soviet system is more democratic than any other. And in reply to foreign critics who object that
the one-party system is undemocratic, he praises the Constitution
because it leaves in force the dictatorship of the working class and
"the present directing position of the Communist Party."[52] Further,
Stalin is on record as holding that proletarian revolution may legitimately be carried out when the proletariat is only a minority of the
population—the Party, of course, being only a minority of the proletariat.

Stalin expresses the contrast between Bolshevism and Western socialism most vividly in his 1934 interview with H. G. Wells, already
mentioned. Wells approaches Stalin from the point of view of a Western
socialist; he states that conceptions of violent class war are obsolete;
leading businessmen are not ruled wholly (or even primarily in many
cases) by the profit motive, and there is therefore no radical conflict
of interest between capital and labor; modern technology makes socialism inevitable through gradual extension of government controls;
hence the need is for intelligent direction, not violent revolution;
Eastern and Western socialists should develop a common language and

[51] *Istoriia* (1938 to present), pp. 40, 45, 135, 337, 343; see also "Ob osnovakh
Leninizma" (1924 to present), pp. 64-75.
[52] "O proekte konstitutsii Soiuza SSR" (1936 to present), *Pravda*, November 26,
1936, p. 3.

work together rather than emphasize their historic antagonisms. Stalin replies with denial on all points and puts the crux of the matter as he sees it thus: "The replacement of one social system by another social system is a complicated and protracted revolutionary process. It is not a merely spontaneous process. . . . No—revolution . . . has always been struggle, an excruciating and cruel struggle, struggle for life and death."

Communists, he continues, do not idealize force and violence; they would gladly dispense with them if the bourgeoisie would consent to turn things over peaceably to the proletariat. But abundant historical experience teaches (as he said to Wells) that "classes which have had their day do not leave the stage of history voluntarily." His history of the Party picks up this theme in describing how the revolutionary period comes after social forces have evolved spontaneously to a certain point:

After the new productive forces have matured, the existing productive relations and their bearers, the ruling classes, turn into that 'insurmountable' obstacle which can be removed only by means of the conscious action of the new classes, by the forcible acts of these classes, by revolution. . . . The masses are welded into a new political army, create a new revolutionary authority, and use it to abolish by force the old system of productive relations and establish the new system. The spontaneous process of development gives place to the conscious action of men, peaceful development to violent upheaval, evolution to revolution.[53]

The 'combat staff' of the new political army is the Communist Party.[54] Effective Communist Party action is Stalin's 'subjective' condition for revolution which, when timed with the 'objective' conditions previously described, actually brings revolution to pass. As he puts it to the Seventeenth Party Congress :

Some comrades think that as soon as there is a revolutionary crisis the bourgeoisie must be in a situation from which there is no way out . . . that the victory of revolution is thus secure. . . . This is a profound mistake. The victory of the revolution never comes of itself. It must be prepared for and won. And only a strong proletarian revolutionary party can prepare for and win it. Moments occur when the situation is rev-

[53] *Istoriia* (1938 to present), p. 125.
[54] "Ob osnovakh Leninizma" (1924 to present), p. 66.

olutionary, the power of the bourgeoisie is shaken to its very foundations, and yet the victory of the revolution does not come, because there is no revolutionary party of the proletariat sufficiently strong and authoritative to lead the masses and take power in its own hands.[55]

World Strategy : The Soviet Union as Base. Before we proceed to examine Stalin's views on how revolution is 'prepared for and won' by the Communist Party, a word of caution is in order. As generals are not accustomed to publish their operational directives, so it is unreasonable to expect Stalin to publish his. From his writings it is possible to reconstruct certain main lines of strategy and tactics, but the writings also contain definite acknowledgment that 'illegal' or underground activities play a major role in Communist operations. Speaking of the revolutionary uses of compromise and reform, he states :

In revolutionary tactics under a bourgeois regime, reform naturally becomes an instrument for disintegrating this regime, an instrument for strengthening revolution. . . . The revolutionary accepts reform in order to use it as a means of meshing the legal work with the illegal work, in order to use it as a cover for the strengthening of the illegal work which aims at revolutionary preparation of the masses for the overthrow of the bourgeoisie.[56]

Therefore it must remain a question to what extent Stalin's published views on Communist strategy and tactics are supplemented or modified by doctrine reserved for the Communist high command.

In any case, Stalin's approach is characteristically military, and it is hardly by accident that his writings are strewn with military figures of speech—tactics and strategy; staff, cadres, vanguards, reserves; strong points, forward positions; advances, assaults, retreats, maneuvers; encirclement, flanking movement, regrouping of forces; and so forth.[57] An early sketch not published until 1947 shows most succinctly the connection between theory and strategy:

[55] "XVII s"ezd" (1934 to present), p. 1. See also "Beseda s pervoi amerikanskoi rabochei delegatsiei" (1927-39), in *Voprosy* (9th ed., 1932), p. 266; *Istoriia* (1938 to present), p. 337.

[56] "Ob osnovakh Leninizma" (1924 to present), p. 63. See also *Istoriia* (1938 to present), pp. 127, 133, 136, 151.

[57] Stalin remarks that he and other younger members of the Central Committee were required by Lenin to study the fundamentals of warfare ("Otvet tov. Stalina na pis'mo Razina," *Bol'shevik*, February 1947, p. 6).

The *theory* of Marxism, studying primarily the objective processes . . . defines the tendency of evolution, points out the class or classes which are inevitably rising to power or which are inevitably falling, must fall. . . . The *program* of Marxism, basing itself on the conclusions of the theory, defines the goal for the movement of the rising class, in this case of the proletariat. . . . *Strategy*, guiding itself by the directives of the program and resting on a calculation of the contending forces, internal . . . and international, defines that . . . general direction along which the revolutionary movement of the proletariat should be directed with a view to achieving the biggest results with the . . . developing correlation of forces.[58]

The program thus defines the objectives at which strategy aims. Stalin distinguishes the 'maximum program'—"socialist revolution, overthrow of the capitalists' rule, establishment of the dictatorship of the proletariat"—from the 'minimum program' formulated for a particular phase of the total process.[59] Stalin writes in *Voprosy* that "strategy has to do with the main forces of revolution and their reserves. It changes with the passage of revolution from one stage to another, remaining essentially without change for the whole period of a given stage." The first stage was 1903 to February 1917, the second March to October 1917. The third stage began after the October Revolution: *"The goal is to consolidate the dictatorship of the proletariat in one country, using it as a base for the overthrow of imperialism in all countries.* Revolution spreads beyond the limits of one country; the epoch of world revolution has begun."[60]

The fundamental, not merely incidental, intention to use the Soviet Union as the base for world revolution has thus been on the record in Stalin's most important doctrinal work, repeatedly republished for mass circulation from 1924 to the present time. In another passage which has had similar authoritative distribution from 1924 to the present Stalin elaborates his view:

The very development of world revolution . . . will be more rapid and more thorough, the more thoroughly socialism fortifies itself in the first

[58] *Sochineniia*, V, 62; see also p. 162.
[59] *Istoriia* (1938 to present), pp. 38, 40; *Sochineniia*, V, 63, 162.
[60] "Ob osnovakh Leninizma" (1924 to present), p. 54 (italics added). See also *Sochineniia*, V, 173-80; "K itogam rabot XIV konferentsii RKP (b)" (1925-34), p. 110.

victorious country, the faster this country is transformed into a base for the further unfolding of world revolution, into a lever for the further disintegration of imperialism.

While it is true that the *final* victory of socialism in the first country to emancipate itself is impossible without the combined efforts of the proletarians of several countries, it is equally true that the development of world revolution will be the more rapid and thorough, the more effective the aid rendered by the first socialist country to the workers . . . of all other countries.

In what should this aid be expressed?

It should be expressed, first, in the victorious country "carrying out the maximum realizable in one country *for* the development, support, awakening of revolution *in all countries.* . . ."

It should be expressed, second, in that the "victorious proletariat" of the one country . . . "after organizing its own socialist production, should stand up . . . *against* the remaining, capitalist world, attracting to itself the oppressed classes of other countries, raising revolts in those countries against the capitalists, in the event of necessity coming out even with armed force against the exploiting classes and their governments."[61]

This passage deserves detailed comment. The supreme aim of world revolution is the logical outcome of Stalin's entire theoretical position as outlined in the present study—notably the thesis that capitalism is a single *world-system* fatally torn by contradictions which can be cured only by a consciously directed socialist revolution. Granted these assumptions, the determination to use the foothold won in the Soviet Union as a base for world revolution is elementary common sense. This outlook is confirmed by many other passages in widely published statements by Stalin.[62] The sole contradictory passages—un-

---

[61] "Oktiabr'skaia revoliutsiia i taktika russkikh kommunistov" (1924 to present), p. 104. The latter part of this passage, including the reference to using armed force, is a quotation from Lenin which Stalin employs also in "K voprosam Leninizma" (1926 to present), p. 142, and in "K itogam rabot XIV konferentsii RKP (b)" (1925-34), p. 122. This repetition in widely circulated works is added evidence that Stalin means every word.

[62] See the statement to Ludwig above, and the vow of fidelity to the principles of the Comintern quoted below; also "Mezhdunarodnyi kharakter oktiabr'skoi revoliutsii" (1927, 1934 to present), in *Voprosy* (11th ed., 1945), p. 179; *Sochineniia* IV, 166, 238, and V, 85, 169, 179; "K itogam rabot XIV konferentsii RKP(b)" (1925-34), p. 132. This list of corroborating passages is by no means exhaustive.

less cunningly interpreted—are remarks made by Stalin to two foreigners, under circumstances where it is obviously to his advantage to convey another impression. For example, he tells Roy Howard in 1936 that the Soviet Union has never had plans for fostering revolution in other countries because exporting revolution is nonsense.[63] The other statement, made to Mr. King, of Reuters, in May 1943, will be described in a moment. These two statements are not republished in *Voprosy* or otherwise for wide and lasting distribution in the Soviet Union. When they are weighed against the mass of contrary evidence on Stalin's views presented above, the only conclusion is that they are misleading.

In 1938 the Party history appears with the revolutionary motto on its title page: "Workers of all countries, unite!" And the introduction declares: "Studying the history of the CPSU (B) strengthens confidence in the final victory of the great cause of the party of Lenin and Stalin, the victory of communism in the whole world." The history also repeats the fundamental quotation from Lenin on the country of socialism 'rising against' the capitalist world after organizing its own production, states that "the victory of proletarian revolutions in capitalist countries is a vital interest of the toilers of the USSR," and quotes Stalin's 'great vow' of 'fidelity to the principles of the Communist International.' All these points, it should be remembered, are made in a work used for mass indoctrination down to the present time [1949].

In 1936 Howard asks Stalin if he has not to some extent abandoned his plans for world revolution. Stalin replies, "We never had such plans and intentions," thus excluding the interpretation that what he is saying to Howard represents in any way a change of mind.[64] He then declares that "we Marxists hold that revolution will occur in other countries too. But it will occur only when the revolutionaries of these countries find it possible or necessary. The export of revolu-

---

[63] "Beseda tovarishcha Stalina s predsedatelem amerikanskogo gazetnogo ob"-edineniia 'Skripps-Govard N'iuspeipers' g-nom Roi Govardom," *Pravda*, March 5, 1936, p. 2.

[64] The denial that the USSR ever had 'such plans and intentions' amounts to denying that it had ever given aid to revolutions abroad, for example to China. The import of the statement for the future can be no greater than its application to the past.

tion—that is nonsense." But this statement says nothing about ways
in which local revolutionaries may be used, directed, and aided by
outside agencies; the only 'export' of revolution which it denies would
be the very crudest kind, which dispensed with forming even a minimum of local Communist leadership. Carefully analyzed, then, Stalin's
remarks turn out to be a sort of legalistic quibble used to convey a
general impression which is in fact false.

It has at times been thought that some of Stalin's statements during
the current period indicated a change of mind on his part with regard
to long-term relations with the 'capitalist' democracies. A careful
search through all his published statements from July 1941 to March
1948 yields only one case which appears to warrant such a belief—
a letter in May 1943 to King, Reuters correspondent (mentioned
above), about the dissolution of the Comintern. The interview with
Stassen merely says that the important point is not whether coexistence
is possible but whether both sides desire it. If 'one side' does not
want cooperation, "the result will be conflict, war."[65] In other words,
if 'one side' does not like the terms of the Soviet Union, it is lacking
in desire to cooperate. Also, when Stassen asks if wartime experience
has changed things, Stalin denies that he ever said the two systems
could not cooperate; he thus implies that his views remain unchanged
and makes it impossible to attribute to his current statements on
cooperation a more generous meaning than to his earlier ones. Stalin's
remark that the postwar international security organization "will be
effective if the great powers ... continue to act in a spirit of unanimity"[66] is another expression of this same conception of 'cooperation'; when queried by Hugh Baillie about the veto, Stalin denies
that the Soviet Union has abused it in the United Nations or the
Council of Foreign Ministers.[67]

But the letter to the Reuters correspondent on the dissolution of
the Comintern is an explicit contradiction of Stalin's earlier statements

[65] "Zapis' besedy tov. I. V. Stalina s deiatelem respublikanskoi partii SShA
Garol'dom Stassenom," p. 1.

[66] "XVII godovshchina velikoi oktiabr'skoi sotsialisticheskoi revoliutsii," *Pravda*,
November 7, 1944, p. 2.

[67] "Otvety tov. Stalina I. V. na voprosy prezidenta amerikanskogo agentstva
Iunaited Press g-na Kh'iu Beili," *ibid.*, October 3, 1946, p. 1.

of revolutionary methods and aims. Here he says that the dissolution of the Comintern is right because, among other reasons:

(a) It exposes the lie of the Hitlerites that 'Moscow' intends to intervene in the life of other states and 'bolshevize' them. Henceforth an end is put to that lie. (b) It exposes the slander of the enemies of communism in the workers' movement to the effect that the Communist parties of the various countries act not in the interests of their own nation but according to orders from outside. Henceforth an end is put to that slander too.[68]

These propositions, reminiscent of the 1936 Howard interview, can be reconciled with Stalin's established revolutionary doctrine only by very special pleading. Since they are made to a foreign correspondent and contain no express disavowal of pertinent basic writings currently republished in quantity in the Soviet Union, the balance of evidence is that they are merely part of the current tactical and propaganda line and do not reflect a fundamental change. The most decisive evidence to this effect is the republication of Stalin's vows of fidelity to Lenin and his cause originally made before the Second Congress of Soviets on January 26, 1924. Toward the close Stalin says that "Lenin was the leader not only of the Russian proletariat, not only of the workers of Europe, not only of the colonial East, but also of the earth's entire toiling world." Then he makes his last vow, set off in bold-faced capitals from the rest of the text: "In departing from us, Comrade Lenin bequeathed to us fidelity to the principles of the Communist International. We swear to thee, Comrade Lenin, that we will not spare our life in order to strengthen and expand the union of toilers of the whole world—the Communist International."[69] In the light of this vow, repeatedly republished, Stalin's real view evidently is that the Comintern was dissolved only in form, not in spirit. Stalin's charge that the United States and Great Britain are

[68] "Otvet tov. I. V. Stalina na vopros glavnogo korrespondenta angliiskogo agentstva Reiter," *ibid.*, May 30, 1943, p. 1.

[69] "Po povodu smerti Lenina," in V. I. Lenin, *Izbrannye proizvedeniia v dvukh tomakh* (4th ed.; Moscow, 1946), I, 8, which in turn refers to Stalin's *O Lenine* (1942), pp. 17-22. The vow is also quoted in *Istoriia* (1938 to present), p. 257. Thus it has been widely circulating in at least three authoritative versions during the current period.

not interested in agreement and cooperation with the USSR, made in the interview by a *Pravda* correspondent, are also to be read against this background.[70] The passages in Stalin's various interviews in which he indicates the possibility or desirability of coexistence and cooperation between capitalist and socialist systems do not really contradict the strategic aim of world revolution because they refer to a temporary tactic.

The second paragraph in the long passage quoted above places the problem of the 'final' victory of socialism in one country within the wider context of world revolution, thus excluding the hypothesis that the more limited objective—involving merely enough additional revolutions to end 'capitalist encirclement' and provide security for the Soviet Union—marks the outer limit of Stalin's program for Communist expansion. Further, the passage quoted indicates that the Soviet Union will first be prepared as a base, and only then, "*after* organizing its own socialist production," will be used more aggressively to aid revolution abroad. This tallies with the predominant absorption of the Soviets with internal affairs during the earlier five-year plans. Further, the phrase does not define the stage at which production is to be considered adequately organized. Hence the prospect of three or more additional five-year plans, as announced in 1938 and again in 1946, may indicate that the base is still not ready for contemplated operations.

Finally, the passage definitely states that armed force will be used against capitalist governments if necessary. There thus is nothing except expediency to limit the aid which Stalin contemplates giving to revolutions abroad. However, the phrase 'if necessary' indicates that armed force is not to be used by preference; ahead of it come propaganda and Communist Party control, by which is meant that the Soviet Union should attract to itself "the oppressed classes of other countries, raising revolts in these countries against the capitalists."[71]

[70] *Pravda*, October 29, 1948.

[71] Stalin's belief in the necessity for strict party discipline on an international and not merely a national scale is illustrated in his speeches in the Comintern in May 1929, in which he castigates members of the American delegation for refusing to accept a decision of the Presidium disciplining American Party leaders; debate and criticism are permissible in advance of decision, he concludes, but once a deci-

The ultimate resort to armed force is a logical development of the Leninist thesis that only consciously led revolution can drive the capitalists from the stage of history, as explained in the preceding section. The assumption that the world has been fundamentally divided into two camps since the October Revolution runs through Stalin's writings from his early days and is grounded in his Marxist philosophy.[72] Stalin pictures the long-range evolution of the two camps as follows :

Most probably, in the course of development of the world revolution, side by side with the centers of imperialism in individual capitalist countries and the system of these countries throughout the world, centers of socialism will be created in individual soviet countries and a system of these centers throughout the world, and the struggle between these two systems will fill up the history of the development of the world revolution.[73]

The systems are expected to be organized around two centers:

Thus in the course of further development of international revolution two centers will form on a world scale: a socialist center, binding to itself the countries that gravitate to socialism, and a capitalist center binding to itself the countries that gravitate to capitalism. The struggle between these two centers for the possession of the world economy will decide the fate of capitalism and communism in the whole world.[74]

The plan to make the Soviet Union the base for world revolution implies that it will be one of the two centers. Evidence will be pre-

sion is made all must accept it, else there can be no 'collective direction.' "O pravykh fraktsionerakh v amerikanskoi kompartii," *Bol'shevik*, January 15, 1930, pp. 8-26.

[72] *Sochineniia*, IV, 232, 380; "Ob osnovakh Leninizma" (1924 to present), pp. 26, 43; "K voprosam Leninizma" (1926 to present), pp. 113, 140; "Itogi pervoi piatiletki" (1933 to present), *Pravda*, January 10, 1933, p. 1; "Privetstvie tov. I. V. Stalina," *ibid.*, September 7, 1947, p. 1. These are only a few of the many passages which reflect a two-world conception.

[73] "Oktiabr'skaia revoliutsiia i taktika russkikh kommunistov" (1924 to present), p. 105.

[74] "Beseda s pervoi amerikanskoi rabochei delegatsiei" (1927-39), p. 287; also reproduced in the introductory section of the previously cited (note 69) popular edition of Lenin's works, *Izbrannye proizvedeniia v dvukh tomakh*, I, 28. See also "K itogam rabot XIV konferentsii RKP (b)" (1925-34), p. 111; "Politicheskii otchët TsK" (1925), *XIV s"ezd: Stenograficheskii otchët*, p. 19; "Ob itogakh iiul'skogo plenuma TsK VKP (b)" (1928-34), p. 338.

sented later that the United States is expected to be the other. The ultimate inevitability of war to the finish between the two camps is made clear in one of Stalin's favorite quotations from Lenin :

We live . . . not only in a state but in a system of states, and the existence of the Soviet Republic side by side with the imperialist states for a long time is unthinkable. In the end either one or the other will conquer. And until that end comes, a series of the most terrible collisions between the Soviet Republic and the bourgeois states is inevitable.[75]

Stalin appended to this forecast of inexorable wars a succinct, "Clear, one would think." Thus Stalin expects not merely one but several world wars before the end of capitalism.

At the very close of the struggle the forces of socialism will be so superior that Stalin foresees an exception to the general rule that revolutionary violence is necessary to overthrow capitalism:

Of course, in the distant future, if the proletariat wins in the most important capitalist countries and if the present capitalist encirclement is replaced by a socialist encirclement, a 'peaceful' path of development is fully possible for some capitalist countries, whose capitalists, in view of the 'unfavorable' international situation, will consider it expedient to make serious concessions to the proletariat 'voluntarily.'[76]

The technique of 'cold revolution,' as it has been called, illustrated recently in eastern Europe, may be interpreted as a variety of 'socialist encirclement' in that it also dispenses with the need for overt violence. In any case, the passage quoted excepts "the most important capitalist countries," and so does not apply to the United States.

Flexibility of Strategy and Tactics. We are now in a position to link Stalin's strategy and tactics with his conception of the 'objective' conditions making for revolution. It is the business of strategy and tactics, he holds, to prepare the 'subjective' condition of revolution —the mobilization of the proletariat and its allies— and bring them into action at the most favorable times and places as determined by the development of the 'objective' conditions.[77] More than this, prep-

---

[75] "K voprosam Leninizma" (1926 to present), p. 140; see also p. 113. Quoted again (1938) in "Otvet t-shchu IVANOVU Ivanu Filippovichu," p. 3.

[76] "Ob osnovakh Leninizma" (1924 to present), p. 32. On socialist encirclement see also *XVIII s "ezd: Stenograficheskii otchët* (1939 to present), pp. 33, 56.

[77] *Sochineniia*, V, 62, 74, 161; "O pravykh fraktsionerakh v amerikanskoi kom-

aration of the 'subjective' conditions really involves gaining leadership of social forces which often in the first place develop spontaneously. Describing the skill shown by the Communist Party in Russia in 1917 in uniting "in one common revolutionary stream such different revolutionary movements as the general democratic movement for peace, the peasant democratic movement for seizure of the landed estates, the movement of the oppressed nationalities for national liberation and national equality, and the socialist movement of the proletariat for the overthrow of the bourgeoisie and the establishment of the dictatorship of the proletariat," Stalin declares that "undoubtedly, the merging of these diverse revolutionary streams in one common, powerful revolutionary stream decided the fate of capitalism in Russia."[78]

In general, despite his comparatively rigid doctrinal framework, Stalin's conception of Communist strategy and tactics is highly flexible. It rests on a continual assessment of the status of forces in both the capitalist and the socialist systems. Thus he writes :

Tactics, guiding itself by the directives of strategy and by the experience of the revolutionary movement . . . calculating at every given moment the state of forces inside the proletariat and its allies (greater or lesser cultivation, greater or lesser degree of organization and class consciousness, presence of particular traditions, presence of particular forms of movement, forms of organization, *basic* and *secondary*), as well as in the camp of the adversary, profiting by the discord and every kind of confusion in the camp of the adversary—marks out those *concrete courses* for winning the wide masses to the proletarian side and leading them to battle stations on the social front . . . which most surely pave the way for strategic successes.[79]

In view of this flexibility, and of the way in which Stalin expects Communist leadership to win control of many movements which originate spontaneously, it must be concluded that the 'objective' conditions of revolution are not fixed quantities in Stalin's thinking, but rather interdependent variables which are to be manipulated to satisfy

partii," *Bol'shevik* (January 15, 1930), pp. 13, 23; "Voprosy sverdlovtsev i otvet t. Stalina," *Pravda*, February 10, 1930, p. 2.

[78] *Istoriia* (1938 to present), p. 204.

[79] "O politicheskoi strategii i taktike russkikh kommunistov" (written 1921, first published 1947), *Sochineniia*, V, 63.

just one equation: revolution occurs where the Communist command concentrates superiority of forces at a point on the capitalist front where the bourgeoisie can be isolated and overwhelmed. In other words, 'revolutionary crises' do not have to be waited for; they can to some extent be organized; and an extremely favorable balance of outside aid can compensate to a considerable degree for a deficiency in favorable internal conditions.

For the period of world revolution, Stalin's grand strategy is to use the Soviet Union as a base linking the proletariat of the West with the movements for national liberation from imperialism in the East into "a single world front against the world front of imperialism." In this way he harnesses two of the major contradictions of capitalism to his chariot—contradictions between proletariat and bourgeoisie, and contradictions between capitalist and colonial countries. The front thus formed is to be used to exploit the third contradiction of capitalism—that between capitalist countries, whose rivalry for spheres of influence must lead periodically to war, the event most propitious for revolution.[80]

One of the chief conditions to which tactics must be adjusted, according to Stalin, is the ebb and flow of the forces favoring revolution. Aggressive tactics should be timed with a rising tide; tactics of defense, the assemblage of forces, and even retreat go with an ebbing tide.[81] The importance of gauging the direction of the tide is illustrated by Stalin's remarks in 1929 concerning a controversy with Bukharin, who apparently held that the 'stabilization of capitalism' was persisting unchanged:

This question, comrades, is of decisive importance for the sections of the Comintern. Is the capitalist stabilization going to pieces or is it becoming more secure? On this the whole line of the Communist parties in their day-to-day political work depends. Are we in a period of decline of the revolutionary movement . . . or are we in a period when the conditions are maturing for a new revolutionary rise, a period of preparing the working class for coming class battles—on this depends the tactical position of the Communist parties.

[80] "Ob osnovakh Leninizma" (1924 to present), pp. 17, 54; *Sochineniia*, IV, 166, 238, 378.
[81] "Ob osnovakh Leninizma" (1924 to present), p. 55; *Sochineniia*, V, 64.

Stalin holds that it is a period of revolutionary upswing.[82]

Stalin's insistence on flexibility of tactics is ground for a very important maxim in the interpretation of his public statements; one must avoid, if possible, mistaking a change in tactics for a change in fundamental doctrine and strategic objectives. The example of a change in tactics often thus mistaken is Stalin's remarks about peaceful coexistence of and cooperation between the socialist and capitalist systems. The whole body of mutually reinforcing propositions in Stalin's philosophy adds up to a veritable religion of conflict and contradiction. This is described as not only inevitable but desirable, until revolution is achieved. Here we find further strong evidence that Stalin's statements on cooperation represent nothing deeper than a tactic.

Stalin first announced a period of 'peaceful coexistence' for proletarian and bourgeois worlds in 1925, saying that the revolutionary movement was ebbing and capitalism achieving a temporary stabilization. But the context of his statement makes plain that he expected peaceful coexistence to be as temporary as the stabilization.[83] In 1927 he stated that capitalist stabilization was coming to an end and that the period of 'peaceful coexistence' was likewise giving way to one of imperialist attacks. But he added that the Soviet Union must continue to pursue a policy of maintaining peace for the following reason:

We cannot forget the saying of Lenin to the effect that a great deal in the matter of our construction depends on whether we succeed in delaying war with the capitalist countries, which is inevitable but which may be delayed either until proletarian revolution ripens in Europe, or until the colonial revolutions come fully to a head, or, finally, until the capitalists fight among themselves over division of the colonies. Therefore the maintenance of peaceful relations with capitalist countries is an obligatory task for us.

The basis of our relations with capitalist countries consists in admitting the coexistence of two opposed systems.[84]

[82] "O pravom uklone v VKP (b)" (1929 to present), *Bol'shevik* (December 1929), p. 20.

[83] *XIV s"ezd: Stenograficheskii otchët*, pp. 8, 10, 17; "K itogam rabot XIV konferentsii RKP (b)," p. 110.

[84] *XV s"ezd: Stenograficheskii otchët*, p. 47.

This concern for peaceful relations in order to build the socialist economy at home should be read in the context of the previous discussion in this paper of the Soviet Union as a base for world revolution; in that light, a peace policy is an intelligible tactic. Stalin continues to advocate it in the years after 1927, while at the same time urging the Communist parties to adopt aggressive tactics in keeping with the end of capitalist stabilization.[85] Thus appears an important variation of tactics on different levels of activity: peaceful coexistence for the Soviet government, preparation for attack by Communist parties.

The peace policy has another tactical function in Stalin's strategy of revolution. He notes how successfully the Communists capitalized on the general popular craving for peace during the October Revolution; accordingly he maneuvers the Soviet Union and the Communist parties into position as apostles of peace, unmasking the imperialist 'warmongers' in order to profit by popular sentiments for peace in the future. Particularly interesting in this connection is the way Stalin combines his peace stand with verbal onslaughts on Social Democratic pacifism as a mere mask of the warmongers.[86]

Apart from their bearing on peace, the tasks of developing trade and obtaining technological assistance from capitalist countries have a direct relationship to building the industrial base of the Soviet Union, especially during the early stage of the five-year plans. Stalin makes several unsentimental and businesslike proposals for improved relations along these lines, particularly with the United States.[87] His fullest and frankest statement on cooperation between Soviet and capitalist worlds is made in 1927, shortly before his announcement that the capitalist stabilization is coming to an end. To the American Workers' Delegation, who asked to what extent such cooperation is possible and whether it has definite limits, Stalin replies:

[85] On aggressive tactics, see "O pravom uklone v VKP (b)" (1929 to present), pp. 15-49 (including passage quoted immediately above in text); "O pravykh fraktsionerakh v amerikanskoi kompartii," pp. 8-26.

[86] "Ob itogakh iiul'skogo plenuma TsK VKP (b)," p. 336; "Otchëtnyi doklad" (1939 to present), p. 15; "Oktiabr'skaia revoliutsiia" (1924 to present), p. 78.

[87] "Gospodin Kempbell priviraet," Bol'shevik (November 30, 1932), p. 12; interview reported by Eugene Lyons, New York Herald Tribune, November 24, 1930, pp. 1, 2.

The matter concerns, obviously, temporary agreements with capitalist states in the field of industry, in the field of trade, and, perhaps, in the field of diplomatic relations. I think that the presence of two opposed systems . . . does not exclude the possibility of such agreements. I think that such agreements are possible and expedient under conditions of peaceful development. . . .

The limits of these agreements? The limits are set by the opposition of the two systems, between which rivalry and struggle go on. Within the limits permitted by these two systems, but only within these limits, agreements are fully possible. . . .

Are these agreements merely an experiment or can they have more or less lasting character? That depends not only on us; that depends also on those who contract with us. That depends on the general situation. War can upset any agreement whatever.[88]

A few pages later the same interview reads: "Thus in the course of further development of international revolution two centers will form on a world scale: a socialist center . . . and a capitalist center. . . . The struggle between these two centers for the possession of the world economy will decide the fate of capitalism and communism in the whole world." This passage places cooperation clearly as a temporary tactic on the way to world revolution. When read against the foregoing as background, Stalin's statements to Howard, Duranty, Lyons, Werth, Elliott Roosevelt, and Stassen, to the effect that the two systems can coexist and compete peacefully, appear not so much inconsistent with his basic principles as merely elliptical: he neglects to specify how long and on what terms. To that extent the effect is misleading, as we have seen, and properly comes under the heading of propaganda.

Revolution in the United States

In a speech in the Comintern in May 1929, Stalin rebukes representatives of the American Communist Party for exaggerating the 'specific traits' of American capitalism. The basis for the activities of all Communist parties, he states, is the 'common traits' of capitalism, which are fundamentally the same for all countries—the specific traits of capitalism in a particular country merely supplement

[88] "Beseda s pervoi amerikanskoi rabochei delegatsiei" (1927-39), pp. 280, 287.

the general traits. This implies that Stalin makes no major exceptions on behalf of the United States in regard to the application
of his theory of capitalism and his objective of world revolution.
In April 1947, Stalin presents an unchanged view in his talk with
Stassen; he even says that the economic systems of the United
States and of Nazi Germany are identical—namely, monopoly capitalism. When Stassen argues that the American system is really very
different, he is politely but firmly parried.

As we have noted, Stalin's portrait of the capitalists paints them
as utterly unprincipled and ruthless men, dominated by the lust for
profits, to which they are willing to sacrifice all else. In his interview with Lyons (intended for publication in America and appealing
for better business relations) he remarks, apropos of the alleged sanc-
tity of the old war debts, which were a stumbling block: "Since when
has the bourgeoisie placed principle above money?" In his report
to the Eighteenth Congress in 1939, he complains of the policies of
the United States and other countries toward Germany and Japan,
and declares: "Far be it from me to moralize on the policy of nonin-
tervention, to talk of treason, of treachery, and so forth. It is naive
to read a moral to people who do not recognize human morality."[89]
To Wells in 1934, he says that American or other capitalists will never
permit abolition of unemployment because they need a "reserve army
of unemployed" to ensure cheap labor. Capitalists are "riveted to profit"
and "see nothing except their own interest." The government is merely
their tool; if Roosevelt seriously threatens private property and the
profit system, they will put in another president.

How does Stalin regard Americans in general? His admiration for
American technological prowess and business efficiency is well known.
To Ludwig in 1931 he also mentions the democratic simplicity of American manners, but he denies 'worship of everything American.' As
far as Soviet sympathies with the majority of any other nation are
concerned, those with the Germans are beyond comparison with 'our
feelings toward Americans.'[90] On no occasion does Stalin appeal to
lasting ties of sentiment or culture as a basis for cooperation with
the United States. Even to Howard in 1936 he specifies that neither

[89] "Otchëtnyi doklad" (1939 to present), p. 14.
[90] "I. Stalin, Beseda s nemetskim pisatelem Emilem Liudvigom," p. 38.

of the rival systems will evolve into the other. "The Soviet system will not grow into American democracy, and vice versa." The utterly unsentimental basis of Stalin's approach to cooperation despite ideological differences is made particularly clear by his statement to Stassen in 1947 that the Soviet Union would have cooperated with Germany as much as with any other capitalist country if Germany had desired. Stalin bids for cooperation on the basis of interest, such as maintaining peace and securing profitable trade.

Stalin has long evinced a belief that proletarian forces are backward in the United States. To the American Labor Delegation in 1927 he comments that American labor leaders are 'reactionary' and 'reformist,' and points to the small fraction of workers who are unionized. He also observes that both political parties are bourgeois, and asks: "Don't you comrades consider that the absence of your own mass workers' party, if only one like the English [Labor Party], weakens the strength of the working class in its political struggle with capitalism?" In 1947 he remarks to Stassen that he sees little difference between Democrats and Republicans. Likewise in speaking to American Communist Party representatives in 1929 he attacks them for 'rightist factionalism,' saying, "It cannot be denied that American life offers an environment which favors the Communist Party's falling into error and exaggerating the strength and stability of American capitalism."[91] He has said nothing since to indicate a change of opinion. Thus such evidence as his writings afford points to an expectation that the United States will be one of the last countries to go Communist.

This conclusion is reinforced by Stalin's views on the American economy. He notes that the United States—'the chief country of capitalism, its stronghold'—is hardest hit by the economic crisis of 1929, and that the crisis of 1937 originates here. But he also observes that the country leads world recovery in 1925 and 1933, and in 1939 he implies that it will pull out of the later crisis.[92] Thus the United States is the center of the capitalist world system, its 'strong-

[91] "O pravykh fraktsionerakh v amerikanskoi kompartii," p. 8.
[92] "XVI s"ezd" (1930-39), p. 1; "Politicheskii otchët TsK" (1925), p. 11; "Politicheskii otchët TsK" (1927), p. 38; "XVII-omu s"ezdu" (1934 to present), *Pravda*, January 28, 1934, p. 1; "Otchëtnyi doklad" (1939 to present), p. 9.

hold,' and, though affected by the general decadence of capitalism, shows some remnants of health in its powers of recovery. As early as 1925 Stalin observes that the center of capitalist financial power is moving across the Atlantic, and describes how the United States, with England as its partner, is becoming the hub of the capitalist system. "Two chief, but opposed, centers of attraction are being formed," he writes, "and, in conformity with this, two directions of pull toward these centers throughout the world: Anglo-America ... and the Soviet Union."[93] In the years immediately following, Stalin sees the United States and England becoming rivals rather than partners, but at no time up to the present has he implied that the United States has ceased to be the center of world capitalism. To Stassen in 1947 he comments on the unique opportunities for rapid economic development enjoyed by this country from the beginning, and also points out that with the elimination of Germany and Japan as competitors it has access to world markets as never before, and thus has opportunity for further development.

Thus Stalin's conception of the United States as the 'stronghold of capitalism' dovetails with his picture of the future course of world revolution. The United States is expected to be the center of the rival world system which finally must clash with the Soviet system until capitalism goes down and socialism conquers the world. This means that Stalin expects revolution in the United States only near the end of the 'epoch of world revolution.'[94] As he declares to the American Commission of the Comintern in 1929, "when a revolutionary crisis has developed in America, that will be the beginning of the end of all world capitalism."

[93] *XIV s"ezd: Stenograficheskii otchët*, pp. 10, 19.
[94] The factor of geographical position obviously supports such a view also. Stalin recognizes that proximity is an important factor in assisting revolution in another country from the Soviet base. Among the unfavorable circumstances of the October Revolution in Russia he mentions "the absence, next to it or in its neighborhood, of a soviet country which it could lean upon. Undoubtedly, a future revolution, in Germany for example, would be in a more favorable situation in this respect, for it has nearby so powerful a soviet country as our Soviet Union." *Voprosy* (11th ed., 1945), p. 79.

The Next Phase

Thus it is probable that Stalin hardly expected revolution to occur in the United States during World War II or its aftermath. But the evidence presented in the present article makes it likely that his perspective on this period was (and is) as follows:

(1) The time for the next harvest of revolution is at hand. The world war, predicted since 1927, has come to pass, and the upheaval it has created will bring to a climax the contradictions of capitalism in a way that will make revolution possible in 'a number of countries in Europe and Asia.'[95] Precisely such revolution is required to guarantee once and for all that the forces of capitalism will not obliterate socialism (even in the USSR itself) and compel the whole process to begin again from scratch. Therefore the minimum revolutionary objective for World War II and its aftermath is to bring enough countries into the Soviet camp to effect such a guarantee.

(2) The 'law of ebb and flow' implies that unless the whole of capitalism collapses under the present revolutionary wave, the surviving remnant will temporarily stabilize itself a few years after the end of the war and an ebb in the tide of revolution will set in. The revolutionary objective for World War II must therefore be consolidated before the tide begins to ebb. This imparts a certain urgency to revolutionary tactics in the immediate postwar period.

(3) Although the Soviet Union has not yet equaled the United States in industrial production per capita, its industrial and military strength has increased greatly since 1928, and with the defeat of Germany and Japan its relative strength among the powers of Europe and Asia will be enormous. Therefore the Soviet Union will be in position to serve as base for much more active fostering of revolutionary movements in other countries, though not ready to establish communism throughout the world. This indicates a much more aggressive tactic toward other countries, but not so aggressive as deliberately to bring on war for world hegemony in the immediate future.

The success of this tactic would depend in part, according to Stalin's theory of revolution, on the extent to which the critical areas were isolated from foreign influences hostile to revolution. This

[95] "XVII s"ezd" (1934 to present), p. 1.

gives a major clue to Stalin's war and postwar policies toward Britain and the United States. Many of them can be regarded as a delaying action: by retarding realization on the part of these countries of what is really going on, then minimizing efforts to intervene as realization gradually dawns, they, in effect, tend to isolate the 'bourgeoisie' in the countries singled out for revolution until Communist control is established. Stalin's profession of nonaggressive war aims served to lull suspicion. So did the dissolution of the Comintern and his comments thereon. So did his statements on the possibility of coexistence and cooperation and the necessity for unanimity among the big powers after the war. These and similar moves imposed a serious reluctance on the part of the Allies to do or say anything that could be construed as a breach in the spirit of wartime collaboration. When at last Allied public opinion began to denounce Soviet or Communist actions, the same statements served as a basis for propaganda counterattack. Stalin launched this attack with his comments on Churchill's speech at Fulton, declaring it a 'dangerous act,' sowing discord among the Allies, harming the cause of peace and security, in short, warmongering.[96] Thereafter those who, like Churchill, object to Soviet policies in eastern Europe and elsewhere are denounced as 'warmongers,' and an attempt is made to mobilize against them the popular craving for peace.

Even the United Nations has to some extent been exploited by Stalin's tactics. The possibility of using the veto to cripple Allied action in revolutionary areas is obvious. But if, as some think, Stalin might prefer a deal based on spheres of influence to the United Nations pattern, such an arrangement could be depended on to further, not to limit, revolutionary operations. Within his sphere Stalin would have a free hand, and Communist action would also continue across the demarcation line into the other sphere.

When Stalin looks to the more distant future, the United States, which has emerged from the last war more truly than ever the 'stronghold of capitalism,' probably continues to figure in his thinking as it has done in his basic writings since the mid-1920s—as the center around which the capitalist system will form for the final war to the

---

[96] "Interv'iu tov. I. V. Stalina s korrespondentom 'Pravdy' otnositel'no rechi g. Cherchillia," *Pravda*, March 14, 1946, p. 1.

death between the two systems.   Meanwhile, Stalin (*Pravda*, February 10, 1946) projects further industrial expansion in the Soviet Union
on a scale which suggests, other factors aside, that the climactic struggle will not be risked before fifteen or twenty years have elapsed.
Stalin's theory of 'ebb and flow' would lead him to expect a new stabilization of capitalism within a few years, followed some years later
by another wave of crisis and revolution generated by capitalism's
inexorable contradictions.   He apparently is timing completion of the
Soviet base of operations for the crest of this next wave.   Tactics of
the moment may swing this way or that, but the Marxist doctrine
to which he is committed is uncompromisingly revolutionary.   In
that doctrinie, world communism is the supreme aim, Soviet power
the major instrument by which it will be achieved.

Russian Imperialism or Communist Aggression?

MICHAEL M. KARPOVICH

If we are to examine the roots of Soviet expansion, we must, first of all, reject the notion that any people is by nature warlike, peace-loving, imperialistic, or nonimperialistic. We need not 'disprove' this peculiar aspect of 'racism.' We need only recall that, from the end of the seventeenth to the middle of the nineteenth century, most of Europe regarded the French as highly belligerent and aggressive, and the Germans as peace-loving and hardly able to defend themselves. From 1870 on the 'primordial aggressiveness' of the German people was discovered; French bellicosity passed into the realm of historical legend. Outside Europe, the British were regarded throughout the nineteenth century as inherently imperialistic; now little remains of Britannia's past glories, but there is increasing talk of American imperialism—and not only in Communist countries.

Obviously, estimates of the imperialistic or nonimperialistic nature of peoples shift with changes in the relation of international forces. For this reason, the question of Russian imperialism can only be discussed in the light of concrete historical data. And in that light, one is struck first, not by the uniqueness of Russia's development, but rather by how closely it parallels that of the other European countries.

Even if one regards ninth-century Kievan Russia as the first attempt to create a Russian empire (as Marx did when he dangled 'the Russian menace' before the eyes of the world on the eve of the Crimean War), one should recognize its resemblance to the slightly earlier but similar attempt by the Carolingians in the West. Both states were

Published in the *New Leader*, June 4-11, 1951.

Michael M. Karpovich, Professor Emeritus of History and former chairman of the Slavic Department at Harvard University, is one of the deans of American scholarship on the Soviet Union.

built on rudimentary political foundations; they proceeded from the subjugation of related ethnic groups to the seizure of alien neighboring territories. Both 'empires' soon distintegrated under the combined pressure of internal and hostile external forces (Asiatic nomads in the East, Arabs and Normans in the West). The early feudal period followed in West Europe; a period of semifeudal decentralization ensued shortly afterward in Russia.

With the formation of the Muscovite empire, the experience of the Russian state not only parallels, but is concurrent with, the growth of national states in the West. The Vasiliis and Ivans who unified 'the Russian lands' were contemporaries of Ferdinand and Isabella in Spain, Louis XI in France, the Tudors in England. In essence, they all pursued the same methods and sought similar 'ideological justifications' for their policies. While the Polish historian Kucharzewski sees something specifically Russian in the aggressiveness, trickery, and hypocrisy of the early Muscovite tsars, Western royal analogies can easily be cited for every example of tsarist political amorality. In the epoch of Machiavelli, most European rulers employed both cunning and force, violated treaties, were merciless with defeated foes. The tsars referred to fictitious rights and doubtful historical traditions; West European 'legalists' invented similar myths. Certainly the notorious Muscovite messianism has a parallel in the idea of restoring the Roman Empire which captivated the West for so long. The rise of Moscow is a chapter in the modern history of Europe as a whole.

. . . .

One feature of Russian expansion, it seems to me, has played a large part in producing exaggerated Western notions of it. Russia, always a continental power, never possessed a formidable navy. Unable to establish scattered colonies overseas, the tsars instead annexed adjoining land. Such expansion is visually more impressive than colonial expansion of the English type. The continuous expanse of Russia, all in one color, cannot be missed on a map; a grasp of the British Empire's dimensions requires a certain mental effort. Marx computed the number of miles the Russian frontiers had advanced since Peter the Great; a simultaneous assessment of the British Empire's growth would have been equally instructive.

The 'Russian menace' began to arouse fear rather late in the Western world, toward the end of the eighteenth century—or coincidentally with the emergence of Russia as a European great power. In Western eyes, the successes of Peter and Catherine in the field of foreign policy were dramatic, if not sensational. Almost without warning, a potent and relatively new factor had arisen to disturb the traditional European balance of power.

. . . .

West European exaggeration of the 'Russian menace' was psychologically understandable, but, in historical perspective, the Russian imperialism of that time was not exceptional or unprecedented. At the beginning of the seventeenth century, the Hapsburgs had been seriously suspected of striving for world domination. By the end of that century, the chief 'enemy of the human race' was Peter the Great's older contemporary, Louis XIV. The aggressive policies of Frederick the Great several decades later led to a European coalition in which Russia participated; Frederick was no less responsible than Catherine for the partition of Poland. And while Prussia's rise, as well as Russia's, contributed to the disruption of the European balance of power, no tsarist expansion ever produced such upheavals on the European continent as France did under Napoleon.

In the nineteenth century, the Near East was a primary objective of European expansion. Before Russia's appearance on the Near Eastern scene, France began an economic, later political, penetration of the Ottoman Empire. Russia's involvement in the Balkans was preceded by Austrian activity there. Even before the nineteenth century, the eastern Mediterranean had become an essential link in the British Empire's chain of communications. Germany and Italy were to join in the game somewhat later. The tsars had company in the Near East.

We note the same picture of general European expansion in the era of so-called 'neo-imperialism,' in the late nineteenth century and in the early twentieth. However objectionable were the tsarist Far Eastern policies which led to the Russo-Japanese War, they were an integral part of the general European imperialism which at one time threatened China's very existence as an independent state. In the initial stages of this Far Eastern expansion, long before the end of the nineteenth century, England and France played a more active role than Russia. In the 1890s, the signal for the assault on China was given by Japan; England, France, Russia, and Germany all took part in the scramble for concessions that followed. During this same period, a considerable part of Africa was partitioned among several European powers; Russia did not participate.

. . . .

From this hasty survey, the inescapable conclusion is that prerevolutionary Russian imperialism was essentially no different from the imperialism of the other great powers. The Russian Empire was a conventional one; its policies were traditional imperialist policies. Neither its emergence nor its expansion needs to be explained by allusions to 'Russian messianism' or to peculiar traits of the 'Russian character.' If there is an illusory identity between prerevolutionary and Soviet foreign policy, it stems from the fact that the same territories often constitute the objects of expansion. Finland, the Baltic states, Poland, Bessarabia, the Balkans, Constantinople, the Dardanelles, Persia, Chinese Turkestan, Mongolia, Manchuria, Korea—these names stud the pages of tsarist diplomatic history as they do the newspapers of our own day, creating an impression of historical continuity. But must one fall into geographic fatalism? After all, when one comes down to it, the Soviet Union still occupies the same space as the Russian Empire did before it; its expansionist tendencies can, therefore, be expected to appear in the same neighboring territories. One can hardly conclude from this that the aims, methods, and general character of both imperialisms are the same.

For just as the Soviet system, or the modern totalitarian state in general, differs radically from traditional nation-states (whether absolute monarchies, constitutional monarchies, or republics), so, too, the foreign policy of such a totalitarian state is something radically and fundamentally new. Postwar Soviet foreign policy's extraordinary territorial scope and dynamism have been referred to often—and rightly so. For it is a 'global' policy, persistently seeking to achieve a number of aggressive aims simultaneously in various corners of the earth. This alone sharply distinguishes Soviet policy from the policy of the tsars, who, as a rule, pursued limited aims and pursued them in a certain sequence.

Peter quickly gave up his struggle with Turkey to concentrate on the struggle for the Baltic. Catherine contented herself with the conquest of the Black Sea coast and readily pigeonholed the famous 'Greek project.' At the Congress of Vienna, Alexander I abandoned his original Polish plan when he encountered the opposition of other powers. Diplomatic pressure alone forced Nicholas I to renounce what Russia had gained from Turkey by the Treaty of Unkiar Skelessi. After the Crimean War and the Congress of Berlin, Russian diplomacy instantly drew the appropriate conclusions from its defeat, temporarily 'put the Near Eastern question on ice,' and concentrated on other problems (in Asia). And after the Russo-Japanese War, Russia divided spheres of influence in the Far East with Japan, concluded an agreement on Central Asian questions with England, and only then moderately and cautiously put forward her Near Eastern aims, attempting to obtain a settlement by negotiation.

This difference between the global activities of the Politburo and the limited activities of the Romanovs is sometimes explained by the Soviet Union's greater military and economic might. But that might should not be exaggerated, just as, in retrospect, the strength of imperial Russia should not be minimized. In relation to the other great powers, Russia under Peter, Catherine, and Alexander I was not militarily. weak.

Another explanation seems sounder. This cites the extraordinarily favorable international situation which was created for the Soviet regime at the end of the Second World War. Disruption of the established balance of power and the collapse of existing institutions is always a temptation for expansion. The chaos at the end of the last war was unparalleled in modern times. And thus, it is said, Stalin had opportunities which the Russian emperors never had.

Yet it seems to me that this also fails to explain fully the dynamism of Soviet policy. The difference between tsarist and Soviet policy is qualitative, not quantitative. The presence of several powerful rivals was not the only reason prerevolutionary Russian policy lacked global or continental scope. Much more important, pre-Communist Russian policy, in contrast to Soviet diplomacy, had no global *aims*.

It did not have these aims because it possessed no *all-embracing political plan*, with an *over-all idea* underlying it. The idea of world revolution underlies an all-embracing Soviet plan, contained in the body of literature the Communists call Marxism-Leninism-Stalinism. The tsars had no such aims or plans.

. . . .

The foreign policy of the tsars was the customary policy of a national state. The Romanov autocracy, unlike the Soviet Union, was neither an 'ideocracy' nor an insurrectionary-totalitarian state, and it is impossible to find a parallel with 'Marxism-Leninism-Stalinism' in its foreign policy. Furthermore, the Russian autocracy never had anything at its disposal even remotely suggestive of a Comintern or Cominform. The difference in aims between the tsars and the Bolsheviks is matched by an equally fundamental difference in methods.

Tsarist Russia's diplomatic techniques differed little from those of the other great powers. Like their Western colleagues, tsarist diplomats thought in terms of balance of power, division of spheres of influence, territorial compensation, political alliances and military coalitions, 'rectification' of strategic frontiers, 'peaceful penetration,' and so on.

While Western publicists (and occasionally Western government officials) did sometimes accuse Russia of 'revolutionary' conduct, these accusations were most often a means of political warfare. Marx's statements on the eve of the Crimean War belong in this category. Marx spoke about "hundreds of Russian agents perambulating Turkey and the Balkans," about Russia's ambition "to unite all branches of the great Slav race under one scepter and to make them the ruling race of Europe," and so forth. Finding facts to support Marx's charges is difficult.

Tsarist diplomats did from time to time employ 'irregular' methods, but considered them deviations from the norm; they never dreamed of elevating them to the status of a global foreign-policy system. And while Marx was accusing Russia of organizing insurrections within the Ottoman Empire, Britain was helping Caucasian mountaineers fight Russian rule. The dispatching of secret agents abroad, the bribing of foreign newspapers and politicians, behind-the-scenes influence exerted on foreign political parties—these methods were used by all European powers at one time or another. The chapters on eighteenth-century secret diplomacy in Sorel's work on Europe and the French Revolution dispel the idea that Russia was the only power to use these techniques. Of course, the same holds true for the nineteenth century.

When Western writers today match up selected facts and assert that tsarist and Soviet diplomacy are continuous, they are essentially doing what apologists for Soviet foreign policy do. These apologists say, "Yes, Russia interferes in the East European countries, but don't America and England do the same in Greece and Iran? Yes, Moscow sends Communist propaganda beyond its frontiers, but doesn't America conduct foreign propaganda, too? Russia is creating puppet governments, but what is America doing in Korea?"

This is the same logic as the matching of prerevolutionary and Communist foreign policies. The trick in both cases is to tear apparently similar facts out of context, and thus obscure a *basic difference in principle* between two different *systems*. It is a classic example of how a difference in quantity becomes a difference in quality. What in one case was a deviation, in the other becomes a norm. The diplomacy of old Russia was part of a world-wide diplomatic tradition. Soviet diplomacy is hostile to, and consciously violates, this tradition; in moments of candor, it justifies the violations on grounds of principle.

Like the Fascist states, the Stalin regime conducts a *diplomacy of civil war*. Its spirit, aims, and methods were created by the Bolsheviks during their struggle for power in Russia and against the Russian people; when the opportunity arrived, they were applied on an international scale. The Comintern and Cominform are not in the same class as past instances of internal intervention by foreign states. With the Communist 'fifth column,' something *fundamentally new* appeared on the historical scene. Anyone who has not fully grasped this is incapable of understanding Soviet foreign policy.

. . . .

It appears to me that an appreciation of the unique Soviet concept of 'security' will go further toward providing an understanding of Soviet foreign policy than comparisons with the tsars.

Traditionally, a nation's external security was guaranteed by political or military agreements, 'rectification' of strategic frontiers, and, where possible in extreme cases, by spheres of influence or protectorates. From this point of view, Russia's security was amply guaranteed, for example, by the relations established with Czechoslovakia after the last war.

Czechoslovakia made all the political and economic concessions Stalin sought. Beneš and Masaryk 'voluntarily' ceded the Carpatho-Ukraine, giving the USSR direct access to Hungary—a vital 'rectification' of the Soviet strategic frontier. The Communists received disproportionate influence in the government. Moscow vetoed Czech participation in the Marshall Plan. Czechoslovakia was virtually a Soviet protectorate even before the *coup* of February 1948.

But Stalin needed this *coup* just the same. He needed it because all he had achieved was still inadequate according to his own concept of 'security.' For, in contrast to the traditional idea, this Soviet concept aims not at the territorial security of the nation but at the political security of the regime in power.

Czechoslovakia was a threat to the Soviet regime because, even in 1947, it retained some democratic freedom internally and in its relations with the non-Communist world. And in Communist eyes, nothing is more dangerous than freedom nearby. Fear of freedom is the essence of the Soviet theory of security. The tyranny established in Russia is not secure until the same tyranny is established over the entire world. This so-called 'triumph of socialism' is the ultimate aim of the party of Lenin and Stalin. Its immediate task is to 'secure' nearby countries which fall under Soviet influence. To provide such 'security,' these countries must be completely Stalinized. The transition from 'people's democracy' to complete Sovietization is an imperative—in Eastern Europe, in China, wherever the Soviets gain a foothold.

. . . .

This is, of course, quite different from the security concept of the tsars. Nicholas I may have preferred the German monarchies to the constitutional regimes of England and France; Alexander III may have hesitated before allying himself with the Third French Republic.

But no Russian diplomat ever imagined that the world triumph of autocracy was needed for Russian security.

. . . .

Among educated circles in Russia, messianism was never too strong. During the reign of Nicholas I, the Slavophile Aksakov complained that so many Russian intellectuals in the provinces supported the 'Westerner' Belinskii, and none shared his own views. A book by Danilevskii, once called 'the bible of Pan-Slavism,' enjoyed some success during the reign of Alexander III, but was completely forgotten by the turn of the century. By that time, Pan-Slavism had become almost the exclusive property of nationalist right-wing groups; among most intellectuals, it aroused little interest.

Messianism, Pan-Slavism, and imperialism in general were alien to most of the Russian intelligentsia from the first quarter of the nineteenth century; before then, outstanding representatives of Russian culture did take pride in Russia's foreign gains. (Pushkin was simultaneously 'the bard of empire and liberty.') But after Pushkin, this attitude steadily declined.

The absence of 'imperial consciousness' among the Russian intelligentsia is a fact. No important work in Russian historical writing deals with the development of the Russian Empire. . . .

Among Russia's liberals and democrats, Paul Miliukov is generally singled out as an imperialist. But his 'imperialism' consisted only in a refusal in 1917 to renounce Russian claims to Constantinople and the Straits, which had been conceded by the Western Allies by treaty. . . . Even Miliukov's moderate 'imperialism' proved unacceptable to the Russian people in the first months after the democratic revolution of March 1917. The revolutionary government immediately proposed a peace without annexations or indemnities—a program which had strong roots in prerevolutionary pacifism and anti-imperialism. In judging the state of mind of the Russian people, one should overlook neither the enthusiasm this program evoked nor the skillful way Lenin exploited it.

History shows that imperialism, like nationalism, never originates among the masses but seeps down to them from the cultural elite. The pre-Communist Russian intelligentsia was predominantly anti-imperialistic, and it is hard to imagine an imperialist spirit among the popular masses. This heritage quite probably has immunized the Russian people against Communist messianism.

There seems to me no basis for the assertion that the Russian people are burning with the desire to impose communism on the world. Former Soviet citizens testify to the contrary. Frederick C. Barghoorn, who served in our Moscow Embassy during the war, declares : "I never met any Soviet people who seemed to take pride in Soviet political or territorial expansion, in Pan-Slavism, or in the extension of Communist power."

In the light of historical experience, this seems more like the Russian national tradition than any mythical 'innate Russian imperialism.' Far from backing Communist aggression abroad, the Russian people yearns for lasting peace, for normal and decent conditions of human life, and, above all, for its own liberation from Communist aggression at home.

Some Soviet Techniques of Negotiation

PHILIP E. MOSELY

There is a deep-seated tradition in Western diplomacy that an effective diplomat should be a two-way interpreter. He must present his own government's policy forcefully to the government to which he is accredited and defend the essential interests of his country. If he is to give intelligent advice to his government, he must also develop a keen insight into the policies of the government with which he deals and become skilled in distinguishing basic interests and sentiments which it cannot disregard from secondary ones which it may adjust or limit for the broader purpose of reaching agreement. Occasionally, as instanced by Woodrow Wilson's criticism of Walter Hines Page, it has seemed as if individual ambassadors became too much penetrated by the viewpoint and interests of the country to which they were sent and less able to press contrary views of their own governments.

No such problem of delicate balance in functions arises to plague the Soviet negotiator. This has been especially true since the great purge of the Commissariat of Foreign Affairs in 1938-39 and the replacement of Litvinov by Molotov in 1939. The new foreign affairs staff was recruited among the middle ranks of Soviet officials, whose entire training had been based on rigid adherence to centralized decisions and who had rarely had informal contacts with life outside the Soviet Union. The present-day Soviet representative can hardly be called a 'negotiator' in the customary sense. He is rather treated as a mechanical mouthpiece for views and demands formulated centrally in Moscow, and is

Published in *Negotiating with the Russians*, edited by Raymond Dennett and Joseph E. Johnson (Boston, 1951).

Philip E. Mosely, until 1955 Director of the Russian Institute of Columbia University, is Director of Studies at the Council on Foreign Relations in New York.

deliberately isolated from the impact of views, interests, and sentiments which influence foreign governments and peoples. Probably the Soviet representative abroad, through fear of being accused of 'falling captive to imperialist and cosmopolitan influences,' serves as a block to the transmission of foreign views and sentiments, rather than as a channel for communicating them to his government.

This does not mean that Moscow is cut off from the flow of public-opinion materials from abroad. On the contrary, it probably receives a very large volume of material, especially clippings of all kinds. On occasion Andrei Vyshinsky quotes triumphantly from some small local newspaper or some relatively obscure 'public figure' to prove that the 'ruling circles' in the United States are hatching some 'imperialist,' 'war-mongering' plot. This practice arouses bewilderment or uneasy merriment in American listeners, whose ears are attuned to the cacophony of conflicting views. In the Soviet way of thinking, the citing of such sources is perfectly logical since it is assumed that nothing happens 'accidentally' and therefore all expressions of opinion are of equal value in exposing the underlying pattern of hostile intention. Incidentally, the diligent Soviet gathering of opinion data appears to rely primarily upon newspapers and their editorial expressions; from the indirect evidence available it seems that very little attention is paid to radio material and to the much more potent role of radio commentators in molding the thinking of the public.

The large amount of opinion material imported daily from abroad appears to be analyzed and digested in Moscow with two purposes in mind. One is to prove that, despite protestations of humanitarian and peace-loving intentions, the adversary is actually preparing an aggressive war of conquest. Thus, isolated expressions of a willingness to go to war in the near future or statements of ability to wage war are gladly built up into a confirmation of the 'imperialist' and 'aggressive' aims of the 'ruling circles' in the United States. Other material is cited to prove that 'the broad masses' in the enemy country are opposed both to war and to all preparation for defense, but are thwarted in giving effect to their attitude by the 'dictatorship of big capital.'

Some students of Soviet policy believe—in my opinion, far too hopefully—that this two-fold use of foreign press material is directed primarily toward molding public opinion within the Soviet Union, in satellite or, rather, 'captive' states, and among the Communist or Communist-influenced faithful elsewhere, and that the Soviet leaders at the center of power have available an objective and factual analysis of foreign events and currents of opinion as a basis for their decisions. No doubt, the Politburo has available many facts and reports which do not enter into the controlled flow of information available to their subjects. And on occasion Stalin, less often Molotov or Vyshinsky, has shown an awareness of facts or opinions widely known abroad yet not imparted to their own people. On more rare occasions they have shown a willingness to make small concessions to those interests, alien as they are to the Soviet way of thinking.

At Potsdam President Truman and Secretary Byrnes presented with great earnestness the resentment felt by Americans at the complete censorship which was being exercised over news reporting from the former German satellites—Hungary, Rumania, and Bulgaria—with the connivance or by orders of the Soviet occupation authorities. They protested that, since the United States was among the victors and was represented on the Allied Control Commissions, American opinion could not understand why American correspondents were prevented from reporting freely on developments in those countries. While Generalissimo Stalin undoubtedly continued to regard conscientious Western correspondents as 'spies' and as a nuisance to be tolerated as little as possible, he accepted President Truman's arguments based on the power position of the victor and agreed, after relatively unacrimonious dispute, to the United States proposal for assuring Western correspondents of freedom to gather and transmit news from the three satellites. The leader of the Soviet regime could accept the Western contentions in this matter, particularly as they left untouched the central power positions of Soviet policy, while subordinate agents would have felt impelled, in harmony with the Soviet concept of centralized manipulation of 'opinion,' to reject them with vehement accusations of ill will.

1

In opening negotiations with any Soviet representatives except Stalin the first problem is to discover whether the representatives have any instructions at all. To discover what those instructions, if any, are requires sitting out the whole course of the negotiation, with its demands, insults, and rigidities and its always uncertain outcome. By comparison, Western representatives are often allowed to exercise a certain amount of discretion. They may facilitate the ultimate attainment of a workable compromise—a generally shared goal of both sides—by giving their 'opposite number' some fairly clear intimation of the 'hard' and 'soft' spots in their instructions. A still further development of this flexible approach to the desired goal of adjustment, one based on a high level of intergovernmental and interpersonal trust, is to discuss in detail, at various stages in their formulation, instructions which are in process of preparation. For example, a staff officer may be able to tell his counterpart what recommendations on a given matter he proposes to make to his superiors and similarly to learn what ones will be made by his 'opposite number' in the other government; if his recommendations are overruled 'higher up,' no reproach is made to him and no official reference can be made to his confidence.

A thorough knowledge on both sides of the respective instructions as they are being worked out enhances the mutual understanding of the interests and forces which underlie the positions taken, eliminates many secondary points of friction, and leaves the larger unagreed issues in clearer view. This pattern of 'continuous' negotiation, preceding and following the principal and formal negotiation, requires continuing consultation and reporting at at least three levels—the expert or 'recommending and drafting' level, the intermediate or 'Assistant Secretary' level, and, finally, the 'ministerial' level. Where, in addition to the ministry of foreign affairs, various other ministries or executive departments, dealing with military, financial, and other matters, are also concerned, there may emerge parallel three-level consultations with those departments on the same informal basis.

A similarly informal and highly effective approach is provided by the 'working party,' a technique which was first cultivated within the British civil service to deal with interdepartmental problems below the level of the cabinet and the cabinet secretariat, and which has been applied very successfully in interallied and even wider international negotiations. Under the 'working party' technique the staffs of experts are given a broadly stated problem to work out, on which each national staff brings to bear a broad picture of the aims and interests of its own government. In the course of its work, facts are established, alternative solutions are considered, and an agreed recommendation may be reached, for presentation to the principal negotiators on both sides. Under this procedure the various staffs operate as experts as much or more than as national representatives, and it is understood that neither side is bound by anything said or tentatively drafted until the report and recommendations as a whole have been considered and approved 'at a political level.'

These and similar techniques or habits of 'continuous negotiation' provide the daily adjustment or lubrication of policy among like-minded and like-purposed Western powers. They are, of course, not practiced by the Soviet government in its dealings with the West. Soviet experts and diplomats cannot participate in an informal day-to-day exchange of information, comments, and tentative recommendations concerning policy. Until Moscow has sent instructions they can say nothing at all, for they may fail to express the exact nuance of thinking or intention which has not yet been formulated at the center, and transmitted to them. After Moscow has spoken they can only repeat the exact formulation given to them, and no variation may be introduced into it unless Moscow has sent the necessary further instructions. The Western habit of continuous negotiation is baffling to the Soviet diplomats, who cannot understand that their Western colleagues have both the opportunity and the responsibility for presenting and even advocating policies within their own governmental operations and that, within a broadly agreed pattern of interests and purposes, they have considerable leeway in finding the most effective, and usually informal, methods of influencing their 'opposite numbers' in foreign ministries or embassies.

The frequently noted 'woodenness' of Soviet negotiation apparently applies in relations with satellite or captive regimes, at least with their governments. Thus, President, then Premier, Gottwald, outwardly the principal leader of the Communist Party of Czechoslovakia, was called on the carpet in Moscow, in early July 1947. He was told by Stalin in person that his government must withdraw its acceptance of the invitation to participate in the conference which was about to meet in Paris to prepare the groundwork for the Marshall Plan of economic aid to European economic recovery. Gottwald had assumed that the government of Czechoslovakia was free to accept this invitation and that the Communist members of the cabinet were free to vote for its acceptance. His dismay, on being confronted with Stalin's absolute and vehement veto, points to the absence, at least at that time, of informal and day-to-day exchanges between the two governments. Similarly, the period preceding the June 1948 break between Moscow and Belgrade was clearly marked by the failure of informal communication between Soviet and Yugoslav policy-makers as well as by the failure of the Soviet embassy to inform Moscow of the probable effects of an attempt to overthrow the leadership of Marshal Tito.

The important network of informal communication among the Western powers, as well as the moderate latitude given to their representatives, makes for a swift pace of negotiation which arouses bewilderment and suspicion among their Soviet colleagues. Since Western foreign ministries are receiving daily a flow of confidential comment on foreign views and intentions, they are forearmed with current analyses and can often give necessary decisions rapidly. Western diplomats also have a substantial latitude to work out agreed positions and drafts, at least on secondary and procedural matters. Thus, their minor differences are often resolved with what seems to their Soviet colleagues like suspicious speed.

Not believing in or not understanding the system of informal communication and limited individual latitude, the Soviet representatives readily fall back on the theory of 'American dictation.' It is easier for them to assert that the United States government has exerted political, military, and financial pressure to force its will upon other governments than to take the trouble to analyze the complex and, to them, unfamiliar and unbelievable system of informal communication which usually lies behind the 'automatic majorities' assembled around United States proposals. They are incredulous when told that such pressure is exerted only rarely and that more often agreement is reached through give-and-take of views, by which no side gets its full position and each gets a part of it.

Sometimes the sole instructions with which a Soviet delegation enters a conference are that it is not to commit itself to anything or sign anything. Oddly enough, the outcome may be fairly pleasant and even profitable. When the British and American governments decided to call a conference, held at Bretton Woods, for the creation of postwar institutions of financial and economic cooperation, the Soviet government at first decided to refrain from participation in it. Probably it saw, at best, no direct gain to itself through setting up international machinery to promote monetary stability and the flow of international investment. At the worst, in accordance with the Soviet philosophy of history, it must have regarded such efforts as a futile and undesirable attempt to stave off the long-predicted 'general crisis of capitalism.' When the Soviet government received the intimation that its refusal even to attend the Bretton Woods conference would discourage the tenderly nurtured growth of interallied cooperation and would provide Goebbels with valuable propaganda material, it reversed its position regarding participation in the conference, but not with respect to joining in arrangements and obligations which might emerge from it, and sent a small but able delegation. Having no direct responsibility for the outcome and probably having no need to annoy 'the center' in Moscow with requests for instructions, members of the Soviet delegation could devote their very considerable ingenuity to helping the progress of the conference, by making many minor but useful suggestions as they went along.

The usual experience with 'uninstructed' Soviet delegations has been the reverse of this. In some negotiations it became clear, after delivery by it of numerous charges and accusations, that the Soviet delegation had no instructions except to 'report back.' In 1944, with the beginning of the liberation of western Europe, it became urgent to make provision for the orderly restoration of inland transportation, both by land and water, and it was hoped that these provisions would be applicable to all European belligerents except the Soviet Union and the United Kingdom. Some countries had been stripped of rolling stock and barges; others held plundered equipment in large quantities. Undestroyed repair facilities would be very unevenly distributed upon the cessation of hostilities; some countries would have considerably more than the necessary minimum of new rails, rolling stock, and bridging material, while others would have none at all. And efficient allocation of urgently needed materials,

which Great Britain, Canada, and the United States were preparing
to supply, required the establishment of some European-wide agency for arriving at agreed but voluntary decisions on these matters.
During the greater part of 1944 American, British, and Soviet delegations negotiated in London for the establishment of an emergency
European Inland Transport Organization.

At least the American and British delegations negotiated with each
other and with the Soviet delegation, with great zeal and energy, but
the Soviet delegation failed to 'negotiate back.' The Western representatives explained over and over again that not only each great
power but each member government would be free to accept or reject
the recommendations of EITO, but that it was hoped that agreed
recommendations, based on a joint study of the facts, would usually
be reached. The Soviet delegates reiterated endlessly that their government could not agree to leave these decisions to any experts. Obviously,
the concept that governments would merely ratify the 'decisions'
reached by experts was both unfamiliar and inconceivable to them.
While the Western negotiators felt that the 'European' character of
the proposed organization was a positive factor, the Soviet delegates
seemed to regard it with great suspicion, which was merely confirmed
when the British delegation expressed a hope that currently neutral
countries would also join EITO after the conclusion of hostilities.
As the discussions with the Russians continued, the American and
British drafts were clarified and gradually began to merge into a single
draft, more or less 'by attrition.' Naturally, this only increased the
uneasiness of the Russians, who could not conceive of any representative
daring to modify the sacrosanct text which had been handed down
to him.

Days and weeks went by with constant meetings. When the Soviet
representatives criticized some aspect of the American or British draft,
the other delegations promptly offered some revision which appeared
likely to meet that particular criticism. So many versions of the various
articles flew around the table that the Russian interpreter was frankly
unable to render them to his own delegation. Without attempting
to grasp the fine nuances as between successive drafting texts the
Soviet delegate proceeded to repeat this or that general criticism,
accusation, or suspicion after each one of them. Firm in a conscious-

ness both of good intentions and of a practical, functional approach
to a vital problem, the Western delegates urged on their Soviet colleagues
the importance of the early creation of EITO, in order that it could
begin urgently needed planning for the recovery of the transportation
system. To this the Russian representative blandly retorted that
'planning' was not possible under capitalism, anyway.

After several weeks of 'negotiation' the American delegation came
to the conclusion that the Soviet delegation was unable to present any
proposals of its own or to accept any British or American proposals.
On the other hand, it was free to raise and repeat any number of criticisms of the other drafts, provided it did not allow itself to be pinned
down to approval of any individual provision or textual wording. It
was clear that the Soviet delegation had long since given up any effort
to record in Russian or to transmit to its own government any of the
numerous modified drafts which had been submitted by the other
two delegations during the course of the negotiation. It was quite probable that the Soviet delegation had been hustled off to London with
no proposals to present and with no detailed instructions except to
report back. Once in London, its members were probably too timid
to make any recommendations or even to ask for new instructions, and
in Moscow the few people who were qualified to handle a question of
this kind were too busy with matters of direct Soviet interest, such as
transforming the Lublin Committee into the government of Poland
or negotiating the Soviet terms for the armistice with Rumania, to
bother their heads or Stalin's head about EITO.

What could be done about this impasse? In relations between
Western countries questions could be asked informally between middle-
ranking members of an embassy and members of the foreign office;
within a few days intentions could be clarified and decisions taken.
Since the Soviet system permits of communication only at the top and
since the 'top-level' channels of communication were badly over-
loaded with more urgent military and political questions, the negotiators for EITO had to find some way to 'muddle through.'

My own analysis of the situation was that the Soviet delegation
would report to its own government only when it had firm American
and British proposals to transmit. Instead of devoting their full effort
to persuading the Soviet delegation to take a position, which it was

not empowered to do, the two Western delegations should now work out their differences and arrive at an agreed draft. But they should do this in front of the Russians, since otherwise the latter would regard Anglo-American consensus as a conspiracy against themselves. In arriving at a single draft the two delegations should take reasonable account of the various general Soviet objections and should point out to the Soviet delegation that they were doing so. The agreed draft should provide fully for Soviet adherence, then or in the future, to EITO, but it should provide for its coming into force without Soviet participation after a waiting period. If it required Soviet participation in order to come into force, and if the Soviet government saw no direct benefit for itself in joining it, it would block the entire agreement merely by not answering various notes and *démarches*. On the other hand, every effort should be made to secure Soviet participation since Soviet refusal would mean that the Soviet zone in Germany and the countries occupied by the Soviet armies would also refrain from joining this useful cooperative effort. However, on balance it seemed that the Soviet government would be more likely to join EITO if it saw that the other allies were prepared, eventually, to go ahead without it after taking every precaution to keep the Soviet government informed at each point in the negotiation.

Neither the full hopes nor the entire fears which inspired the EITO negotiators were fulfilled. The question of Soviet participation dragged along until the Potsdam Conference of July 1945. Then, in one of the occasional moments of good feeling between the storms, the British delegation raised the question and urged Soviet participation in EITO. After some whispered consultations, in which Mr. Vyshinsky was seen to shake his head with some vigor despite an effort at impassivity, Generalissimo Stalin turned back to the table and without further discussion or questions announced that the Soviet government would join EITO. This step, however, did not result in the Soviet government relaxing its demands for rolling stock, equipment, barges, tugs, cranes, repair tools, and so forth, in countries occupied or 'liberated' by it; it also contributed nothing in the question of whether Germany would be treated as an economic unit or whether the Soviet zone would, as turned out to be the case, be regarded solely as a Soviet appendage.

2

By far the most frequent situation is one in which the Soviet negotiators are bound by detailed instructions rigidly pressed. Each point at issue, large or small, then becomes a test of will and nerves. Instead of striving to reduce the number of points of friction and to isolate and diminish the major conflicts of interest, the Soviet negotiator often appears to his exasperated Western colleague to take pride in finding the maximum number of disputes and in dwelling on each of them to the full. Even during the wartime period of relative cooperation it was noticeable that each decision to convene a three-power conference was followed by the piling up of disputes and grievances, as well as by the rapid fabrication of Soviet accomplished facts. Thus the decision to hold the Yalta Conference was followed swiftly by the unilateral Soviet recognition of the Lublin Committee as the legitimate government of Poland. While arrangements were being made to hold the Potsdam Conference, at which Poland's territorial gains in the west would presumably be determined by three-power decision, the Soviet government proceeded to turn over to Polish administration a large part of the Soviet zone. This action was, of course, an assertion of the Soviet Union's exclusive role in eastern Europe, in disregard of a political agreement to determine the western boundary of Poland jointly, and in violation of the three-power agreement defining the zones of occupation in Germany.

The closely related technique of playing up grievances was also well illustrated at Potsdam. Bitter and prolonged Soviet attacks upon the presence of British troops in Greece, the Dodecanese, Syria and Lebanon took up much time and energy. When the Western negotiators had been worn down by these wrangles, the Soviet negotiators could face with greater equanimity the American and especially the British protests against the brutal assertion of Soviet hegemony in Hungary, Rumania, and Bulgaria. By their tactics the Soviet leaders had encouraged their militant supporters in Greece, had upheld their reputation for hostility to 'colonialism' in the Middle East, and had fought off any coordinated Western program for loosening their grip on the three satellites.

At the same time, without fanfare, they secured what at the time promised to be a long extension of the occupation of Iranian Azerbaijan.

In 1942, when the Soviet Union and Britain had promised Iran to withdraw their troops from Iranian soil 'six months after the conclusion of hostilities,' the Soviet Union had been at war with Germany and not with Japan. At Potsdam, when the Soviet Union was still not at war with Japan, it rejected the British assumption that the six months' period should be counted from the surrender of Germany and insisted, against Western objections, that the period should be counted from the surrender of Japan! The best military advice at the time was that the war with Japan might end late in 1946 or in 1947. By occupying Iranian Azerbaijan for so many additional months, the Soviet forces, which had already cut it off from control by Teheran, could expect to complete the assimilation of this area into the ranks of the 'people's democracies.' Thus the wrangles over the role of British troops in the eastern Mediterranean had effectively covered up a drastic and unreasonable reinterpretation of an international agreement, made without even consulting Iran, which was a signatory to it.

The treasuring of grievances, real or imaginary, within a cycle of themes for negotiation is paralleled within the individual negotiation by the use of disconcerting ripostes and of accusations of bad faith. One of the most important issues which confronted the Moscow Conference of Foreign Ministers in October 1943 was whether the Czechoslovak government-in-exile should conclude a twenty-year defensive alliance with the Soviet Union alone, or whether the building of any regional systems of postwar guarantees against a revival of German aggression should be postponed until the three major allies could resolve the problem by joint decision. As early as February 1942 the Soviet government had proposed twenty-year bilateral treaties of mutual defense against Germany to the Polish, Czechoslovak, and Yugoslav governments-in-exile. Only the Beneš government had accepted the proposal, and of the three governments concerned it alone was allowed by the Soviet government to return to its homeland, only to be overthrown in its turn by a Communist seizure of power in February 1948. The British and American viewpoint was that this and similar problems should be postponed until after the defeat of Germany, until the governments-in-exile had returned to their countries and had received a direct mandate from their peoples to undertake long-range commitments, and until the postwar system of international

security could be worked out on the basis of the contemplated organization of the United Nations.

The Czechoslovak government was eager to cooperate with both
East and West and hoped to have the support of both. However,
in accordance with military prospects, it looked to the Soviet forces
to enable it to return to its country, and it had a mandate from the
underground at home to accept Soviet support for its postwar security.
Enthusiasm for Slav solidarity, Russia's ambiguously encouraging
support of Czechoslovakia at the Munich crisis, in contrast to its abandonment by Britain and France, the desire to dissociate itself from the
Polish-Soviet territorial dispute and to avoid the kind of internecine
struggle which was tearing Yugoslavia apart were factors which encouraged the Beneš government to sign the Soviet alliance, which
had been ready in draft form for many months, but it wished to do
so only with the approval of the British and American governments,
or at least with their express acquiescence.

It was against this background that the issue was taken up by the
conference of foreign ministers, but the issues were not threshed out in
detail. Early in the discussion a concrete issue of fact arose between
Eden and Molotov. In a conciliatory fashion Eden began by saying,
"I may be mistaken, but..." Before he could complete his sentence
Molotov broke in harshly, "You *are* mistaken." His abrupt riposte
was effective. Eden's presentation was disrupted. By this tactic, and
by constant accusations that the Western powers were trying to rebuild
a *cordon sanitaire* in eastern Europe, Molotov succeeded in evading any
probing discussion of the nature and purpose of the Soviet program
of building up a security belt of its own and won British approval
and American acquiescence for the first step, the conclusion of the
Soviet-Czechoslovak alliance, which was signed at Moscow two months
later.

A similar attempt to use accusations of evil intentions to gain a Soviet
point occurred during the negotiations of April-July 1945 over the
arrangements for the occupation and control of Austria. In planning
the zones of occupation the American, British, and French delegations
maintained that, as had been arranged in the agreement on zones of
occupation in Germany, zonal boundaries should follow existing provincial or *Länder* frontiers. Any other procedure would involve com-

plicated and detailed reshuffings of administrative, police, rationing, housing, and other arrangements. The Soviet delegation, however, refused to follow the precedent which had been applied in the drawing of the German zones and insisted on canceling all changes in administrative boundaries 'which had been made since the annexation by Germany in 1938.

The reason was simple enough. The *Land* of Vienna had undergone a long overdue expansion after the *Anschluss*. If the more extended post-1938 *Land* of Vienna were placed under four-power control, the province of Lower Austria, which was to be under Soviet occupation, would be reduced by that much in area, population, and resources. It must be said, in all fairness, that the Western position was genuinely based on the factor of administrative convenience and was not motivated directly by a desire to constrict the area of Soviet control. However, this was probably not appreciated by the Soviet negotiators, as the Western delegations were also insisting, and insisted successfully after many weeks of heated discussions, on rejecting the Soviet demand to occupy large parts of Styria and Carinthia and on limiting the Soviet zone to Lower Austria and Burgenland.

During the long and tedious debates over the question of adopting the pre-1938 or post-1938 boundaries of the *Land* of Vienna the favored argument of the Soviet delegation was that by urging the use of the post-1938 provincial boundary the United States representative 'was promoting Fascism.' After hearing the changes rung on this charge for several sessions and many hours I calmly pointed out that, unlike certain other governments, my government had not given political recognition to the Nazi seizure of Austria, that the Allied authorities in Austria would have enough to do in effecting the separation of Austria from Germany and in eradicating Nazism without wasting time in reshuffling minor administrative boundaries, and that I was unmoved by the charge of 'promoting Fascism' since I was on record as having pointed out the warlike and aggressive dangers of German Fascism as early as 1930. This particular argument was thereupon dropped by the Soviet delegation, a factor which helped to improve the tone and quality of later deliberations on the arrangements for Austria. In the end the agreement established the *Land* of Vienna within its narrower pre-1938 boundaries, but it did so only in return for numerous concessions which were made by the Soviet delegation from its original and hard-fought demands.

3

During the course of negotiation it is often clear that the Soviet negotiators are under compulsion to try for a certain number of times to secure each Soviet point, no matter how minor. After trying up to a certain point and finding that the demand cannot be put through, the Soviet representative has often given in, only to turn to the next item in dispute, over which a similarly prolonged period of deadlock ensues. What is not clear, however, is whether the number or duration of these tries has been prescribed in advance by instruction or whether it is left to the judgment of the individual Soviet negotiator to decide when he has built up a sufficiently impressive and protective record of having beaten his head against a stone wall.

A good example of the 'head-against-stone-wall' technique developed rather early in the negotiations of 1945-46 over the Yugoslav-Italian boundary. At the first meeting of the Council of Foreign Ministers, held at London in September 1945, almost the only item of agreement was a brief instruction to the Deputies to the effect that the boundary "should be in the main the ethnic line leaving a minimum under alien rule." When the Deputies began their work at Lancaster House, in January 1946, the Soviet delegation began a strong campaign, lasting for some six weeks of almost daily argument, to remove the words 'in the main.' The issue was fought over in long meetings of the four-power Commission for the Investigation of the Yugoslav-Italian Boundary, and from there it was carried into long, numerous, and even more tense meetings of the Deputies.

The three words which aroused Soviet ire were extremely important. If the boundary was to follow 'the ethnic line,' it would reach the sea between Monfalcone and Trieste, leaving Trieste with its large Italian majority and the coastal strip of Western Istria within Yugoslavia. In the triangle Monfalcone-Gorizia-Trieste the ethnic boundary between Italian and Slovene villages is clearly marked and has hardly varied in several hundreds of years. On the other hand, if the boundary was to be 'in the main the ethnic line,' the commission would have to give considerable weight to the claims of the Italian majorities in Trieste and in the coastal strip of Istria, offsetting against them the Slovene national character of several small villages in the coastal strip between Monfalcone and Trieste. If the words 'in the main' were omitted, it was hardly necessary to send out an investigating commission at all, with its attendant wave of turbulence, terrorization, kidnapings, and murders, and the 'ethnic line,' pure and simple, could be drawn in Lancaster House.

During the weeks of intensive debate tension mounted around the green-topped table. As usual, Soviet intransigence turned the dispute into a test of staying power. In view of the fact that public opinion still continued to regard any failure to reach speedy agreement with the Soviet government as primarily the fault of American or British 'reactionaries,' rather than attributing any part of it to the 'all-or-nothing' Soviet attitude, it was not clear how long the Western delegations would hold out against the Soviet demand that the boundary issue be prejudged one-hundred-percent in favor of the Soviet position. In an effort to win the Soviet delegation over to a compromise the Western delegations offered to remove from the purview of the boundary commission Fiume, the islands of the Quarnero, and the primarily Yugoslav-inhabited parts of Venezia Giulia; they did insist that the formula 'in the main' be retained and that the commission be free to investigate the Italian and mixed areas within the region. Finally, 'enough was enough,' even for Soviet negotiators enamored of indefinite repetition, and the Deputies suspended their meetings without agreement on the terms of reference.

Now, at last, the Soviet delegation had, reluctantly, to inform Moscow that the Western Deputies refused to budge on this basic issue of rewriting the formula which had been approved by the Council of Foreign Ministers. This put up to the Soviet government the question of taking the responsibility for an indefinite deadlock in the negotiation of the peace treaties. After two days of marking time the Soviet delegation asked to have a meeting of the Deputies and proceeded, without outward resentment, to approve the final Western-backed version of the commission's terms of reference, retaining the key words, 'in the main the ethnic line.' One basic factor in the Soviet decision to recede from its stubbornly pressed demand must have been that Anglo-American forces were stationed in Trieste, Pola, and the Isonzo valley. If Yugoslav or Soviet forces had been in possession, the deadlock would probably have been allowed to continue indefinitely.

While Western representatives are usually given some leeway to negotiate and always may refer back to their governments with recommendations and suggestions which, they believe, may advance their task, they can sometimes arouse a sympathetic response, on minor matters, in their Soviet colleagues by making it clear that there are certain points on which they cannot budge. A situation of this kind arose during the discussions of 1944 in London concerning the terms of the armistice with Bulgaria. After the Soviet Union had declared war on Bulgaria and its troops had occupied the country, the initiative in drafting the terms of the armistice passed to the Soviet delegation to the European Advisory Commission. The Russian representatives now argued for extremely favorable terms for the Bulgarians, although the latter had inflicted great and needless sufferings on both Greece and Yugoslavia. It was clear that the Soviet negotiators regarded every gain for Bulgaria, which they now regarded as a Soviet client, as a gain for the Soviet Union.

In particular, the Soviet representatives strongly opposed any suggestion that the Bulgarians, who were then eating very well and had, over the last few months, accumulated large supplies of foodstuffs which could no longer be shipped to Germany because of the breakdown in transportation, should be required to deliver reparations. On the other hand, all of Greece was suffering severely from lack of foodstuffs and some parts were on the verge of acute starvation, while the situation was serious in many parts of Yugoslavia. In order to provide a bare minimum of food, very tight Allied supplies and shipping were being diverted to Greece, and of course American, British, and Canadian taxpayers were meeting the bill for this aid. The Soviet negotiators brushed aside all these considerations, based on the community of the Allied war effort, and argued that since Bulgaria had declared war on Germany and was now fighting on the side of the Allies, it was wrong to discourage its new-found zeal by requiring the payment of reparations even through deliveries in kind. No such consideration had prevented the Soviet government, a few weeks before, from imposing vast and indefinite obligations of reparation and restitution upon Rumania, whose defection to the Allied side was a genuinely important contribution to the war against Germany.

Finding that debate around the table failed to budge the Soviet representatives, I sought them out for a private talk. I explained that if Bulgaria escaped the payment of all reparations in kind the burdens of the American government would be increased by just that much, that approval and review by the Congress of all appropriations was a basic part of our governmental procedure, that failure to impose on Bulgaria the payment of reparations might lead to an investigation, and that I might then be punished. At the word 'punished,' a sympathetic gleam of understanding came into the eyes of my Soviet colleagues, and on the following day they agreed to insert the provision for payment of reparation in kind into the terms of the armistice. It is hardly necessary to record that, in any case, the enforcement of the terms of the armistice lay primarily in the hands of 'the Allied (Soviet) High Command' in Bulgaria, and that, according to one report, for the authenticity of which I cannot vouch, Bulgarian deliveries to Greece under the terms of the armistice amounted to one broken-down wagon and two slat-ribbed cows!

4

One of the main pitfalls in wartime Anglo-American negotiations with the Soviet Union was the tendency to rely upon reaching an 'agreement in principle,' without spelling out in sufficient detail all the steps in its execution. After long and strenuous debates, studded with charges, accusations, and suspicions, it was undoubtedly a great relief to reach a somewhat generally worded agreement and to go home. Prodded by manifold public and party duties, anxious to prove to themselves and to their people that current agreements and postwar cooperation with the Soviet government were genuinely possible, facing 'deadlines' with respect to the expectations of legislatures and of public opinion, the Western leaders often approached these negotiations under serious disadvantages. Wooed rather than the wooer, able to deal at leisure with the manipulation of their public opinion at home, facing no deadlines, the Soviet leaders had many advantages. In this situation the Western powers sometimes gained the 'principle' of their hopes, only to find that 'in practice' the Soviet government continued to pursue its original aims.

At Yalta the Soviet government agreed, after very lengthy argument and stubborn resistance, to participate in a reconstruction of the Polish government which would, it appeared, permit the survival of some political freedom for the great non-Communist majority of the people. By delays and quibblings over the execution of the 'agreement in principle' during the next few months, the Soviet government secured about ninety per cent of the original position with which it had come to Yalta and thus strengthened beyond challenge the small Communist minority in its dominant control of the country. At Yalta the Soviet government also agreed, in return for sweeping territorial and other concessions, to deal only with the Chinese National government as the representative of China. By turning over territory, administration, and Japanese arms to Chinese Communist forces, the Russians nullified, in the areas where their forces were dominant, the principal and vital *quid pro quo* which they had promised at Yalta. When British, Canadian, and American negotiators come to an 'agreement in principle,' they often haggle to a fare-thee-well over the implementation of an arrangement which may still be distasteful to each of them. However, they remain within the framework of the principle to which they have agreed, or else they frankly ask to reopen the agreement in principle and to renegotiate it on the grounds that further consideration has shown that they cannot carry it out. It has remained for the Soviet representatives to assert that they are carrying out 'an agreement in principle' by doing just the reverse 'in practice.'

Except for a scant handful of legal consultants who were trained in general jurisprudence and international law prior to the great revolution of 1927-29 in Soviet academic life, Soviet representatives usually show little comprehension of the legal problems which arise in seeking agreements among nations or in meeting the constitutional requirements of democratic states, and special obstacles have arisen not infrequently from this cause. During the Paris sessions of the Council of Foreign Ministers there was one amusing instance of this difficulty. The Soviet delegation appeared rather puzzled over the presence of Senator Tom Connally and the late Senator Arthur H. Vandenberg among the American delegation. Senator Vandenberg upset them particularly. After some especially outrageous tirade by Molotov he would take his un-smoked cigar from his mouth and grin across the table most engagingly, as if to say, "Well, well, that *is* a new angle !"

One afternoon, as we were leaving the conference hall for tea, a member of the Soviet delegation, taking me by the arm, asked, after one or two hurried preliminaries, why the Senators were there. I quickly gave him a three-minute sketch of the background and working of the bipartisan foreign policy and explained that the peace treaties, on which the Council was working, could be ratified by the President only upon the advice and consent of the Senate, and of two-thirds of the Senate, at that. And since (using Soviet terms for clarity) American parties were 'undisciplined,' affirmative action by the Senate would require approval and support by influential leaders of both parties. My Soviet colleague was frankly amazed to learn of this responsibility of the Senate. " You don't mean that the Senate would refuse to ratify a treaty that your governement had signed ?" he asked. To that I could only reply that the Senate had often refused to act at all or had acted negatively on treaties negotiated and submitted to it by the executive.

In 1944, in the work of the European Advisory Commission, a difficult legal problem arose during the preparation of the Instrument of Un-conditional Surrender which was to be imposed by the three, later four, powers at the time of the final surrender of the German government and the German High Command. Should those forces which would be surrendered in this final act, in distinction from those who surrendered or were captured during hostilities, be declared prisoners-of-war, or not ? After detailed discussions with military and legal experts the American and British delegations were instructed to oppose declaring such German and other enemy personnel to be prisoner-of-wars, while the Soviet government insisted that they be so declared.

From the American and British viewpoint there was a whole series of difficulties involved in this. The final surrender might suddenly place from three to six million German armed personnel in their custody, with the legal requirement to furnish them with food, housing, clothing, and medical care according to the respective standards applied by the American and British armies to their own troops on a garrison footing. This was not physically, financially, or politically feasible. Furthermore, in the unprecedented situation in which Germany would cease to be a sovereign state there was no way of knowing how long this tremendous burden might continue. It would also mean that the legally necessary provision for the German forces would place them in a greatly favored position as against the liberated populations of our own allies in Europe. Finally, there was considerable legal doubt as to whether a prisoner-of-war could be tried for war crimes aside from the previously established crimes of war. It was clear that the Soviet Union was faced by no such difficulties. Its personnel had been subjected by the Nazis to great cruelty and even to mass extermination, and it was not bound by any international conventions in its treatment of German prisoners taken during or at the close of hostilities.

For some five months this problem was a serious block in the way of completing an agreed Instrument of Unconditional Surrender. The Soviet delegation insisted day after day that the German forces must be declared prisoners-of-war. The American and British delegations explained over and over again why they were unwilling to do this, though they were willing, and proposed fairly early in the negotiation, that provision be made that each of the three, later four, commanders-in-chief be free to declare or not to declare prisoners-of-war those German forces which came under his control at the final surrender. In attacking both the position of the two Western delegations and the compromise which they had offered, the Soviet representatives continually accused the latter of 'promoting German militarism,' 'fostering Nazism,' and so forth.

Finally, Soviet consent to the proposed compromise formula was secured by drawing up a fairly detailed statement of the difficulties which the Soviet proposal raised, translating it into Russian, and persuading the Soviet delegation to send it to Moscow, despite the reluctance of the Soviet negotiators to appear even to question the correctness of their original instructions to which they had held so stubbornly. Even at the very end the Soviet delegation remained unconvinced that there was any real legal difficulty involved for the Western powers but were persuaded finally that there was 'nothing bad' in this final compromise for the Soviet position.

5

In this as in numerous other instances Soviet negotiators, even when under some pressure to reach agreement, have shown that they are in mortal terror of violating any part, minor or major, of their instructions, and are extremely reluctant to report to Moscow that they cannot get every point and every wording in their own drafts. Making recommendations for even slight changes in their instructions exposes them to serious risks. It means that they consider their own superiors slightly less than omniscient. It may mean that they can be accused of giving undue weight to the viewpoint of another government and thus of 'falling captive to imperialist insinuations.' The result is that, even when, in a given question, the Soviet negotiator is committed to the desirability of achieving agreement, he is unable to take any initiative in finding a reasonable meeting ground of viewpoints and he is usually extremely reluctant even to present to his own government suggestions for compromise or reconciliation of differences which originate in other delegations.

A widespread lack of ease in using English or French commonly adds a good deal to the difficulties of the Soviet negotiator. Russian linguists have done pioneer work in the development of effective teaching of languages. Most of the newer methods which have been developed in the United States during and since the war for the intensive teaching of languages were familiar twenty years ago in the best Soviet institutes. But relatively few Soviet representatives abroad have received adequate training in languages at a sufficiently early age, and almost none have had the experience of living informally in a foreign culture at an impressionable period of their development. Since the great purge of the Soviet foreign service at the end of the 1930s the staff has been recruited primarily from among administrators and engineers, with a sprinkling of professors. Until they entered upon their new careers the newer Soviet diplomats had no need or incentive to learn a foreign language effectively, and once entered upon it they have no time or permission to relax and absorb not only a language but the culture or way of thought which is expressed in mastering it. This places a special burden on foreign negotiators to phrase their proposals and texts in a form which can be rendered exactly into Russian, if they wish their own positions to be understood.

Russian, particularly in its Soviet usage, lends itself even less readily than English to the disciplined clarity of French, the unequaled language of diplomacy. Dictionary renditions are often downright misleading. According to dictionaries and pre-Soviet usage, *predlagat'* means 'to propose'; in Soviet usage, carried over from Communist Party practice, it means 'to direct,' to give an instruction which cannot be disobeyed. On occasion I have seen a Soviet negotiator fall into a rage because an inoffensive 'propose' was turned into *predlagat'* in the translation. The word *soiuz* in Russian means both an 'alliance' between two independent states and a complete 'union' into a single state. *Blagorazumnyi* is as near as Russian comes to 'reasonable,' and the Russian word has none of the overtones or undertones of its English meaning.

The Russian word *vlast'* is usually rendered as 'authority,' but *vlast'* connotes a complete power of disposal, not a limited 'authority.' This difficulty was illustrated in an abortive attempt, in April 1945, to negotiate an agreement concerning the future status of Allied newspaper and radio correspondents in Germany. The key provision of a draft agreement, which had been drawn up in the War Department for negotiation in the European Advisory Commission, was that the correspondent was to be subject 'to the full authority' of the commander-in-chief who issued credentials to him in his own zone. When I received this draft, with the instruction to begin negotiations at once for its acceptance by the four governments, I pointed out to Washington that in the Soviet interpretation of this provision an American correspondent who entered the Soviet zone could be tried by a secret Soviet court and sentenced by purely administrative procedure to a term in a concentration camp because some article which he had written ten years earlier in America was regarded as 'inimical to the security and strength' of the Soviet Union. My objections were overruled and my suggested redraftings, designed to avoid this risk, were brushed aside. I received a peremptory instruction to circulate the draft agreement and to urge its adoption.

For more than fifteen months the Soviet delegation had, time and again, been extremely slow in responding to American and British proposals, and it was usually unable to give any indication of whether it would ever be able to negotiate. In this case, however, Moscow acted with great alacrity. Within less than a week the Soviet delegation indicated that it wished to begin negotiations on the following day on the American draft agreement. It was clear that the Soviet foreign office liked the War Department's draft and that it was ready to accept it with minor changes. With no time for further argument with Washington about the dangerous draft, I wired that I expected to be asked to clarify some of the wording of the draft. If, for example, I should be asked to define 'full authority,' I proposed to state that its meaning was that the commander-in-chief had 'full authority in matters of accrediting and disaccrediting' foreign correspondents in his zone.

A few hours later the European Advisory Commission began its first and only session on the draft agreement. The Soviet representative offered a few minor textual improvements in the American draft and then declared that he was prepared to conclude it at once. It was now my turn to explain that by 'full authority' the draft meant only 'full authority in matters of accrediting and disaccrediting' correspondents. After this the Soviet representative rapidly lost interest in the draft, and the subject was not discussed again in the commission, which had many other urgent matters to struggle with.

One of the difficulties of Soviet-Russian vocabulary is that the word 'compromise' is not of native origin and carries with it no favorable empathy. It is habitually used only in combination with the adjective 'putrid.' 'Compromise for the sake of getting on with the job' is natural to American and British people, but it is alien to the Bolshevist way of thinking and to the discipline which the Communist Party has striven to inculcate in its members. To give up a demand once presented, even a very minor or formalistic point, makes a Bolshevik-trained negotiator feel that he is losing control of his own will and is becoming subject to an alien will. Therefore any point which has finally to be abandoned must be given up only after a most terrific struggle. The Soviet negotiator must first prove to himself and his superiors that he is up against an immovable force. Only then is he justified in abandoning a point which plainly cannot be gained and in moving on to the next item, which will again be debated in an equally bitter tug-of-wills.

The Soviet negotiator must try to force the acceptance of his entire proposal. Hence he regards each provision and phrase as equally important. The Bolshevik is trained to feel that ideology must be 'monolithic' at any given time, even though it may change from time to time. In one period it may be wrong for a 'good Bolshevik' to shave every day and to wear a necktie; at another time he will be reprimanded for neglecting these amenities. The important thing is to have a complete answer to past, present, and future and to insist, against all contrary evidence, that this answer is, always has been, and must ever be, the same. This attitude gives rise to the, to the Westerner absurd, insistence on periodically rewriting the history of the Party, of Russia, and of the world and on rewriting it each time to uphold some new 'infallible' dogma.

The Western negotiator is usually able to envisage a series of minor shifts in his own and other positions. He is 'pluralistic' in his approach to a solution, in the adjustments of democratic decision-making at home, and in seeking adjustments of interests and views among nations. The Soviet negotiator is worried, puzzled, scornful, and suspicious when the Western negotiator tries out a series of minor variations to see if the opposing positions cannot be brought closer together. To him it means only that the Western representative was 'not serious' in the first place. If he is willing to shift so quickly from his original position, it must mean that he did not hold it in earnest to begin with and that he can eventually be forced all the way over to the Soviet position, provided the Soviet negotiator will only display 'principled steadfastness' long enough and vigorously enough.

The Western representative tends to assume that a minor concession here or there will facilitate achieving the common aim of cooperative action. He does not necessarily look for an immediate *quid pro quo* for each minor concession. At a later stage in the negotiation his partner will remember the facilitating concession and will yield something in turn. To him 'good will' is both a lubricant of the negotiating process and a valuable intangible by-product. The Soviet negotiator takes a minor concession as a sign that his principles are stronger and his will is firmer than those of his opponent. He does not believe in 'good will.' He trained to assume the ill will of the 'capitalist environment.' If an 'imperialist' negotiator asserts his will for peace, it means, at the best, that he is consciously in favor of peace but is unconsciously a tool of uncontrollable forces which work for war and for the final clash between 'two worlds.' At the worst, it means that he is trying to deceive and gain time while mouthing words of 'peace.' To a Bolshevik even a momentary 'loss of vigilance' may have fatal consequences. The Soviet diplomat feels himself like a traveler by night in the forest who must be constantly on the watch for the smallest sound or sight of treachery. He must be unceasingly on guard against his own human tendency to 'fall into complacency' and thus to underestimate the dangers which surround both him and the regime which he serves.

Soviet diplomacy is also monolithic in its method of operation and in its reactions to outside events or internal changes of stress. The American practice is to subdivide authority extensively, both at home and in foreign dealings. A military mission in Moscow, trying to work out plans for military coordination, would have nothing to say about the arrangements or conditions for Lend-Lease. A political negotiation, aiming to preserve the freedom of choice for an East European nation, would have no relation to another mission which might be deciding which German ships should be transferred to the Soviet Union, and all of them would have no relation to a decision concerning military and economic aid to China. No such autonomy or fragmentation of authority is felt in the Soviet conduct of its foreign policy. While it is probable that little background information on policy is communicated by Moscow to its representatives abroad, beyond that which they need individually in order to carry out their instructions, it is pretty clear that underlying attitudes are communicated rapidly to them. Thus, a negotiation over the status of Tangier bogs down in Paris; this may be a repercussion of a crisis which has arisen in Vienna or of a note delivered in Warsaw. Bolshevist mythology is full of 'chain-reaction' concepts of causality. With the clumsy force of centralized wisdom Moscow attempts to meet this assumed universal causal interdependence ('nothing is accidental') with its confidence in its own ability to manipulate events in accordance with its own Leninist-Stalinist dialectic, which it regards as a unique instrument for both foreseeing and bringing about the future.

6

This is a grim picture. The Soviet negotiator is tight as a spring, deeply suspicious, always trying to exert the Soviet will power outward and to avoid reflecting non-Soviet facts and aspirations inward, a rigid agent knowing only the segment of policy which he must carry out with mechanical precision. Does this mean that negotiation in any real sense of the term is impossible? Admitting that negotiation under these conditions is a very limited affair and very difficult and unrewarding, it may still be both possible and essential. But it requires a special approach. Naturally, a knowledge of Russian in its Soviet nuances is important. It is equally important to understand the role of the Soviet negotiator in relation to his own government and to its ideology. The Department of State has carried on a far-sighted policy of equipping a substantial number of its representatives through language and area training and through service in missions in the Soviet-dominated areas to deal with Soviet problems, and as these young men mature in experience they will fill an important need. The Army and Air Force have also done a good deal along this line.

In the absence of informal channels of communication with Soviet representatives it is important for an American delegation to be able to determine whether the Soviet negotiators have no instructions, have definite instructions, or merely have instructions to build up a propaganda position. A well equipped negotiator can go much more thoroughly into the range of Soviet intentions if he follows the discussion in the original, without being handicapped by the opaque veil of translation. In addition he should review each document exchanged or each statement made in the light of its clear rendering into Russian. It is unfortunate, for example, that many American public figures continually speak of the need for an 'aggressive policy' to counteract Soviet pressures, when they mean an 'energetic' or 'vigorous' policy. In Russian 'aggressive' means only 'intending to commit or engaged in committing aggression,' and the colloquial American use of 'aggressive' inevitably receives a sinister meaning in Russian translation, which is the form in which documents must be utilized by all but a handful of Soviet negotiators and policy-makers.

In conducting negotiations with Soviet representatives it is important to adopt in the beginning a single clear position, one which can be upheld logically and politically during long discussions. The Soviet delegation will not report this position as the final and strongly held one until they have had a chance to attack it from all sides. Indefinite repetition of arguments must be accepted as an inevitable preparation to negotiate. The American negotiator is inclined to make a single presentation and then to become impatient when the Soviet response makes it plain that the Soviet representative either has not understood it or does not believe it. The Soviet negotiator, of course, does not believe what he hears, but he listens for undertones of firmness or uncertainty which tell him whether or not he is shaking the determination of his adversary. Strong but controlled feeling, rather than impatience or anger, is an effective way of giving him his answer to this question. When a position is firmly established it is often advantageous to prepare a special memorandum, accompanied by a clear and idiomatic translation into Russian, in order to be sure that one's own position is adequately reported to Moscow, the only spot at which new instructions are likely to be initiated. Oral statements of position may or may not be reported, but it is probable that every bit of written material is carefully transmitted. If some part of the English memorandum does not lend itself to clear rendering into Russian, it is useful to rewrite the English version until it can be rendered without ambiguity, for while Russian can express any thought, it does not lend itself flexibly to a literal rendering of an English concept or phrase.

Once a position has been worked out, the non-Soviet negotiator must be prepared to uphold it in detail, and for a long time. The technique of constantly trying out variant versions, which works well in the Western style of negotiation, only confuses the Soviet representative, who suspects some new trick in each new variant and must subject each in turn to exhaustive interpretation. Constantly modifying one's position or the way in which it is expressed means also that the Soviet negotiator is at a loss to know what version is based on bedrock and should therefore be reported to Moscow. Even slight shifts in position or wording increase his belief that the adversary's position is a shaky one and thus encourage him to hold out that much longer for the full Soviet position. Western negotiators are usually in a position to accept slight adaptations, but even the slightest variation must be reported back to Moscow for decision there.

Since Western negotiators are generally free, in the light of previous instructions and their knowledge of their governments' over-all policies, to comment at once on new proposals or statements made during the course of negotiation, they often assume that Soviet negotiators have a similar latitude and accordingly press them to express their views. When so pressed, the Soviet negotiator is always free to raise innumerable objections and criticisms. He is not free to express concordance with any part of a proposal on which he has not received instructions from Moscow. Even the 'program statements' of Soviet negotiators must be reviewed or written in Moscow before they can be delivered, and therefore Soviet statements at conferences often seem to have little relation to the immediately preceding statements of other delegations.

When a negotiation is actually under way, it is useful to avoid pressing the Soviet delegation to commit itself on a new proposal or draft. During the active negotiations carried on in the European Advisory Commission, whenever a new proposal or even a redraft was first presented, it was my habit to ask questions which would clarify its meaning and implications and then to take the initiative, even if I had adequate instructions, in saying that I would have to consult my government before commenting on it, thus relieving the Soviet delegation of the onus of either declining to comment on it or else of building up a whole series of negative statements against the proposal. Then, on occasions when I had instructions on the new point at issue, I would go at once to the Soviet delegation and inform its members in detail of the American position. This meant that Moscow had before it, at the same time, the proposal and the American position on it. When there was a certain underlying desire to reach agreements, this procedure was often effective, or so it seemed, in reducing the number of divergences by providing full background on the problem before Moscow had taken a firm position, which could later be modified only by a long and exhausting tug-of-wills. Such informal discussions, conducted in Russian, also offered an occasion for learning or sensing the often unforeseen Russian objections and suspicions and for attempting to remove or alleviate them at an early stage.

When stating a position it is well to be sparing in the use of general or broadly stated principles, and when such principles are an essential part of the position it is necessary to remember that they are not shared by the Soviet negotiator. Broad statements of principle can, however, be effectively anchored in the historic experience of one's own people and, explained in that setting, they can have a certain impact on Soviet thinking. Soviet policy-makers may then accept them as a fact which must be taken into account, even though they do not believe in them or share them.

Wherever possible it is more useful to state one's position in terms of a definite material interest, as in the case of the question of Bulgaria's obligation to provide reparation to Greece and Yugoslavia. Soviet-trained negotiators pride themselves on identifying material interests and can therefore more readily visualize them as facts to which a certain adjustment can be made.

This can be illustrated from the problem of the Soviet treatment of American prisoners-of-war who were overrun in the Soviet advance into eastern Germany. Despite the agreement for mutual assistance in collecting, caring for, and repatriating each other's prisoners-of-war, the agreement never received halfway adequate implementation on the Soviet side, and great and unnecessary hardships were inflicted by the Soviet attitude on American and other Western prisoners. The Soviet authorities could not understand that it was a normal and automatic principle, for Americans, to give every possible care, on an American standard, to fellow countrymen who had been taken captive. Soviet prisoners, overrun by their own armies, were given only the meager standard of care which falls to the lot of the ordinary Soviet population, and in addition they were subjected to special disabilities until they could prove that they had not, in some measure, surrendered voluntarily to the Germans. If the American authorities had emphasized that liberated American prisoners must be well cared for because they were needed immediately in the war against Japan—which was not the case—the Soviet authorities would probably have given much better cooperation in caring for and transporting them, as they would have been impressed by the direct material interest involved.

Is it worthwhile to dwell on these experiences or to talk about negotiating at all? Even during the wartime alliance against the common menaces of Germany and Japan negotiations with the Soviet government were extremely difficult and frustrating, and, aside from the advantage of having established the United Nations, even before the end of the war, as a 'forum for the opinions of mankind,' none of the wartime agreements on postwar cooperation has worked out as was hoped, even against hope. Since the war the Soviet government has striven by all the means in its extensive arsenal to gain and retain every advantage for its side, regardless of the fact that thereby it quickly dissipated a very large reservoir of good will and aroused the deep alarm of all nations which lay beyond its direct control. In a period of Soviet expansion and of hope for further expansion, negotiation could have only the purpose of confusing and dividing the nations which opposed its pressure, and since the war the Soviet purpose in negotiating has not been to reach agreements with strong opponents but to intimidate weaker and adjacent countries and to undermine the stamina of its principal potential adversaries.

Protected by two oceans and remote from the direct origins of previous world wars, Americans have been accustomed to ignore the rising storm and then, once it had burst upon them, to work solely for victory over the immediate menace. Thus, they tend to feel a sharp dichotomy between 'war' and 'peace.' When at peace they are reluctant to think of the possibility of war. When at war they concentrate solely on winning the war, as if it were a grim football match, and refuse to worry about the peace which is the goal of war. Through Lenin and Stalin Soviet thinking has fully absorbed the Clausewitz maxims that national strength and strong alliances determine the effectiveness of national policy in peace, and that in war one must never lose sight of the aims of policy for which it is waged. To the Soviet way of thinking, conflict is inherent in the development of 'capitalist' society, and cannot be wished out of existence by 'subjective good will.'

Within this ongoing history of conflict, however, Soviet tactics and techniques are not inflexible. Soviet policy toward the outside world has varied markedly during the past thirty-four years. True, the outward pressure of Soviet power has marked and seared the post-1945 years, and the building of a reliable counterforce is only now under way in Europe. The outline of a similar counterforce cannot yet be discerned in Asia. In Western policy the building of 'positions of strength' and the use of negotiation must go hand in hand. Building of strength and negotiating cannot be regarded as alternatives or as opposites. They must be teamed. Negotiation without strength and determination behind it is frustrating, dangerous and may be suicidal. On the other hand, when strength has been built, refusal to negotiate may precipitate a colossal struggle, which would be fought as a cruel civil war in many parts of the world—the very conflict which Western strength is being fashioned to avert.

For the time being negotiation of those issues which are negotiable between the Soviet Union and the West is, generally speaking, in abeyance. But the art of policy will be to recognize, from a position of strength, future potentialities of negotiation, not with an expectation of bringing about a lasting or world-wide relaxation of Soviet ambitions, but as a means of alleviating individual sources of tension and thus of strengthening the free world. And if negotiation must go in harness with consistent and purposeful building of strength, the art and technique of international dealings must also be broadened to take full account of the peculiar character of the Soviet approach to negotiation.

The Psychology of Soviet Foreign Policy

ROBERT C. TUCKER

The story of Soviet foreign policy in the recent past is epitomized in the biblical adage, "Pride goeth before a fall." The high-water mark of pride was set at the time of the Twentieth CPSU Congress in early 1956.

In a speech before the assembled delegates Anastas Mikoyan declared:

Striking are the successes of Soviet foreign policy, especially in the past year. Here too the directing collective of the party has injected a fresh new current, pursuing a high-principled, active, and flexible foreign policy expressed in calm tones and without invective. . . . Certain ossified forms have been cast aside in the work of our diplomacy. . . . Let those swaggering Americans who boast of their wealth of today, their 'American way of life,' join a contest with us in this field, and they will see where more is done for the good of the people, and whose way of life proves better.

The mood of the leaders was confident and self-assured. Stalin, praise be, is dead and gone, it seemed to say. The new collective administration has taken matters in hand. It has set the wrongs to right, corrected the errors, banished the terror, gone out into the world. It has ended the stagnation and charted a new course big with promise, especially in foreign affairs. Thus, the horizons of possibility seemed wide and beckoning. To paraphrase a Russian proverb, the sea itself looked to the Kremlin no more than knee-deep.

So confident, in fact, was the attitude that it now seemed expedient to set the Congress straight on certain disagreeable facts out of the past, and Khrushchev revealed in closed session a part of the story

Published in *Problems of Communism* (May-June 1957). Copyright, 1957, by the RAND Corporation.

Robert C. Tucker, formerly editor of the Joint Press Reading Service in Moscow and now Associate Professor of Government at Indiana University, wrote this article while a consultant of the RAND Corporation.

of Stalin's dark record of evil. This speech was the beginning of the fall. By the year's end, the Soviet army was suppressing a popular revolution in Hungary. Poland was launched on the troubled waters of national communism. Foreign Communist parties were in deep difficulties. The USSR was morally isolated again in Europe and large parts of Asia. And various people around the world were speaking seriously of such things as the dissolution of the Soviet empire and the beginning of the end of the Soviet regime.

The author's purpose here is to search for some of the deeper forces and factors at work behind this historic sequence of Russian pride and fall. What are the spiritual roots of the predicament in which the Soviet regime clearly finds itself today? Basically, the problem is to deepen our understanding of what Stalinism meant and the way in which Stalin's death caused change in Soviet policy. On one important aspect, the change had to do with the matter of persuasion. The new Soviet foreign policy which Mikoyan spoke of so proudly in early 1956 was, in a distinctly un-Stalinist sense, a diplomacy of persuasion; and it is just this diplomacy of persuasion which later suffered a shattering setback. But how are we to account for the shift in the Soviet orientation toward persuasion? The view to be developed in these pages holds that it was not simply a matter of shifting tactics but that it had a psychological origin. The crucial fact is that Stalin's death occasioned a psychological revolution in Soviet foreign policy. The meaning of this proposition will be expanded in what follows.

Stalinism and the Cold War

First, let us briefly reconsider the classic period of the cold war. The final chapter in Stalin's life, from the end of World War II to his death in early 1953, was the culminating period of Stalinism in all departments of Soviet life and policy. And in foreign policy, Stalinism means cold war.

Before hostilities ended, Stalin was embarked upon a grandiose endeavor of empire-building in countries coming under the sway of Soviet forces. Contrary to later Soviet propaganda, very little in the way of a spontaneous revolutionary process took place there. In fact, Stalin's policy had by now come to frown on spontaneous revolutionary movements, as was shown, for example, by Tito's wartime difficulties with Moscow. What Stalin wanted to do—and succeeded in doing—in most of Middle Europe can best be described by the Nazi term *Gleichschaltung*, which connotes a process of forcibly bringing a foreign area *under* control and *into* conformity. Middle Europe, along with North Korea, and later, China and North Vietnam, came to constitute parts of an enormous, expanded Soviet control-sphere with its center in Moscow.

As this process of *Gleichschaltung* developed in 1944 and 1945, stiffening Western reaction and eventual efforts by the United States and Britain to counteract it were met with Soviet intransigence and, increasingly, Soviet hostility. A set pattern of belligerency came to pervade all aspects of Soviet relations with Western and other countries, and especially with the United States.

In Zhdanov's report at the founding meeting of the Cominform in Warsaw in September 1947, Stalin issued a kind of official declaration of permanent Soviet cold war against the West. From then on until his death, the pattern of belligerency remained rigidly in force. The expressions ran a gamut from hate propaganda and diplomacy of invective to warlike acts such as the blockade of Berlin and systematic shooting down of United States aircraft, and finally to outright war by proxy in Korea. An enormous growth of international tension ensued. The director-general of Soviet belligerency all through this period was Stalin himself. Among the totalitarian despots of this century, he was the supreme practitioner of cold war.

So far as the motivation of Soviet foreign policy during this period is concerned, it is essential to distinguish between its formal and operative aims. A formal aim is the object one declares oneself to be seeking; an operative aim is the object implicit in what one actually does. The two may or may not coincide.

The discrepancy between them has rarely been more glaring than it was in Stalin's foreign policy during the cold war. The 'strengthening of peace' was constantly proclaimed as a Soviet aim; but Soviet actions were blatantly inconsistent with the notion of strengthening peace. Another aim frequently if not always unequivocally declared was that of promoting the cause of the world revolution and the liberation of peoples from the 'capitalist system of exploitation.' Here too a discrepancy appeared, although less obviously. Stalin, as already suggested, had grown deeply hostile to spontaneous revolutionary processes of every kind, including social revolutions from below. He still talked revolution, but he showed in many ways that the revolutionist in him had given way to the hidebound reactionary, enamored of the values of stability, authority, and order. In his essay on linguistics in 1950 he anathematized the Marxian notion that development always takes place through periodic upheavals or 'explosions.' The very idea of revolutionary explosions had become profoundly distasteful to him.

As for the liberation of peoples from 'capitalist exploitation,' it is hard to believe that this was Stalin's operative aim, since the Soviet system is one of state monopoly capitalism and the most exploitative in modern history. Nor could his aim have been simply to replace private capitalism with state capitalism or nationalized economies—had it been, he would logically have softened the Soviet attitude toward Britain and other European countries which began to nationalize their economies after the war. And he would not have feuded as he did with Tito's Yugoslavia, where Soviet principles of state capitalism had been carried farther after the war than in most of the satellite states.

The crucial operative aim for Stalin was *control*. This is the conclusion dictated by Stalinist behavior as distinct from the official Stalinist image of that behavior. The operative aim, implicit in all that Stalin did, was to get control of territory and people, and to absolutize that control by every available means, the principal one being police terror.

Examination of the whole postwar process of Soviet *Gleichschaltung* of foreign lands bears out this judgment about the operative aim. Critical confirmation is afforded by the Stalin-Tito conflict. The issue was Tito's refusal to permit Yugoslavia to be incorporated into the Soviet command and control structure. Tito was among the Communist leaders most antagonistic to private capitalism. It was not any deviation on this score that underlay the break but rather Tito's resistance to Stalin's claim to absolute Soviet control of Yugoslavia. The consequence was a Soviet 'little cold war' against Belgrade for as long as Stalin lived; the moment he died, it began to slacken.

The Stalinist ideology of cold war reflected this operative aim of total control indirectly in its image of international reality. This image dichotomized the globe into two 'worlds,' called the 'Soviet camp of peace, socialism, and democracy' and the 'American camp of capitalism, imperialism, and war.' The political universe was divided cleanly into the white world of Soviet socialist progress and the black world of American capitalist reaction. Stalin had enunciated such a conception of a polarized political universe, with Russia and America as the two antagonistic poles of power, as early as 1927. Twenty years after, it reappeared as the Soviet *working conception* of international reality; that is, it was acted out in terms of actual foreign policy. A Soviet document of 1948 stated:

The struggle of the two camps now determines the fate of the whole world, the fate of mankind. This struggle emerges more and more as the chief moving force of the development of our age toward communism. Here lies the basic content of the political struggle of our time.[1]

The relation between the two-world image and the drive for total control can be stated very simply: the working criterion of 'belongingness' to the one world or the other was the criterion of Soviet control. Consequently, the Stalinist definition of the character of a given country's regime turned essentially on the question: Does it constitute a part of the Soviet control-sphere? If so, it was socialist and democratic; if not, capitalist and fascist. The Yugoslav regime, for example, underwent metamorphosis almost overnight in 1948 from a 'people's democracy' into a 'police regime of the fascist type.' Its actual institutional structure had not, of course, changed at all; but its relation to the Soviet control structure had, and this was crucial for Stalin.

There was no geographical or political space between the two worlds, no room for neutralism, no possibility of a 'third force,' no such thing as nonalignment. Political neutrality in the cold war was just a blind. The pretense of neutrality might be tolerated very grudgingly in a marginal case, such as Finland's, but never admitted in principle. The notion of an 'uncommitted nation' or 'third force' was nothing but a crude political myth devised for devious Western purposes. The Soviet document already quoted said:

The 'third line' or 'third force' concocted by the right-wing socialists is in fact nothing other than a cover for the policy of defense of capitalism

---

[1] Ts. A. Stepanian, "Neodolimoe dvizheniie k kommunizmu," *Voprosy filosofii*, No. 2 (1948), p. 87.

and fight against communism. In our epoch there is not, and cannot be, a 'third force.' . . . Two forces, two camps, exist throughout the world.[1]

One of the most fateful political consequences of the captivity of Stalinist policy to this conception was the attitude taken in the Kremlin toward the new Asia. Next to the cold war itself, the most important historical fact of the period following World War II was the political emergence of Asia from Western tutelage. There was no way to square this fact with the logic of the Stalinist drive for total control and the two-world image associated with it. For this would mean recognizing Asia as a 'third force' or a space between the worlds. Consequently, Stalin, and therefore Stalinist policy, denied the fact, legislated it out of existence. This was one of the key issues of the famous Varga controversy in 1947. In a book written before the end of the war, the Soviet economist Eugene Varga had spotted the new trend, the changing relationship of Europe and Asia. On Stalin's orders, the book was condemned, and its author forced to recant what he knew to be absolutely true. The real facts about the new Asia were purged along with Varga. The newly won national independence of India, Burma, the Philippines, and other former Western dependencies was pronounced a 'fiction,' a cunning imperialist device for continuing to exercise control over these countries without appearing to do so. According to the logic of the drive for control, they could not be considered 'liberated' so long as they had not yet been incorporated into the Soviet control-sphere. Not having changed worlds in this way, they had to remain integral parts of the black world, *de facto* colonies which the West held on to with the help of 'antinational ruling circles,' puppets such as Nehru, U Nu, and others.

Thus, Stalinist policy was predicated on an official delusion of continued Asian bondage to the West. There was no essential change in this regard until Stalin died. There is every reason to believe that most of the men around Stalin were quite aware of the delusive character of this image of the new Asia, and the image of the external world generally. They could see that it was nothing but an externalized portrait of Soviet-bloc reality, and that the external world was not *really* like that. Some, it seems, were painfully conscious of the resulting detriment

[1] *Ibid.*, p. 86.

to Soviet Russia's interest as a great power. In effect, the image blocked off the new Asia as a profitable field for Soviet power politics, constraining policy to costly and risky ventures such as the aggression by proxy in Korea. But the men around Stalin could do nothing, or next to nothing, to correct the situation so long as he was alive and in autocratic control. Few situations could illustrate more convincingly the potential importance of the personality factor in foreign policy.

Illusions and Realities

This brings us back to the question of persuasion. Foreign policy in the normal course of events is largely an activity of intergovernmental persuasion. Persuasion aims at influencing other governments to do or not to do certain things, such as concluding a treaty, settling a dispute, joining or not joining an alliance. The basis of appeal is mutuality of interest. Recognition of the other government's interest in its own continued existence and security is always necessarily presupposed.

The Stalinist politics of cold war were not politics of persuasion, and the foregoing discussion suggests the reason why. When the operative aim is total control, persuasion is not a fit instrument of policy; one form or another of aggression is necessitated. Save for the marginal case, Soviet diplomacy withered on the vine during the years 1945 to 1953; the whole range of intergovernmental activities of persuasion by conventional means was excluded.

In the case of Yugoslavia, to take it again as an illustration, there was no possibility of negotiating the issue of total Soviet control. The Tito regime might be persuaded to do all sorts of things in the Soviet interest. The one thing it could not be persuaded to do was to part with its independence, but this was precisely Stalin's demand. Following Stalin's death, the Soviet government began to pursue a policy of persuasion vis-à-vis Belgrade, and it is still doing so. The precondition of this, however, was a drastic scaling down of Moscow's demand upon Tito, a change of the operative aim from total control to a relationship of influence. A similar change occurred in the motivation of Soviet policy toward other areas of the non-Soviet world, with similar results in the form of efforts to persuade. What underlay this change was a lessening of the felt *need* for control. This, in turn, was a consequence of the fact that when Stalin died the peculiar needs of his personality ceased to determine the motivation of Soviet foreign policy.

Paradoxically, Stalinist policy in the cold war placed the greatest emphasis on international propaganda. Since propaganda is ordinarily regarded as an instrument par excellence of persuasion, how explain the fact that propaganda claimed so much Soviet attention and effort at the very time that policy all but excluded international persuasion in the sense defined? The question is too complex for adequate treatment here. But one important aspect of the answer lies in the two-world fantasy. It saw the black world as inwardly bifurcated, in contrast to the white world, which was monolithic. As the previously quoted ideologist of Stalinism put it, "Two forces, two camps, exist in any capitalist country." The second camp in the black world consisted of all those who belonged—in attitude, in thought, and in deed—to the white world, who regarded themselves as *its* citizens living in a foreign land, and who, therefore, submitted to Soviet control voluntarily.

The Stalinist designation for such persons was 'proletarian internationalists.' The nucleus of the universal fraternity of spiritual citizens of the Soviet Union was, of course, the membership of foreign Communist parties. But the fraternity was not confined to this circle. *Anybody could belong.* The decisive test of belonging was laid down by Stalin in 1927. "He is an internationalist," said Stalin then, "who unreservedly, unhesitatingly, and unconditionally is prepared to defend the USSR, because the USSR is the base of the world revolutionary movement."[3] This reasoning was further elaborated during the period of the cold war. A statement of 1948, for example, refined it as follows:

At the present time the sole and decisive criterion of proletarian revolutionary internationalism is: *for or against the USSR*, the fatherland of the international proletariat. . . . *Only he is a genuine internationalist who carries his sympathy, respect, recognition to the point of practical and maximum aid, support, and defense of the USSR by every means and in various forms.*[4]

Note carefully that the criterion for admission to the white camp in the black world was not intellectual; that is, it was not the acceptance of an idea or set of ideas as such. It was rather an act of total self-

[3] I. V. Stalin, *Sochineniia*, X (Moscow, 1948), 51.
[4] Stepanian, p. 86.

identification with the Soviet system. It was the participation in a cult, the cult of the USSR, regarded by definition as the repository of the socialist idea. The criterion did not say: Believe in socialism, accept the socialist idea. It said: Believe in the USSR as the fatherland of socialism, accept whatever it tells you as the sacred truth, and do whatever it bids you for its sake.

This difference is more significant than it may seem. It must be borne in mind in analyzing the traumatic effect of Khrushchev's denunciation of Stalin on thousands of Soviet sympathizers abroad. It also throws light on Stalinism's thinly veiled distrust and contempt for intellectuals. The intellectual is suspect precisely because of his devotion to ideas and principles as such. Every true totalitarianism —whether Stalin's or Hitler's or any of the others—tries to set up complete loyalty and devotion *to itself*, to the system and the Leader, as the only ultimate principle.

Returning to the question about propaganda, it is not hard to see why so much effort was expended in this field during the very years when so little attempt was being made at international persuasion. The principal function of the international propaganda was to preserve and foster the cult of the USSR, and for this reason it may be regarded as essentially an extension of Soviet internal propaganda to the foreign field. The purpose was not to persuade the audience through an appeal to the intellectual faculties; it was rather to indoctrinate participants in the cult, to train 'internationalists.' That is, it presupposed the surrender of the critical faculties, the will to believe, the prior emotional self-identification *in toto* with the object of the cult, the USSR.

Given such identification, everything might be credible, no lie too big to be swallowed as gospel truth. If Moscow, for example, said that the Americans were waging germ warfare in Korea, this—to the participant in the cult—had to be true *because Moscow said so*. Hence, the basic task of the international propaganda was to furnish continual new material for the cult, to hold aloft day in and day out the glorious, glowing image of Soviet reality and at the same time to besmirch to the utmost the image of the enemy camp. The inner content of the cold war propaganda can therefore be epitomized in ten words: The Soviet world is white; the American world is black. The vital importance of the Iron Curtain as a protective shield for this two-world fantasy is obvious.

It has been suggested above that the two-world conception was a reflex of the Stalinist drive for total control, which operated at its high point during the period of the cold war. However, the argument now indicates that the relation between these two phenomena was an inter-active one. On the one hand, the felt need for absolute control reinforced the image of the world as split in two. But on the other hand, this image, and particularly the projection of the Soviet world as glisteningly white, greatly reinforced the need for control, dictating, for example, all the devices of control summed up in the phrase 'Iron Curtain.' Thus, one very important contributing motivation for the Stalinist control drive was the urge to make an illusion about Russia seem real.

The actual fact was that Russia had become in the Soviet period a powerful, industrialized country with an enslaved, miserable, poverty-stricken population, with an economy best described as state monopoly capitalism, and with a political system of the fascist police-state variety; and the empire was an extension of all this to captive peoples abroad. In the official illusion, however, the USSR appeared as the realization of man's dream of social utopia, a land of progress and prosperity, where all the economic problems were solved or in process of solution, where culture was in flower, where freedom and justice prevailed, where nearly everybody was happy; and the empire was just an extension of all these benefits to grateful peoples on the periphery.

This was no mere Potemkin village; it was a *Potemkin Russia*, fabricated not out of wooden facades but out of words and pictures and mass spectacles in Red Square. Absolute centralized control was necessary in order to make the illusion *appear* to be true. The discrepancy between the Potemkin Russia and the real Russia could be hidden from view so long as the MVD terror machine operated to keep everything under control, to see to it that nobody revolted, that few if any people got in or out, that everyone in Russia and the satellites pretended to be living in the Potemkin world, that no one spoke the truth out loud, and that articles and books and films complied with the dictates of 'socialist realism'; that is, that they depicted the illusion.

But from whose view would the discrepancy be hidden by such means? Not, certainly, from the ordinary Soviet citizen's; he realized what kind of Russia he was living in, and that it had nothing in common with the heavenly system portrayed in the propaganda. The Soviet and satellite peoples knew all about the discrepancy, knew much more about it than their well-meaning friends in the West who were trying to enlighten them on the point. The bureaucracy knew about it. Even high up in the Politburo much was known about it. For whom, then, was the big show staged? In part it was staged for the 'proletarian internationalists' abroad, to keep them comfortably deluded. But the enormous investment of effort that this enterprise of political stagecraft entailed was undertaken mainly for another reason: the crucial spectator was Stalin. It was he who imperatively needed the Potemkin Russia. The same force of neurotic self-idealization which underlay the Stalin cult also underlay the cult of the USSR. The latter had become an extension of the former: the idealized Russia was a background panorama for the figure of the idealized Stalin.

A passage in Khrushchev's secret report to the Twentieth Congress gives us an interesting glimpse into Stalin's need for the Potemkin Russia. Khrushchev spoke of the agricultural situation, which was going from bad to worse in Stalin's final years:

All those who interested themselves even a little in the national situation saw the difficult situation in agriculture, but Stalin never even noted it. Did we tell Stalin about this? Yes, we told him, but he did not support us. Why? Because Stalin never traveled anywhere. . . . He knew the country and agriculture only from films. And these films had dressed up and beautified the existing situation in agriculture. Many films so pictured kolkhoz life that the tables were bending from the weight of turkeys and geese. Evidently, Stalin thought that it was actually so.

Clearly, Khrushchev is not a very good psychologist. He says that Stalin remained ignorant of the crisis in Soviet agriculture because he never traveled anywhere. The point is true but trivial. For it only raises the question: What kept him from traveling around or taking other steps to learn the real state of affairs? The answer is to be found in Stalin's stringent need for the idealized image of Russia, one aspect of which was the image of kolkhoz prosperity. Naturally, police terror could not produce more grain, nor build houses for the workers, nor outstrip the United States in technology, nor make the Soviet people happy and contented and the satellite peoples grateful to Russia and Stalin. But it could make it *seem* as though all this was so, and that was its essential function.

The key requisite was total control. Stalinist policy, internal as well as external, was harnessed to a prodigious effort to act out for Stalin an official illusion about Russia and the world. That is why Stalinism rested on Stalin and why his death marked a decisive turn in Russian history and world politics. It knocked the psychological prop out of the structure of Stalinist policy. It removed the motivating source of the politics of megalomania. A stream of changes followed swiftly.

The Aftermath

This psychological revolution forms the proper starting point for an analysis of Soviet policy in the post-Stalin period. In one aspect, it is a story of official Russia's move to readjust to the real world. In another, it is a story of the failure to carry through the readjustment, and especially of ignorance or disregard of the full extent of popular disaffection in Russia and the satellites. The Malenkov policy, a pale Soviet version of what we have come to call 'national communism,' seemed to reflect some awareness of this; but it fell under the onslaught of Khrushchev, in whom the mentality of the provincial party official-dom finds its classic expression.

Khrushchev was able and willing to admit that Soviet agriculture was in a mess, that the bureaucratic administration was grossly over-centralized, that Soviet intellectual life was stagnating in its isolation from the world, that the terror had been terribly costly in terms of national progress, and so on. But he would not admit, or could not see, certain other realities, such as the fact that most Russians are heartily sick of such things as Five-Year Plans, the priority of heavy industry, the sacrifice of the present to a future which never comes, and that they will not cooperate voluntarily with a regime which endeavors to reform in the interests of *its* efficiency rather than *their* welfare. The present beginnings of an opposition movement from below are the confirmation of this.

Readjustment to the realities of the external world was not so in-hibited. After an interlude of relative quiet under Malenkov, the Soviet regime embarked on a dynamic new policy designed to reshape the inter-national environment. This was no longer a policy of cold war in the classic Stalin sense. The cold war pattern of total belligerency subsided in favor of the slogan of *détente,* the meeting at the summit, and the challenge to peaceful competition of systems. However, the new policy also was fundamentally anti-Western and anti-American from the start. It was addressed in large part to the breaking up of the Western alliance system, which Stalin's cold war had brought into existence and constantly solidified. It was only the shift of motivation, the subsiding of the drive for total control consequent upon Stalin's death, which made it possible for this to become an operative as distinguished from merely a declared aim of Soviet foreign policy. No longer harnessed to the obsession with absolute control, the new policy expressed an expansionism of Soviet influence, a quest, as it were, for more Finlands rather than more Mongolias, more Afghanistans rather than more Albanias. It found its most fertile field in the Middle East, where it allied itself with the forces of a malignant anti-Western nationalism.

All this was accompanied by a change in the official Soviet image of the world, ratified by the Twentieth Party Congress. The compulsion to dichotomize the image of the world was no longer operative. The two-world conception faded out, giving way to the picture of *one* world in which two rival systems of states, the socialist and the capitalist, compete for a preponderance of world influence. This was no longer a Stalinist world of 'capitalist encirclement.' On the contrary, territories contiguous to the Soviet orbit were now seen as fields for the penetration of Soviet capital, Soviet know-how, Soviet arms, and Soviet ideas. Moscow gave the new Asia the political recognition which Stalin had withheld. This new world of Soviet foreign policy was a world which did not exclude political neutrality, or third forces, or the notion of an uncommitted nation. For countries outside the Soviet bloc, there were alternate roads to socialism, even a parliamentary road. The right-wing socialists were, after all, right-wing socialists. Tito's Yugoslavia was not a capitalist-fascist degeneration, merely a wayward form of people's democracy.

In short, Stalin's successors reintegrated the political universe. The world as projected on the new political map was not a stark contrast in black and white. There were various shades of gray in the non-Soviet part of it, and the gray areas were the focus of the new expansionism of influence. A non-Soviet nation unaligned with the Western military system and friendly to the USSR was now described as a 'peace zone.'

The ambitious new policy envisaged the eventual transformation of the whole of the Eurasian continent into one immense 'peace zone,' that is, one big zone of preponderant Soviet influence.

When influence is the operative aim, persuasion is a logical means. Hence the new policy placed tremendous emphasis upon the function of persuasion. The revival of diplomacy and trade, the sponsoring of cultural and technical exchange, the encouragement of official contacts at many levels, the drive to normalize relations with many countries, and the participation in previously boycotted international bodies were, from this point of view, ways of persuading countries that they could do business safely and profitably with the USSR. Many of the major acts of Soviet foreign policy in 1955 were intended primarily as acts of persuasion. From the standpoint of detaching middle nations from dependence upon the Western security system, it was imperative to persuade them that the world was safe for nonalignment. The Soviet motivation in bringing about the Geneva summit conference was closely linked with this ulterior aim of persuasion. Austria was evacuated, and the long-delayed treaty signed, largely in order to make of this country a showcase of Soviet willingness to coexist with small neutrals in its vicinity, the idea being to persuade other countries that they too could be Austrias and flourish in peace.

Finally, changes of Soviet policy in Eastern Europe were partly inspired by this aim of persuasion. If independent countries were to be persuaded to disalign themselves from the West and enter into close relationships with the Soviet Union, something had to be done about the satellites; at the very least they had to be made to look less satellitish. One step to be taken was the partial undoing of the *Gleichschaltung*. Another was the creation of the Warsaw treaty system as a NATO-looking device for retention of Soviet military control of the whole area after control by police terror was relaxed. Further, the potential appeal of Titoism to semi-autonomous Soviet dependencies in Eastern Europe had to be neutralized, and this, it seemed, could best be done by making friends with Tito, or at least making it *appear* that friendship was restored. Then Titoism could cease being a symbol of anti-Russianism and its disruptive force would be negated.

This was the point at which the new policy of international persuasion began to get ahead of itself. Ironically, the trouble sprang in part from the old habit of blinking the distinction between appearance and reality, in this case between the appearance and reality of a Soviet entente with Tito. It was a momentous miscalculation to suppose that a mere façade of entente would serve the Soviet purpose adequately. Actually, it contributed to the ripening of the conditions which produced the explosion of popular wrath in Hungary. The whole boldly conceived policy of international persuasion came to grief in this explosion. The spectacle of Hungary displayed the Soviet regime to the world as the repressive, imperialist, and antipopular dictatorship that it is. Some countries which had been objects of the new expansionism of influence drew back. Others at least began to have second thoughts about doing much political business with the USSR. The scheme of transforming Eurasia into a zone of preponderant Soviet influence suffered an incalculable setback. The great campaign to persuade culminated in a crisis of Soviet persuasion.

The crisis involves far more than a diplomatic debacle. It was the impact of Khrushchev's secret attack on the Stalin cult that set the train of events rolling toward the Hungarian catastrophe and the breakdown of the new diplomacy. Another consequence of the anti-Stalin speech, however, was to cut off the path of orderly political retreat. In the act of destroying the Stalin myth, Khrushchev pulled down the whole structure of illusion about Stalin's Russia. The cult of the USSR, on which the claim to the allegiance of 'proletarian internationalists' had been based, was fused with the cult of Stalin. They stood or fell together. Khrushchev's speech inadvertently struck them both down. By revealing what Stalin was, he in effect informed all participants in the cult of the USSR that the country which they had lovingly looked upon as the 'socialist fatherland' had for twenty years been a fascist despotism similar to Hitler's. The reverberations of this thunderbolt are still resounding around the world.

Recently there have been tendencies to turn back, to reestablish control, to resume the posture of cold war, even to take a nostalgic new look at old Stalin. Khrushchev extols Stalin's virtues in the 'struggle against imperialism.' The key idea, says *Pravda*, is the idea of 'proletarian internationalism.' For example, 'proletarian internationalists' know that the Hungarian revolution was really a 'counterrevolutionary *putsch*' and that the Soviet armed intervention and bloody suppression of it were really 'aid for the cause of socialism and people's democracy.' What the Hungarians did only *appeared* to be a national revolt, and what the Soviet army did only *appeared* to be an intervention. On what grounds should 'proletarian internationalists' take this view of the facts? Primarily, on the ground that the USSR is the 'socialist fatherland' of the workers. We see what this means. It is a call to restoration of the broken structure of illusion.

This is a strategic reaction. But it is no solution for the enormous dilemma in which Soviet policy finds itself today, for in reality there can be no going back now. The way back is blocked beyond a very narrow point. The revival of Stalin's methods may be possible to a certain extent. But Stalinism, as this essay has attempted to show, is not just a matter of 'methods.' Nor will propaganda help, no matter how great the effort. The Potemkin Russia of Stalinism is gone beyond recall. Stalin's death, Khrushchev's attack on Stalin, and all the events that followed have seen to that.

Over a century ago, the Russian thinker Belinskii wrote: "It is time for us to stop *seeming*, and start *being*." It is a good text for today's Russians. The future of Russia, one likes to hope, belongs to those forces in Russian society who will not tolerate official blurring of the distinction between appearances and reality.

The Sources of Soviet Conduct

X

The political personality of Soviet power as we know it today is the product of ideology and circumstances: ideology inherited by the present Soviet leaders from the movement in which they had their political origin, and circumstances of the power which they now have exercised for nearly three decades in Russia. There can be few tasks of psychological analysis more difficult than to try to trace the interaction of these two forces and the relative role of each in the determination of official Soviet conduct. Yet the attempt must be made if that conduct is to be understood and effectively countered.

It is difficult to summarize the set of ideological concepts with which the Soviet leaders came into power. Marxian ideology, in its Russian-Communist projection, has always been in process of subtle evolution. The materials on which it bases itself are extensive and complex. But the outstanding features of Communist thought as it existed in 1916 may perhaps be summarized as follows: (a) that the central factor in the life of man, the fact which determines the character of public life and the 'physiognomy of society,' is the system by which material goods are produced and exchanged; (b) that the capitalist system of production is a nefarious one which inevitably leads to the exploitation of the working class by the capital-owning class and is incapable of developing adequately the economic resources of society or of distributing fairly the material goods produced by human labor; (c) that capitalism contains the seeds of its own destruction and must, in view

Reprinted by special permission from *Foreign Affairs* (July 1947). Copyright by Council on Foreign Relations, Inc., New York.

The famous "X" was subsequently identified as George F. Kennan, former United States Ambassador to the USSR and author of several volumes on American and Soviet foreign policy.

of the inability of the capital-owning class to adjust itself to economic change, result eventually and inescapably in a revolutionary transfer of power to the working class; and (d) that imperialism, the final phase of capitalism, leads directly to war and revolution.

The rest may be outlined in Lenin's own words:

Unevenness of economic and political development is the inflexible law of capitalism. It follows from this that the victory of socialism may come originally in a few capitalist countries or even in a single capitalist country. The victorious proletariat of that country, having expropriated the capitalists and having organized socialist production at home, would rise against the remaining capitalist world, drawing to itself in the process the oppressed classes of other countries.[1]

It must be noted that there was no assumption that capitalism would perish without proletarian revolution. A final push was needed from a revolutionary proletarian movement in order to tip over the tottering structure. But it was regarded as inevitable that sooner or later that push be given.

For fifty years prior to the outbreak of the Revolution, this pattern of thought had exercised great fascination for the members of the Russian revolutionary movement. Frustrated, discontented, hopeless of finding self-expression—or too impatient to seek it—in the confining limits of the tsarist political system, yet lacking wide popular support for their choice of bloody revolution as a means of social betterment, these revolutionists found in Marxist theory a highly convenient rationalization for their own instinctive desires. It afforded pseudoscientific justification for their impatience, for their categoric denial of all value in the tsarist system, for their yearning for power and revenge, and for their inclination to cut corners in the pursuit of it. It is therefore no wonder that they had come to believe implicitly in the truth and soundness of the Marxist-Leninist teachings, so congenial to their own impulses and emotions. Their sincerity need not be impugned. This is a phenomenon as old as human nature itself. It has never been more aptly described than by Edward Gibbon, who wrote in *The Decline and Fall of the Roman Empire*: "From enthusiasm to imposture the step is perilous and slippery; the demon of Socrates affords a memorable

[1] V. I. Lenin, "O lozunge Soedinennykh Shtatov Evropy" (August 1915), in *Izbrannye proizvedeniia v dvukh tomakh* (4th ed.; Moscow, 1946), I, 732.

instance how a wise man may deceive himself, how a good man may deceive others, how the conscience may slumber in a mixed and middle state between self-illusion and voluntary fraud." And it was with this set of conceptions that the members of the Bolshevik Party entered into power.

Now it must be noted that through all the years of preparation for revolution, the attention of these men, as indeed of Marx himself, had been centered less on the future form which socialism[2] would take than on the necessary overthrow of rival power which, in their view, had to precede the introduction of socialism. Their views, therefore, on the positive program to be put into effect, once power was attained, were for the most part nebulous, visionary, and impractical. Beyond the nationalization of industry and the expropriation of large private capital holdings there was no agreed program. The treatment of the peasantry, which according to the Marxist formulation was not of the proletariat, had always been a vague spot in the pattern of Communist thought; and it remained an object of controversy and vacillation for the first ten years of Communist power.

The circumstances of the immediate post-Revolution period—the existence in Russia of civil war and foreign intervention, together with the obvious fact that the Communists represented only a tiny minority of the Russian people—made the establishment of dictatorial power a necessity. The experiment with 'War Communism' and the abrupt attempt to eliminate private production and trade had unfortunate economic consequences and caused further bitterness against the new revolutionary regime. While the temporary relaxation of the effort to communize Russia, represented by the New Economic Policy, alleviated some of this economic distress and thereby served its purpose, it also made it evident that the 'capitalist sector of society' was still prepared to profit at once from any relaxation of governmental pressure, and would, if permitted to continue to exist, always constitute a powerful opposing element to the Soviet regime and a serious rival for influence in the country. Somewhat the same situation prevailed with respect to the individual peasant who, in his own small way, was also a private producer.

[2] Here and elsewhere in this paper 'socialism' refers to Marxist or Leninist communism, not to liberal socialism of the Second International variety.

Lenin, had he lived, might have proved a great enough man to reconcile these conflicting forces to the ultimate benefit of Russian society, though this is questionable. But, be that as it may, Stalin and those whom he led in the struggle for succession to Lenin's position of leadership were not the men to tolerate rival political forces in the sphere of power which they coveted. Their sense of insecurity was too great. Their particular brand of fanaticism, unmodified by any of the Anglo-Saxon traditions of compromise, was too fierce and too jealous to envisage any permanent sharing of power. From the Russian-Asiatic world out of which they had emerged they carried with them a skepticism as to the possibilities of permanent and peaceful coexistence of rival forces. Easily persuaded of their own doctrinaire 'rightness,' they insisted on the submission or destruction of all competing power. Outside of the Communist Party, Russian society was to have no rigidity. There were to be no forms of collective human activity or association which would not be dominated by the Party. No other force in Russian society was to be permitted to achieve vitality or integrity. Only the Party was to have structure. All else was to be an amorphous mass.

And within the Party the same principle was to apply. The mass of Party members might go through the motions of election, deliberation, decision, and action; but in these motions they were to be animated not by their own individual wills but by the awesome breath of the Party leadership and the overbrooding presence of 'the word.'

Let it be stressed again that subjectively these men probably did not seek absolutism for its own sake. They doubtless believed—and found it easy to believe—that they alone knew what was good for society and that they would accomplish that good once their power was secure and unchallengeable. But in seeking that security of their own rule they were prepared to recognize no restrictions, either of God or man, on the character of their methods. And until such time as that security might be achieved, they placed far down on their scale of operational priorities the comforts and happiness of the peoples entrusted to their care.

Now the outstanding circumstance concerning the Soviet regime is that down to the present day this process of political consolidation has never been completed and the men in the Kremlin have continued to be predominantly absorbed with the struggle to secure and make absolute the power which they seized in November 1917. They have endeavored to secure it primarily against forces at home, within Soviet society itself. But they have also endeavored to secure it against the outside world. For ideology, as we have seen, taught them that the outside world was hostile and that it was their duty eventually to overthrow the political forces beyond their borders. The powerful hands of Russian history and tradition reached up to sustain them in this feeling. Finally, their own aggressive intransigence with respect to the outside world began to find its own reaction; and they were soon forced, to use another Gibbonesque phrase, 'to chastise the contumacy' which they themselves had provoked. It is an undeniable privilege of every man to prove himself right in the thesis that the world is his enemy; for if he reiterates it frequently enough and makes it the background of his conduct, he is bound eventually to be right.

Now it lies in the nature of the mental world of the Soviet leaders, as well as in the character of their ideology, that no opposition to them can be officially recognized as having any merit or justification whatsoever. Such opposition can flow, in theory, only from the hostile and incorrigible forces of dying capitalism. As long as remnants of capitalism were officially recognized as existing in Russia, it was possible to place on them, as an internal element, part of the blame for the maintenance of a dictatorial form of society. But as these remnants were liquidated, little by little, this justification fell away; and when it was indicated officially that they had been finally destroyed, it disappeared altogether. And this fact created one of the most basic of the compulsions which came to act upon the Soviet regime: since capitalism no longer existed in Russia and since it could not be admitted that there could be serious or widespread opposition to the Kremlin springing spontaneously from the liberated masses under its authority, it became necessary to justify the retention of the dictatorship by stressing the menace of capitalism abroad.

This began at an early date. In 1924 Stalin specifically defended the retention of the 'organs of suppression,' meaning, among others, the army and the secret police, on the ground that "as long as there is a capitalist encirclement there will be danger of intervention with all the consequences that flow from that danger." In accordance with that theory, and from that time on, all internal opposition forces in

Russia have consistently been portrayed as the agents of foreign forces of reaction antagonistic to Soviet power.

By the same token tremendous emphasis has been placed on the original Communist thesis of a basic antagonism between the capitalist and socialist worlds. It is clear, from many indications, that this emphasis is not founded in reality. The real facts concerning it have been confused by the existence abroad of genuine resentment provoked by Soviet philosophy and tactics and occasionally by the existence of great centers of military power, notably the Nazi regime in Germany and the Japanese government of the late 1930s, which did indeed have aggressive designs against the Soviet Union. But there is ample evidence that the stress laid in Moscow on the menace confronting Soviet society from the world outside its borders is founded not in the realities of foreign antagonism but in the necessity of explaining away the maintenance of dictatorial authority at home.

Now the maintenance of this pattern of Soviet power, namely, the pursuit of unlimited authority domestically, accompanied by the cultivation of the semi-myth of implacable foreign hostility, has gone far to shape the actual machinery of Soviet power as we know it today. Internal organs of administration which did not serve this purpose withered on the vine. Organs which did serve this purpose became vastly swollen. The security of Soviet power came to rest on the iron discipline of the Party, on the severity and ubiquity of the secret police, and on the uncompromising economic monopolism of the state. The 'organs of suppression,' in which the Soviet leaders had sought security from rival forces, became in large measure the masters of those whom they were designed to serve. Today the major part of the structure of Soviet power is committed to the perfection of the dictatorship and to the maintenance of the concept of Russia as in a state of siege, with the enemy lowering beyond the walls. And the millions of human beings who form that part of the structure of power must defend at all costs this concept of Russia's position, for without it they are themselves superfluous.

As things stand today, the rulers can no longer dream of parting with these organs of suppression. The quest for absolute power, pursued now for nearly three decades with a ruthlessness unparalleled (in scope at least) in modern times, has again produced internally, as it did externally, its own reaction. The excesses of the police apparatus have fanned the potential opposition to the regime into something far greater and more dangerous than it could have been before those excesses began.

But least of all can the rulers dispense with the fiction by which the maintenance of dictatorial power has been defended. For this fiction has been canonized in Soviet philosophy by the excesses already committed in its name; and it is now anchored in the Soviet structure of thought by bonds far greater than those of mere ideology.

2

So much for the historical background. What does it spell in terms of the political personality of Soviet power as we know it today?

Of the original ideology, nothing has been officially junked. Belief is maintained in the basic badness of capitalism, in the inevitability of its destruction, in the obligation of the proletariat to assist in that destruction and to take power into its own hands. But stress has come to be laid primarily on those concepts which relate most specifically to the Soviet regime itself: to its position as the sole truly socialist regime in a dark and misguided world, and to the relationships of power within it.

The first of these concepts is that of the innate antagonism between capitalism and socialism. We have seen how deeply that concept has become imbedded in foundations of Soviet power. It has profound implications for Russia's conduct as a member of international society. It means that there can never be on Moscow's side any sincere assumption of a community of aims between the Soviet Union and powers which are regarded as capitalist. It must invariably be assumed in Moscow that the aims of the capitalist world are antagonistic to the Soviet regime and therefore to the interests of the peoples it controls. If the Soviet government occasionally sets its signature to documents which would indicate the contrary, this is to be regarded as a tactical maneuver permissible in dealing with the enemy (who is without honor) and should be taken in the spirit of *caveat emptor*. Basically, the antagonism remains. It is postulated. And from it flow many of the phenomena which we find disturbing in the Kremlin's conduct of foreign policy: the secretiveness, the lack of frankness, the duplicity, the wary suspiciousness, and the basic unfriendliness of purpose. These phenomena are there to stay, for the foreseeable future. There can be variations of degree and emphasis. When there is something the Russians want from us, one or the other of these features of their policy may be thrust temporarily into the background; and when that happens there will always be Americans who will leap forward with gleeful announcements that 'the Russians have changed,' and some who will even try to take credit for having brought about such 'changes.' But we should not be misled by tactical maneuvers. These characteristics of Soviet policy, like the postulate from which they flow, are basic to the internal nature of Soviet power and will be with us, whether in the foreground or the background, until the internal nature of Soviet power is changed.

This means that we are going to continue for a long time to find the Russians difficult to deal with. It does not mean that they should be considered as embarked upon a do-or-die program to overthrow our society by a given date. The theory of the inevitability of the eventual fall of capitalism has the fortunate connotation that there is no hurry about it. The forces of progress can take their time in preparing the final *coup de grâce*. Meanwhile, what is vital is that the 'socialist fatherland'—that oasis of power which has been already won for socialism in the person of the Soviet Union—should be cherished and defended by all good Communists at home and abroad, its fortunes promoted, its enemies badgered and confounded. The promotion of premature, 'adventurist' revolutionary projects abroad which might embarrass Soviet power in any way would be an inexcusable, even a counterrevolutionary act. The cause of socialism is the support and promotion of Soviet power, as defined in Moscow.

This brings us to the second of the concepts important to contemporary Soviet outlook. That is the infallibility of the Kremlin. The Soviet concept of power, which permits no focal points of organization outside the Party itself, requires that the Party leadership remain in theory the sole repository of truth. For if truth were to be found elsewhere, there would be justification for its expression in organized activity. But it is precisely that which the Kremlin cannot and will not permit.

The leadership of the Communist Party is therefore always right, and has been always right ever since in 1929 Stalin formalized his personal power by announcing that decisions of the Politburo were being taken unanimously.

On the principle of infallibility there rests the iron discipline of the Communist Party. In fact, the two concepts are mutually self-supporting. Perfect discipline requires recognition of infallibility. Infallibility requires the observance of discipline. And the two together go far to determine the behaviorism of the entire Soviet apparatus of power. But their effect cannot be understood unless a third factor be taken into account: namely, the fact that the leadership is at liberty to put forward for tactical purposes any particular thesis which it finds useful to the cause at any particular moment and to require the faithful and unquestioning acceptance of that thesis by the members of the movement as a whole. This means that truth is not a constant but is actually created, for all intents and purposes, by the Soviet leaders themselves. It may vary from week to week, from month to month. It is nothing absolute and immutable—nothing which flows from objective reality. It is only the most recent manifestation of the wisdom of those in whom the ultimate wisdom is supposed to reside, because they represent the logic of history. The accumulative effect of these factors is to give to the whole subordinate apparatus of Soviet power an unshakable stubbornness and steadfastness in its orientation. This orientation can be changed at will by the Kremlin but by no other power. Once a given Party line has been laid down on a given issue of current policy, the whole Soviet governmental machine, including the mechanism of diplomacy, moves inexorably along the prescribed path, like a persistent toy automobile wound up and headed in a given direction, stopping only when it meets with some unanswerable force. The individuals who are the components of this machine are unamenable to argument or reason which comes to them from outside sources. Their whole training has taught them to mistrust and discount the glib persuasiveness of the outside world. Like the white dog before the phonograph, they hear only the 'master's voice.' And if they are to be called off from the purposes last dictated to them, it is the master who must call them off. Thus the foreign representative cannot hope that his words will make any impression on them. The most that he can hope is that they will be transmitted to those at the top, who are capable of changing the Party line. But even those are not likely to be swayed by any normal logic in the words of the bourgeois representative. Since there can be no appeal to common purposes, there can be no appeal to common mental approaches. For this reason, facts speak louder than words to the ears of the Kremlin; and words carry the greatest weight when they have the ring of reflecting, or being backed up by, facts of unchallengeable validity.

But we have seen that the Kremlin is under no ideological compulsion to accomplish its purposes in a hurry. Like the Church, it is dealing in ideological concepts which are of long-term validity, and it can afford to be patient. It has no right to risk the existing achievements of the revolution for the sake of vain baubles of the future. The very teachings of Lenin himself require great caution and flexibility in the pursuit of Communist purposes. Again, these precepts are fortified by the lessons of Russian history: of centuries of obscure battles between nomadic forces over the stretches of a vast unfortified plain. Here caution, circumspection, flexibility, and deception are the valuable qualities; and their value finds natural appreciation in the Russian or the oriental mind. Thus the Kremlin has no compunction about retreating in the face of superior force. And, being under the compulsion of no timetable, it does not get panicky under the necessity for such retreat. Its political action is a fluid stream which moves constantly, wherever it is permitted to move, toward a given goal. Its main concern is to make sure that it has filled every nook and cranny available to it in the basin of world power. But if it finds unassailable barriers in its path, it accepts these philosophically and accommodates itself to them. The main thing is that there should always be pressure, increasing constant pressure, toward the desired goal. There is no trace of any feeling in Soviet psychology that that goal must be reached at any given time.

These considerations make Soviet diplomacy at once easier and more difficult to deal with than the diplomacy of individual aggressive leaders like Napoleon and Hitler. On the one hand, it is more sensitive to contrary force, more ready to yield on individual sectors of the diplomatic front when that force is felt to be too strong, and thus more rational in the logic and rhetoric of power. On the other hand, it cannot be easily defeated or discouraged by a single victory on the part of its opponents. And the patient persistence by which it is animated means that it can be effectively countered not by sporadic acts which represent the momentary whims of democratic opinion but only by intelligent long-range policies on the part of Russia's adversaries—policies no less steady in their purpose, and no less variegated and resourceful in their application, than those of the Soviet Union itself.

In these circumstances it is clear that the main element of any United States policy toward the Soviet Union must be that of a long-term, patient, but firm and vigilant containment of Russian expansive tendencies. It is important to note, however, that such a policy has nothing to do with outward histrionics—with threats or blustering or superfluous gestures of outward 'toughness.' While the Kremlin is basically flexible in its reaction to political realities, it is by no means unamenable to considerations of prestige. Like almost any other government, it can be placed by tactless and threatening gestures in a position where it cannot afford to yield even though this might be dictated by its sense of realism. The Russian leaders are keen judges of human psychology, and as such they are highly conscious that loss of temper and of self-control is never a source of strength in political affairs. They are quick to exploit such evidences of weakness. For these reasons, it is a *sine qua non* of successful dealing with Russia that the foreign government in question should remain at all times cool and collected and that its demands on Russian policy should be put forward in such a manner as to leave the way open for a compliance not too detrimental to Russian prestige.

3

In the light of the above, it will be clearly seen that the Soviet pressure against the free institutions of the Western world is something that can be contained by the adroit and vigilant application of counterforce at a series of constantly shifting geographical and political points, corresponding to the shifts and maneuvers of Soviet policy, but which cannot be charmed or talked out of existence. The Russians look forward to a duel of infinite duration, and they see that already they have scored great successes. It must be borne in mind that there was a time when the Communist Party represented far more of a minority in the sphere of Russian national life than Soviet power today represents in the world community.

But if ideology convinces the rulers of Russia that truth is on their side and that they can therefore afford to wait, those of us on whom that ideology has no claim are free to examine objectively the validity of that premise. The Soviet thesis not only implies complete lack of control by the West over its own economic destiny; it likewise assumes Russian unity, discipline, and patience over an infinite period. Let us bring this apocalyptic vision down to earth, and suppose that the Western world finds the strength and resourcefulness to contain Soviet power over a period of ten to fifteen years. What does that spell for Russia itself?

The Soviet leaders, taking advantage of the contributions of modern technique to the arts of despotism, have solved the question of obedience within the confines of their power. Few challenge their authority, and even those who do are unable to make that challenge valid as against the organs of suppression of the state.

The Kremlin has also proved able to accomplish its purpose of building up in Russia, regardless of the interests of the inhabitants, an industrial foundation of heavy metallurgy, which is, to be sure, not yet complete but which is nevertheless continuing to grow and is approaching those of the other major industrial countries. All of this, however, both the maintenance of internal political security and the building of heavy industry, has been carried out at a terrible cost in human life and in human hopes and energies. It has involved the neglect or abuse of other phases of Soviet economic life, particularly agriculture, consumers' goods production, housing, and transportation.

To all that, the war has added its tremendous toll of destruction, death, and human exhaustion. In consequence of this, we have in Russia today a population which is physically and spiritually tired. The mass of the people are disillusioned, skeptical, and no longer as accessible as they once were to the magical attraction which Soviet power still radiates to its followers abroad. The avidity with which people seized upon the slight respite accorded to the Church for tactical reasons during the war was eloquent testimony to the fact that their capacity for faith and devotion found little expression in the purposes of the regime.

In these circumstances, there are limits to the physical and nervous strength of people themselves. These limits are absolute ones, and are binding even for the cruelest dictatorship, because beyond them people cannot be driven. The forced labor camps and the other agencies of constraint provide temporary means of compelling people to work longer hours than their own volition or mere economic pressure would dictate; but if people survive them at all they become old before their time and must be considered as human casualties to the demands of dictatorship. In either case their best powers are no longer available to society and can no longer be enlisted in the service of the state.

Here only the younger generation can help. The younger generation, despite all vicissitudes and sufferings, is numerous and vigorous; and the Russians are a talented people. But it still remains to be seen what will be the effects on mature performance of the abnormal emotional strains of childhood which Soviet dictatorship created and which were enormously increased by the war. Such things as normal security and placidity of home environment have practically ceased to exist in the Soviet Union outside of the most remote farms and villages. And observers are not yet sure whether that is not going to leave its mark on the over-all capacity of the generation now coming into maturity.

In addition to this, we have the fact that Soviet economic development, while it can list certain formidable achievements, has been precariously spotty and uneven. Russian Communists who speak of the 'uneven development of capitalism' should blush at the contemplation of their own national economy. Here certain branches of economic life, such as the metallurgical and machine industries, have been pushed out of all proportion to other sectors of economy. Here is a nation striving to become in a short period one of the great industrial nations of the world while it still has no highway network worthy of the name and only a relatively primitive network of railways. Much has been done to increase efficiency of labor and to teach primitive peasants something about the operation of machines. But maintenance is still a crying deficiency of all Soviet economy. Construction is hasty and poor in quality. Depreciation must be enormous. And in vast sectors of economic life it has not yet been possible to instill into labor anything like that general culture of production and technical self-respect which characterizes the skilled worker of the West.

It is difficult to see how these deficiencies can be corrected at an early date by a tired and dispirited population working largely under the shadow of fear and compulsion. And as long as they are not overcome, Russia will remain economically a vulnerable, and in a certain sense an impotent, nation, capable of exporting its enthusiasms and of radiating the strange charm of its primitive political vitality but unable to back up those articles of export by the real evidences of material power and prosperity.

Meanwhile, a great uncertainty hangs over the political life of the Soviet Union. That is the uncertainty involved in the transfer of power from one individual or group of individuals to others.

This is, of course, outstandingly the problem of the personal position of Stalin. We must remember that his succession to Lenin's pinnacle of pre-eminence in the Communist movement was the only such transfer of individual authority which the Soviet Union has experienced. That transfer took twelve years to consolidate. It cost the lives of millions of people and shook the state to its foundations; the attendant tremors were felt all through the international revolutionary movement, to the disadvantage of the Kremlin itself.

It is always possible that another transfer of pre-eminent power may take place quietly and inconspicuously, with no repercussions anywhere. But again, it is possible that the questions involved may unleash, to use some of Lenin's words, one of those 'incredibly swift transitions' from 'delicate deceit' to 'wild violence' which characterize Russian history, and may shake Soviet power to its foundations.

But this is not only a question of Stalin himself. There has been, since 1938, a dangerous congealment of political life in the higher circles of Soviet power. The All-Union Party congress, in theory the supreme body of the Party, is supposed to meet not less often than once in three years. It will soon be eight full years since its last meeting.[3] During this period membership in the Party has numerically doubled. Party mortality during the war was enormous, and today well over half of the Party members are persons who have entered since the last Party congress was held. Meanwhile, the same small group of men has carried on at the top through an amazing series of national vicissitudes. Surely there is some reason why the experiences of the war brought basic political changes to every one of the great governments of the West. Surely the causes of that phenomenon are basic enough to be present somewhere in the obscurity of Soviet political life, as well. And yet no recognition has been given to these causes in Russia.

[3] [Written in 1947. The next congress was not held until 1952. — A.D.]

It must be surmised from this that even within so highly disciplined an organization as the Communist Party there must be a growing divergence in age, outlook, and interest between the great mass of Party members, only so recently recruited into the movement, and the little self-perpetuating clique of men at the top, whom most of these Party members have never met, with whom they have never conversed, and with whom they can have no political intimacy.

Who can say whether, in these circumstances, the eventual rejuvenation of the higher spheres of authority (which can only be a matter of time) can take place smoothly and peacefully, or whether rivals in the quest for higher power will not eventually reach down into these politically immature and inexperienced masses in order to find support for their respective claims. If this were ever to happen, strange consequences could flow for the Communist Party: for the membership at large has been exercised only in the practices of iron discipline and obedience and not in the arts of compromise and accommodation. And if disunity were ever to seize and paralyze the Party, the chaos and weakness of Russian society would be revealed in forms beyond description. For we have seen that Soviet power is only a crust concealing an amorphous mass of human beings among whom no independent organizational structure is tolerated. In Russia there is not even such a thing as local government. The present generation of Russians have never known spontaneity of collective action. If, consequently, anything were ever to occur to disrupt the unity and efficacy of the Party as a political instrument, Soviet Russia might be changed overnight from one of the strongest to one of the weakest and most pitiable of national societies.

Thus the future of Soviet power may not be by any means as secure as Russian capacity for self-delusion would make it appear to the men in the Kremlin. That they can keep power themselves, they have demonstrated. That they can quietly and easily turn it over to others remains to be proved. Meanwhile, the hardships of their rule and the vicissitudes of international life have taken a heavy toll of the strength and hopes of the great people on whom their power rests. It is curious to note that the ideological power of Soviet authority is strongest today in areas beyond the frontiers of Russia, beyond the reach of its police power. This phenomenon brings to mind a comparison used by Thomas Mann in his great novel *Buddenbrooks*. Observing that human institutions often show the greatest outward brilliance at a moment when inner decay is in reality farthest advanced, he compared the Buddenbrook family, in the days of its greatest glamour, to one of those stars whose light shines most brightly on this world when in reality it has long since ceased to exist. And who can say with assurance that the strong light still cast by the Kremlin on the dissatisfied peoples of the Western world is not the powerful afterglow of a constellation which is in actuality on the wane? This cannot be proved. And it cannot be disproved. But the possibility remains (and in the opinion of this writer it is a strong one) that Soviet power, like the capitalist world of its conception, bears within it the seeds of its own decay, and that the sprouting of these seeds is well advanced.

4

It is clear that the United States cannot expect in the foreseeable future to enjoy political intimacy with the Soviet regime. It must continue to regard the Soviet Union as a rival, not a partner, in the political arena. It must continue to expect that Soviet policies will reflect no abstract love of peace and stability, no real faith in the possibility of a permanent happy coexistence of the socialist and capitalist worlds but rather a cautious, persistent pressure toward the disruption and weakening of all rival influence and rival power.

Balanced against this are the facts that Russia, as opposed to the Western world in general, is still by far the weaker party, that Soviet policy is highly flexible, and that Soviet society may well contain deficiencies which will eventually weaken its own total potential. This would of itself warrant the United States entering with reasonable confidence upon a policy of firm containment, designed to confront the Russians with unalterable counterforce at every point where they show signs of encroaching upon the interests of a peaceful and stable world.

But in actuality the possibilities for American policy are by no means limited to holding the line and hoping for the best. It is entirely possible for the United States to influence by its actions the internal developments, both within Russia and throughout the international Communist movement, by which Russian policy is largely determined. It is not only a question of the modest measure of informational activity which this government can conduct in the Soviet Union and elsewhere, although that, too, is important. It is rather a question of the degree to which the United States can create among the peoples of the world generally the impression of a country which knows what it wants, which is coping successfully with the problems of its internal life and with the responsibilities of a world power, and which has a spiritual vitality capable of holding its own among the major ideological currents of the time. To the extent that such an impression can be created and maintained, the aims of Russian communism must appear sterile and quixotic, the hopes and enthusiasm of Moscow's supporters must wane, and added strain must be imposed on the Kremlin's foreign policies. For the palsied decrepitude of the capitalist world is the keystone of Communist philosophy. Even the failure of the United States to experience the early economic depression which the ravens of the Red Square have been predicting with such complacent confidence since hostilities ceased would have deep and important repercussions throughout the Communist world.

By the same token, exhibitions of indecision, disunity, and internal disintegration within this country have an exhilarating effect on the whole Communist movement. At each evidence of these tendencies, a thrill of hope and excitement goes through the Communist world, a new jauntiness can be noted in the Moscow tread, new groups of foreign supporters climb on to what they can only view as the band wagon of international politics, and Russian pressure increases all along the line in international affairs.

It would be an exaggeration to say that American behavior unassisted and alone could exercise a power of life and death over the Communist movement and bring about the early fall of Soviet power in Russia. But the United States has it in its power to increase enormously the strains under which Soviet policy must operate, to force upon the Kremlin a far greater degree of moderation and circumspection than it has had to observe in recent years, and in this way to promote tendencies which must eventually find their outlet in either the breakup or the gradual mellowing of Soviet power. For no mystical, messianic movement—and particularly not that of the Kremlin—can face frustration indefinitely without eventually adjusting itself in one way or another to the logic of that state of affairs.

Thus the decision will really fall in large measure in this country itself. The issue of Soviet-American relations is in essence a test of the over-all worth of the United States as a nation among nations. To avoid destruction the United States need only measure up to its own best traditions and prove itself worthy of preservation as a great nation.

Surely, there was never a fairer test of national quality than this. In the light of these circumstances, the thoughtful observer of Russian-American relations will find no cause for complaint in the Kremlin's challenge to American society. He will rather experience a certain gratitude to a Providence which, by providing the American people with this implacable challenge, has made their entire security as a nation dependent on their pulling themselves together and accepting the responsibilities of moral and political leadership that history plainly intended them to bear.

The Durability of Soviet Despotism

BERTRAM D. WOLFE

At every turn the historian encounters the unpredictable: contingency; historical accident; biological accident intruding itself into history, as when the death of a history-making person brings a change of direction; changes of mood; emergence of new situations; sudden leaps that seem to turn an accretion of little events into a big one ; the complicated interaction of multiple determinants on every event; the unintended consequences of intended actions.

Still, history is not *so* open that any event is just as likely as any other. As in the flux of things we note continuing structures, as in biology we note heredity as well as variation and mutation, so in history there is an interrelation between continuity and change.

Though all lands go through a history, and all orders and institutions are subject to continuous modification and ultimate transformation, there are some social orders or systems that are more markedly dynamic, more open, more mutable, even self-transforming, while others exhibit marked staying powers, their main outlines continuing to be discernibly the ·same through the most varied vicissitudes.

It may be difficult to determine except in retrospect just when a system may be said to change in ways so fundamental as to signify its transformation; still, it is possible and necessary to distinguish between self-conserving and self-transforming systems, between relatively open and relatively closed societies, and between changes so clearly of a secondary order that they may be designated within-system changes, and those so clearly fundamental that they involve changes in the system or basic societal structure. That this distinction

Published in *Commentary* (August 1957). The essay is a condensation of the author's paper presented at the St. Antony's Conference on Changes in Soviet Society, held in June 1957 at Oxford.

Bertram D. Wolfe is the author of *Three Who Made a Revolution, Khrushchev and Stalin's Ghost,* and other books on the USSR.

may in practice be hard to make, that there may be gradations and borderline cases and sudden surprises, does not relieve us of this obligation. Merely to reiterate endlessly that all things change, without attempting to make such distinctions, is to stand helpless before history-in-the-making, helpless to evaluate and helpless to react.

If we look at the Roman Empire, say from the time of Julius Caesar to the time of Julian the Apostate, or perhaps from Augustus to Romulus Augustulus, we can perceive that for three or four centuries, despite its many vicissitudes and changes, it continued in a meaningful and determinable sense to be the Roman Empire. In similar fashion we can easily select a good half millennium of continuity in the Byzantine Empire. Or if we take one of the most dynamic regions, Western Europe, in one of its more dynamic periods, we can note that monarchical absolutism had a continuity of several centuries. This is the more interesting because monarchical absolutism, though it was one of the more stable and monopolistically exclusive power systems of the modern Western world, was a *multi-centered system* in which the monarch was checked and limited by his need of support from groups, corporations, and interests that were organized independently of the central power: the castled, armed, and propertied nobility; the Church with its spiritual authority; the burghers of the wealthy fortified towns.

It is the presence of these independent centers of corporate organization that makes Western monarchical absolutism an exception among the centralized, long-lasting power systems. It was these limiting forces that managed to exact the charters and constitutions, the right to determine size and length of service of armed levies, size and purpose of monetary contributions, thus ultimately transforming the absolute monarchy into the limited, constitutional monarchy of modern times. And it is from our own Western history, with its exceptional evolution, that we derive many of our unconscious preconceptions as to the inevitability, sweep, and comparative ease of change. To correct our one-sided view it is necessary to compare the characteristics of multi-centered Western absolutism with other, more 'complete' and 'perfected' forms of single-centered power and despotism.[1]

---

[1] This comparison is a central part of Karl A. Wittfogel's *Oriental Despotism: A Comparative Study of Total Power* (Yale, 1957). His attention is centered on

In the *samoderzhavie* of Muscovy we find a more truly single-centered power structure, stronger, more completely centralized, more monopolistic, more despotic, more unyielding in its rigid institutional framework than was the absolutism of Western Europe. The tsar early managed to subvert the independent boyars and substitute for them a state-service nobility. The crown possessed enormous crown lands and state serfs. Bondage, both to the state and to the state-service nobility, was instituted by the central power and adjusted to the purposes of the recruiting sergeant and the tax-gatherer. When the Emancipation came, in the nineteenth century, it was a state-decreed 'revolution from above' (Alexander's own words for it), and carried with it state supervision and the decreeing of collective responsibility to the village *mir*.

To this universal state-service and state-bondage, we must add the features of Caesaro-papism: signifying a tsar and a state-dominated church. And the administrative-military nature of the Russian towns checked the rise of an independent burgher class.

Industrialization, too, was undertaken at the initiative of the state. From Peter I to Nicholas II, there were two centuries of state-ordained and -fostered industrialization: the state-owned and -managed basic industry—mining, metallurgy, munitions, railroad construction and operation—and some commercial monopolies, all crowned with a huge state banking and credit system.

The rudiments of a more multi-centered life were just beginning to develop in this powerful, single-center society when World War I added to the managerial state's concerns the total mobilization of men, money, materials, transport, and industry.

The 'model' country in this new form of state enterprise was wartime Germany. The system of total management by the state for total war has been variously, but not very intelligibly, termed 'state capitalism' and 'state socialism.' In any case, Lenin was quick to welcome this development as the 'final transition form.' In it, as

the countries in which "the state became stronger than society" because of the need to undertake vast state irrigation and flood control works by *corvée* organization of the entire population, with the consequent assumption of enormous managerial functions. But his study is full of insights into modern, industry-based totalitarianism highly suggestive for the purposes of our theme.

in the heritage from the tsarist managerial autocratic state itself, he found much to build on in making his own transition to the new totalitarianism.

From Ivan the Terrible on, for a period of four centuries, "the state had been stronger than society" and had been ruled from a single center as a military, bureaucratic, managerial state. Amidst the most varied vicissitudes, including a time of troubles, wars, conquests, invasions, peasant insurrections, palace revolutions and revolutions from above, the powerful framework endured. Weakenings of the power structure, even breaches in it, were followed by a swift 'restoration' of its basic outlines. When the strains of a world war finally caused its collapse, there came a brief interlude of loosening of the bonds. Then Lenin, even as he revolutionized, likewise 'restored' much of the four-century-old heritage. Indeed, it was this 'socialist restoration of autocracy' which Plekhanov had warned against, as early as the 1880s, as a danger inherent in the longed-for Russian revolution. He admonished the impatient Populists that unless all the bonds were first loosened and a free 'Western' or 'bourgeois-democratic' order were allowed to develop and mature, the seizure of power by would-be socialists could not but lead to a restoration of Oriental, autocratic despotism on a pseudo-socialist foundation with a pseudo-socialist 'ruling caste.' Things would be even worse, he warned Lenin in 1907, if this new 'Inca ruling caste of Sons of the Sun' should make the fatal mistake of nationalizing the land, thus tightening even more the chains that bound the peasant to the autocratic state.

The term 'Oriental despotism' applied to Russia in the course of this controversy among Russian socialists serves to remind us that there are yet more durable social formations with even greater built-in staying powers than those we have so far noted. These reckon their continuity not in centuries alone but even in millennia. As a Chinese historian once observed to me : "Your Renaissance was a fascinating period. We had seven of them." If we substitute restoration for renaissance, in the sense of both restoration of vigor and restoration of basic structure, he was right. For though China suffered upheavals, invasions, conquests, falls of dynasties, rebellions, interregnums, and times of trouble, a Chinese villager or a Chinese official of the nineteenth century, if transported to the China of two thousand or more years ago, would have found himself in a familiar institutional and ideological environment.

With the exception of Western monarchical absolutism, what all these enduring social structures had in common was a single power center, a managerial state, a lack of independent social orders and forms of property, an absence of checks on the flow of power to the center and the top, and an overwhelmingly powerful, self-perpetuating institutional framework.

Modern totalitarianism, I believe, is one of these comparatively closed and conservative societies, with a powerful and self-perpetuating institutional framework calculated to assimilate the changes which it intends and those which are forced upon it, in such fashion that —barring explosion from within or battering down from without— they tend to remain *within-system* changes in an enduring system.

At first glance the word conservative may seem out of place in speaking of a society that is organized revolution. And indeed there is a striking difference between Communist totalitarianism and all previous systems of absolute, despotic, undivided (and, in that sense total) power. For whereas despotism, autocracy, and absolutism were bent on preserving the *status quo*, Communist totalitarianism is dedicated to 'the future.' This powerful institutional structure which tolerates no rival centers of organization has a vested interest in keeping things in flux. The omnipotence of state and ideology is maintained by carrying on a permanent revolution. Like Alexander's, it is a revolution from above. But unlike Alexander's, its aim is nothing less than to keep a society atomized and to create, as rapidly and as completely as the recalcitrant human material and the refractory surrounding world will permit, a new man, a new society, and a new world.

Like the earlier systems referred to, it possesses a state that is stronger than society. Like them, it represents a system of total, in the sense of undivided, power. Like them, it lacks any organized and institutionalized checks on the flow of power to the top. Like them, it possesses a state-centered, state-dominated, state-managed, and, for the first time, a completely state-owned economy.

But if the other societies are distinguished by the high specific gravity of state ownership, state control, and state managerial function within the total activity of society, under Communist totalitarianism state ownership and state managerialism aspire to be total in a new sense. In the other cases, we have been contemplating total power in the sense of undivided power: power without significant rival centers of organization. But now, to the concept of *undivided power*, we must add that of *all-embracing power*.

No longer does the state limit itself to being 'stronger than society.' It now strives to be *coextensive* with society. Whereas the earlier power systems recognized certain limitations on their capacity to run everything, leaving room, for example, for pocket-handkerchief farms and the self-feeding of the *corvée* population, for private arts and crafts unconnected with the managerial concerns of the state, for certain types of private trade, and even finding room for village communal democracy under the watchful eye of the state overseer—what Wittfogel has aptly called 'beggars' democracy' —the new totalitarianism strives to atomize society completely, to coordinate the dispersed villages into its centralized power system, to eliminate even the small private parcel of the *kolkhoznik*, already reduced from a 'pocket handkerchief' to a mere swatch.

For the first time a total-power system in the earlier sense of undivided and unchallenged power aspires to be totalist or totalitarian in the further sense of converting the state-stronger-than-society into the state-coextensive-with-society.

We cannot deduce much from a comparison with other modern totalitarianisms. For historical and physical reasons Italian Fascism was more totalist in aspiration than in realization. And, though Nazism and Stalinist Communism suggestively moved toward each other, Nazism did not last long enough to complete its evolution. But it did live long enough to dispose of certain illusions concerning the supposed incompatibility of totalitarianism with certain aspects of modern life.

Thus it is widely held that the monopoly of total power and the attempt to embrace the totality of social life and activity are incompatible with the complexity of modern industry and advanced technology. But Germany adopted totalitarianism when it was the foremost country of Europe in industry and technology.

Indeed, it is precisely modern technology, with its all-embracing means of communication, its high-speed transmission of commands and reports and armed force to any point in a country, its mass-communication and mass-conditioning techniques and the like, which for the first time makes it possible for total (undivided) power to aspire to be totalist (all-embracing) power. That is what Herzen foreboded when he wrote: "Some day Jinghis Khan will return with the telegraph." If total power tends to arise wherever the state is stronger than society, totalitarian power can aspire to prevail over a great area and in great depth only where the state is both stronger than society and in possession of all the resources of modern technology.

Closely akin to the illusion of the incompatibility of totalitarianism with modern technology is the view that totalitarianism is 'in the long run' incompatible with universal literacy, with advanced technological training, and with widespread higher or secondary-school education. Once more it is Germany that serves to remind us that one of the most highly literate and technologically trained peoples in the history of man adopted totalitarianism. Nay more, modern totalitarianism *requires* that everybody be able to read so that all can be made to read the same thing at the same moment. Not the ability to read, but the ability to choose between alternative types of reading, is a potential—and only a potential—liberating influence.

2

When Stalin died in 1953, Bolshevism was fifty years old. Its distinctive views on organization, centralization, and the guardianship or dictatorship of a vanguard or elite date from Lenin's programmatic writings of 1902 (*Where to Begin; What Is to Be Done?*). His separate party machine, which he controlled with an authoritarian hand, dates from the Bolshevik-Menshevik split of 1903 in the Russian Social Democratic party.

During these fifty years Bolshevism had had only two authoritative leaders, each of whom set the stamp of his personality upon it. Lenin, as we have suggested, inherited much from tsarist autocracy, yet his totalitarianism is different in principle from the old Muscovite despotism. He regarded himself as an orthodox Marxist, building upon and enlarging some aspects of Marx's conceptions while ignoring, altering, or misrepresenting others. His Marxism was so different from Marx's that a not unfriendly commentator, Charles Rappoport, called it *Marxisme à la Tartare*. Stalin's Leninism, in turn, differed enough from Lenin's that we might term it *Marxisme à la mode caucasienne*. Yet there is discernibly more continuity between Stalin and Lenin than between Lenin and Marx. The changes Stalin introduced involved the continuation and enlargement of certain elements in Lenin's methods and conceptions, along with the alteration of others. He inherited and used, now in Leninist, now in his own 'Stalinist' fashion, an institutional framework involving a party machine, a state machine, a doctrine of infallibility, an ideology, and the determination to extend the totalization of power, to transform the Russian into the 'New Communist Man,' and win the world for Communism.

With Stalin's death, once more there are new leaders or a new leader. It is impossible to believe that this new personal imprint will not make alterations in Stalinism as Stalin did in Leninism.

But it seems to me useful, after four years of unsystematic talk about changes, that we should remind ourselves that the 'new men' are not so new, that they have inherited a going concern, and that actually we are confronting changes within a single-centered, closed, highly centralized society run by a power that is both undivided and all-embracing. And we should remind ourselves, too, that such societies as I have classed it with have tended to exhibit built-in staying powers and a perdurability despite changes like the death of a despot, an oligarchical interregnum, or a struggle for succession.

These 'new men' are, of course, Stalin's men. They would not now have any claim to power over a great nation were it not that they managed to be the surviving close lieutenants at the moment of Stalin's death. It is my impression that they are smallish men. There is a principle of selection in personal despotisms which surrounds the despot with courtiers, sycophants, executants, and rules out original and challenging minds. This almost guarantees a crisis of succession where there is no system of legitimacy, until a new dictator emerges. Moreover, the heirs are no longer young (Khrushchev is sixty-three), so that a fresh crisis of succession may well supervene before the present muted and restricted crisis is over.

I would not write these 'smallish men' too small, however, for when you have a sixth of the earth, 200,000,000 population, and a total state economy and a great empire to practice on, you learn other trades besides that of courtier or faction lieutenant. Even so, not one of them at present exhibits the originality and the high charge of energy and intellect that characterized Lenin, or the grosser but no less original demonic force of Stalin.

Whenever a despot dies, there is a universal expectation of change. The new men have had to take account of it, and have taken advantage of it to introduce changes which the old tyrant made seem desirable even to his lieutenants: they have taken advantage of the expectation of change to rationalize elements of a system which has no organized, independent forces which might change it from below, and to make limited concessions while they are consolidating their power. But the institutional framework they have inherited is one they intend to maintain.

Some parts of this power machine are now more than a half century old, others date from 1917, others from the consolidation of the Stalinist regime in industry, agriculture, politics, and culture in the thirties. But even these last have been established for more than two decades.

What the epigoni have inherited is no small heritage: a completely atomized society;[2] a monolithic, monopolistic party; a single-party state; a regime of absolute force supplemented by persuasion or by continuous psychological warfare upon its people; a managerial bureaucracy accustomed to execute orders (with a little elbow room for regularized evasion); a centrally managed, totally state-owned and state-regulated economy including farms, factories, banks, transport and communications, and all trade, domestic and foreign; an established dogmatic priority for the branches of industry which underlie the power of the state; a bare subsistence economy for the bulk of the producers; a completely statized and 'collectivized' agriculture which, though it has never solved the problem of productivity, threatens to reduce even the small parcel to a mere 'garden adornment'; a powerful, if one-sided, forced-tempo industry centralized even beyond the point of rationality from the standpoint of totalitarianism itself; the techniques and momentum of a succession of Five-Year Plans, of which

[2] This does not apply to the Soviet empire but only to the Soviet Union. In general I have omitted any consideration of the empire here.

the present is the sixth; a completely managed and controlled culture (except for the most secret recesses of the spirit which even modern technology cannot reach); a monopoly of all the means of expression and communication; a state-owned system of 'criticism'; an infallible doctrine stemming from infallible authorities, interpreted and applied by an infallible party led by an infallible leader or a clique of infallible leaders, in any case by an infallible 'summit'; a method of advance by zigzags toward basically unchanging goals; a system of promotion, demotion, correction of error, modification of strategy and tactics and elimination of difference by fiat from the summit, implemented by purges of varying scope and intensity; a commitment to continuing revolution from above until the Soviet subject has been remade according to the blueprint of the men in the Kremlin and until Communism has won the world.

It is in this heritage that these men were formed. In this they believe. It is the weight and power and internal dynamics of this heritage that in part inhibit, in part shape such changes as these men undertake, and enter as a powerful influence into the changes which they make involuntarily.

It would require a separate study to attempt an inquiry into what is fundamental to totalitarianism, so that a change in it would represent a 'change in the system,' and what is of a more superficial order, so that a change may readily be recognized as a 'within-system' change.[3] Here we shall have to limit ourselves to a glance at a few post-Stalin political developments. The first change that obtrudes itself is 'collective leadership.'

The Party statutes do not provide for an authoritative leader, a dictator or *vozhd'*. Just as this, the most centralized great power, still professes to be federal, a mere union of autonomous republics, so the Party statutes have always proclaimed party democracy and collective leadership.

---

[3] At the Oxford Conference to which this paper was presented, Leonard Schapiro offered a brief and simple criterion of distinction between within-system changes and changes in the system. He said: "Any changes which leave undisturbed the monopoly of power by the party and its leaders may be regarded as a 'within-system' change. Any firm limitation upon this monopoly of power would represent a 'change-in-the-system.'"

It was not hard to predict that Stalin's orphaned heirs would proclaim a collective leadership at the moment of his death, even as they began the maneuvers that led to the emergence of a still narrower ruling group (triumvirate, duumvirate) and a muted struggle for the succession. Stalin, too, for a half decade found it necessary to proclaim a collective leadership and pose as its faithful wheelhorse, and took a full decade before he killed his first rivals.

Stalin's successors had the same reasons as he for proclaiming the collective leadership of the Politburo, and some additional ones as well. The harrowing and demoralizing experiences of the thirties, the signs of the beginnings of a new mass purge (in the 'poison doctors' case') a few months before Stalin's death, the terror that gripped even his closest collaborators, and their justified fears of each other —all combined to make necessary the proclamation of a 'collective leadership.'

There is nothing inherently incompatible with total, undivided power, nor with totalitarian, all-embracing power, in the rule of an oligarchy, or in an interregnum between dictators or despots. What is noteworthy here is the swiftness with which the first triumvirate (Malenkov, Molotov, Beria) were demoted, compelled to confess unfitness, and, in the case of Beria, killed. It took Stalin ten years to shed the blood of potential rivals or aspirants to power; Beria disappeared in a few months. In less than two years the skeptical were obliged to recognize that Khrushchev was 'more equal than the others' and was making all the important programmatic declarations.[4] Those who follow the Soviet press can perceive that Khrushchev is already the *Khoziain* (Boss), though not yet the *Vozhd'* (Führer, Duce, Charismatic Leader).

This is not to say that Khrushchev must necessarily emerge as the undisputed and authoritative leader in the sense that either Stalin or Lenin was. Combinations and counterforces in the oligarchy and limitations in his own capacity may check or slow or, in view of his age, even nullify the manifest trend. But triumvirates, duumvirates, directories are notoriously transitional in the succession to a despot where there is no legitimacy in providing a successor, and no checks

---

[4] For a time Bulganin made the 'purely' economic pronouncements, but that period seems to have ended with the Twentieth Congress.

against the flow of power to the top. Moreover, the whole dynamics of dictatorship calls for a personal dictator, authoritarianism for an authority, infallible doctrine for an infallible interpreter, totally militarized life for a supreme commander, and centralized, undivided, all-embracing, and 'messianic' power for a 'charismatic' symbol and tenant of authority. Unless the 'collective leadership' should broaden instead of narrowing as it already has, unless power should flood down into the basic units of the Party (which was not the case even in Lenin's day) and then leak out into self-organizing corporate bodies independent of the state, restoring some initiative to society as against the state—in short, unless the whole trend of totalitarianism is not merely slowed (as may be expected during an interregnum) but actually reversed, there is good reason to regard a 'directory' or a 'duumvirate' as transitory.

Both purge and terror were instituted by Lenin and 'perfected' and 'over-perfected' by Stalin. Leaving on one side the purely personal element (paranoia and relish for vengeance), both purge in the Party and terror in society as a whole serve many of the 'rational' purposes of the totalitarian regime: the establishment of the infallibility of the Party, of its summit, and its doctrine; the maintenance of the Party in a 'state of grace' (zeal, doctrinal purity, fanatical devotion, discipline, subordination, total mobilization); the atomization of society as a whole; the breaking up of all non-state conformations and centers of solidarity; the turnover in the elite, demotion of dead-wood and promotion of new forces; the supplying of scapegoats for every error and for signaling a change of line; the maintenance of the priority of heavy industry, of forced savings for capital investment, of unquestioned command and relative efficiency in production, of 'collectivization' in agriculture, of control in culture, and a number of similar objectives of the totalist state.

All of these institutions have been so well established that to a large extent they are now taken for granted. Stalin himself promised in 1939 that there would never again be a mass purge. Except in the case of the army and the Jewish writers, the purge became physically more moderate, until, with increasing marks of paranoia, Stalin gave every sign of opening another era of mass purge a few months before his death. The first thing the heirs did as they gathered round the corpse was to call off the purge, both because it had no 'rational' purpose and because it had threatened to involve most of them.

But it would be a mistake to believe that the 'moderated' purge can be dispensed with. In the preparation of the Twentieth Congress the heirs showed how well they had mastered the 'Leninist norms,' according to which every congress since the Tenth had been prepared for by a prior purge of the party organization. All the regional secretaries and leading committees were 'renewed,' 37 per cent of those who attended the Nineteenth Congress disappeared from public view, 44 per cent of the Central Committee failed to be elected as delegates or to be re-elected to the new Committee. All we can say is that the purge today resembles those of Stalin's 'benign' periods or of Lenin's day. Yet the liquidation of Beria and at least twenty-five of his friends shows that the techniques of the blood purge have not been forgotten. That the Party ranks breathe easier and are glad of the self-denying ordinance of the leaders in the struggle for position we do not doubt. But there is no evidence that the Party ranks ordered this change, or could do so, or would venture to try.

The terror in society as a whole has also diminished. No longer are there such bloody tasks as forced collectivization to carry through. Habitual obedience, the amnesties and concessions of an interregnum, the shortage of manpower for industry, agriculture, and the army because of continued expansion, and the deficit of wartime births that should now have been reaching the labor age—these and many other things account for the fact that artists and writers, workmen and peasants and managers do not at this moment feel that public reproof (which they are very quick indeed to heed) must necessarily be followed by incarceration in the concentration camp. In a time of manpower shortages, the fact that the concentration camp is the most wasteful and least productive way of exploiting manpower is especially felt. The camps are gentler now, yet they are there. Their size is shrinking, yet no one dares to propose their abolition or even to take public notice of them. Even as this paper is being prepared, at least one new class of young people, the rebellious student youth, is being moved in increasing numbers into the camps.

The police has been downgraded and, in a regime so in need of naked force, the army has been upgraded, i.e., given more internal political functions. The public prosecutors have been given more control of trials and pretrial inquisitions—like making the fox the guardian of the chicken-coop. There are some other minor legal reforms. Above all there has been much fuss made about a promise to codify and regularize the laws.

Recodification of the criminal laws was begun during Stalin's lifetime. A new code was promised 'within sixty days' by Lavrentii Beria when his star seemed in the ascendant. It has not been promulgated yet, four years after Stalin's and almost four years after Beria's death. Sight unseen, we can predict that the new code will not touch the foundations of the totalist state: it will not alter the subservience of courts and laws and prosecutors and judges and police to the will and purposes of the oligarchy or the single leader. It is necessary to re-member that any total power, and *a fortiori* any totalist power, may obey its own laws whenever it suits it to do so without giving those laws power over itself or making them into limitations upon its powers. A power center that is both legislator and administrator, and judge and enforcer and even self-pronounced infallible 'critic' of its own acts, may declare any activity it pleases a crime. In the Soviet Union, even loyalty to the underlying principles on which the state itself was founded has been declared a degrading crime and punished with in-credible cruelty. How easily this totalist state may set aside its laws and negate its most solemn and 'binding' promises is evidenced anew —after the proclamation of 'socialist legality'—by the sudden repu-diation by the 'workers' state' of the state debt owed to the workers themselves, without so much as the possibility of anybody making a murmur. The owners of the repudiated bonds, in which they had invested their now wiped out compulsory savings, were even obliged to hold meetings and pass resolutions in which to express their delight at being expropriated.

The longer such a regime endures the more it has need of regulariza-tion of the duties and expectations of its subjects, even as it keeps up undiminished its powers of sudden reversal and unpredictable and unlimited intervention. The only guarantee against a totally powerful state is the existence of non-state organizations capable of effective con-trol of or effective pressure on the governmental power. Otherwise, to attempt to check, or limit, or even question is to invite the fury of exemplary punishment.

"Betwixt subject and subject," Locke wrote of the defenders of despotism,

they will grant, there must be measures, laws, and judgments for their mutual peace and security. But as for the ruler, he ought to be absolute, and is above all such circumstances; because he has the power to do more hurt and wrong, it is right when he does it. To ask how you may be guarded from harm or injury on that side . . . is the voice of faction and rebellion. . . . The very question can scarcely be borne. They are ready to tell you it deserves death only to ask after safety.

It is well for us to remember that the most despotic rulers have on occasion handed down elaborate law codes. The famous and in many ways justly admired Roman Code was compiled and proclaimed only after the emperor himself had become a god, no longer subject to question or limitation, only to worship. Though laws must multiply and be regularized so that the subjects may know what is expected of them and what they can count on in their relations with each other wherever the central power is unaffected, the lack of independent courts, of independent power groups or corporate bodies, of an independent press and public opinion, deprives these laws of any binding force upon the rulers. In Communist totalitarianism, the place of imperial divinity is taken by the infallibility of doctrine, the dogmatic untouchability of the dictatorship, the infallibility of the masters of the infallibile doctrine, and by such spiritual demiurges as 'revolutionary consciousness,' 'historical necessity,' and 'the interests of the revolution and of the people.' Those who *know* where History is going surely have the right and duty to see to it that she goes there.

"The scientific concept, dictatorship," Lenin reminds us with beautiful simplicity, "means neither more nor less than unlimited power, resting directly on force, not limited by anything, not restricted by any laws or any absolute rules. Nothing else but that."

And to Commissar of Justice Kurskii, when he was elaborating the first legal code, Lenin wrote :

[My] draft is rough . . . but the basic thought, I hope, is clear: openly to set forth the proposition straightforward in principle and straightforward politically (and not merely in the narrow juridical sense) which motivates the *essence* and *justification* of terror, its necessity, its limits.

The court should not eliminate the terror—to promise that would be either to deceive oneself or to deceive others—but should give it a foundation and a legalization in principle, clearly, without falsification and without embellishment. It is necessary to formulate it as broadly as possible, for only a revolutionary consciousness of justice and a revolutionary conscience will put conditions upon its application in practice, on a more or a less broad scale.

In these regards the new men do not have to 'return to Leninist norms,' for they have never been abandoned for a moment.

If we can hope for, even perhaps count on, the diminution of the apocalyptic element in the ideology of a going, long-lasting society, we must remind ourselves that Leninism was peculiar in that its central 'ideas' were always ideas about organization and they have been strengthened rather than weakened in the course of time.

Bolshevism was born in an organizational feud about the definition of a party member, and who should control a paper (*Iskra*) which should act both as guardian of the doctrine and organizational core of the party. "Give me an organization," Lenin wrote at the outset of his career as a Leninist, "and I will turn Russia upside down." The organization he wanted, he explained, must be one in which 'bureaucratism' prevailed against 'democratism,' 'centralism' against 'autonomy,' which "strives to go from the top downward, and defends the enlargement of the rights and plenary powers of the central body against the parts." When at the 1903 Congress an exalter of the Central Committee urged that it should become the 'omnipresent and one,' the all-pervasive, all-informing and all-uniting 'spirit,' Lenin cried out from his seat: "*Ne dukh, a kulak* (Not spirit, but fist)!" The idea of the rule of the elite, the idea of a vanguard party, the idea of the hatefulness of all other classes and the untrustworthiness of the working class, the idea that the working class too required a dictator or overseer to compel it to its mission—it is amazing to note that these 'ideas' about organization form the very core of Leninism as a special ideology. Far from 'eroding' or growing 'weak' and merely 'decorative,' it is just precisely these structural principles which have grown and expanded, and become systematized.

Resentments, discontent, longing for a less oppressive regime and an easier lot exist under despotisms, autocracies, total-power states, and totalist states, even as in other social orders. Indeed, whenever hope or expectation stirs they are apt to become endemic and intense. The problem of 'statecraft' in a despotism is that of preventing the discontent and longing from assuming *organized* form. Since the totalist state penetrates all social organizations and uses them as transmission belts (destroying whatever organization it cannot assimilate to its purposes and structure), it is particularly adapted to keeping discontent fragmented and unorganized.

By 1936, Lenin's central idea of an elite, single-centered dictatorship had gotten into the 'most democratic constitution in the world' as Article 126, which proclaimed the Party to be "the vanguard of the working people and the leading core of all organizations, both social and state." And last summer, when Khrushchev and the rest were summing up the discussion over Stalin, they declared in *Pravda*: "As for our country, the Communist Party has been and will be the *only master* of the *minds*, the *thoughts*, the *only spokesman, leader, and organizer* of the people" (my italics).

It is foolhardy to believe that they did not mean it, self-deluding to persuade ourselves that the forces pressing for concessions within the country are likely to find the road open to separate and effective corporate organization, which is the condition precedent to the development of a limited, multi-centered state and a society which is stronger than it.

Even before Stalin died, we got evidence that the spirit of man is wayward and not as easily subjected as his body—the mass desertion at the war's end; the escape of millions who 'voted with their feet' against totalitarianism; the two out of three 'Chinese volunteers' in the Korean prison camps who preferred exile under precarious and humiliating 'displaced person' conditions to return to their native scenes and homes. Since Stalin's death there have been East Berlin and Pilsen, Poznań and Vorkuta, Warsaw and Budapest, to prove that men will sometimes stand up unarmed to tanks and cannon and machine guns. They have proved too that the armies of the conquered lands have never been the pliant instruments of the Kremlin that fainthearted men thought they were.

We have seen that forty years of *Gleichschaltung*, corruption, and terror have not rooted out of the artist the ineradicable notion that sincerity to his creative vision is more to be desired than *partiinost'* and *ideinost'*. We have seen that the youth—although the fainthearted had thought they would be turned off the conveyer belt as 'little monsters'—are born young still, and therefore plastic, receptive, questioning, capable of illusion and disillusion, of 'youthful idealism' and doubt and rebellion. Now the expulsions among the university youth are for the first time providing a pariah elite as a possible leadership to future undergrounds which may form under even this most efficiently regimented of societies.

I have never for a moment ceased to cast about for grounds of hope: that weaker heirs might make less efficient use of the terrible engines of total power; that a struggle or series of struggles for the succession might compel a contender to go outside the inner circles and summon social forces in the lower ranks of the Party or outside of it into some sort of independent existence; that the army, disgraced as no other in all history by the charge that it gave birth to traitors by the thousands in its general staff, might develop sufficient independence from the Party to make it a rival power center or an organized pressure body; that intellectuals, technicians, students might somehow break through the barriers that hinder the conversion of discontent into an organized, independent force.

But if I put the emphasis on the nature of the Soviet institutional framework and its built-in staying powers, it is by way of bending the stick in order to straighten it out. For the Western world has found it hard (or so it has seemed to me) to gaze straight and steadily at the head of Medusa, even if only in the reflecting shield of theoretical analysis. Brought up in a world of flux and openness, we find it hard to believe in the durability of despotic systems. Our hopes and longings are apt to betray us again and again into a readiness to be deceived by others or to deceive ourselves. And the 'journalistic' nature of our culture has made us too ready to inflate the new because that alone is 'news,' while we neglect to put it into its tiresomely 'repetitious' historical and institutional setting.

From the NEP to Socialism in One Country; from the Popular Front and Collective Security to the Grand Alliance and One World; from Peaceful Coexistence to the Geneva Spirit—the occupational hazard of the Western intellectual has been not to read too little but to read too much into planned changes, involuntary changes, and even into mere tactical maneuvers and verbal asseverations.

Each has been hailed in turn as the softening of the war of the totalist state on its own people and the world, as the long awaited 'inevitable change' or 'fundamental transformation'; 'the sobering that comes from the responsibilities of power'; the 'response to the pressure of the recognition of reality'; the growing modification of totalist power by 'a rationalist technocracy'; the sobering 'effect of privilege upon a new privileged class'; the 'rise of a limited and traditionalist despotism'; a 'feeling of responsibility to Russia as against World Revolution'; the 'quiet digestion period of a sated beast of prey' no longer on the prowl; the 'diffusion of authority which could lead to a constitutional despotism'; the 'mellowing process that sooner or later overtakes all militant movements'; the second thoughts on the struggle for the world which have come at long last 'from a recognition of the universal and mutual destructiveness of nuclear war'; the 'inevitable work of erosion upon the totalitarian edifice.' (Each of these expressions is quoted from some highly respected authority on Soviet affairs in the Anglo-Saxon world.)

Because of the nature of our mental climate and our longings, because too of the injection of 'revolutionary methods' into diplomacy in a polarized and antagonistic world, the danger does not lie in a failure on our part to watch for change nor in a failure to 'test'—though generally without sufficient skepticism—the meaning of each verbal declaration. No, 'the main danger,' as the Communists would say, has not lain in insensitivity to hope, but in too ready self-deception.

When Hitler's attack on Russia threw Stalin into our camp during World War II, I wrote an article, entitled "Stalin at the Peace Table," which contended that there would be no peace table and general settlement as after other wars and that the peace would be settled piecemeal by the strategic acts of the war, so that, if the war were not planned accordingly, there would be no decent peace. The illusions of the Grand Alliance were such that this view could not get a hearing.

This is not surprising in the case of a Cassandra who is merely a cloistered writer on totalitarianism and Soviet affairs. But Winston Churchill, participating in the directing councils of the Grand Alliance tried to get an agreement on a strategy for the joint occupation and liberation of the Balkans and Eastern Europe and even he could not prevail against the overpowering Grand Alliance illusions of wartime Britain and America. As a result, where the Soviet Army was in sole occupation, there are conquered countries. Where there was joint occupation, there is a divided Germany and a divided Korea. Where the Soviet Army was not admitted, there is a Japan free to criticize its occupier and remake its own destiny. Thus our trying to understand and estimate Soviet totalitarianism is no mere exercise in sociological abstraction or historical generalization. For literally every judgment about the nature of totalitarianism and the scope of the changes in it is fraught with significance for the fate of millions of men.

The Challenge of a Stable Russia

ALEX INKELES

Well before Stalin's death we were already launched on one of the great debates of our time. Could the Soviet system survive the death of the supreme dictator, and, if it did, what would be the nature of its future development? At least five years after Stalin's death the Soviet system still seems very much with us. There are those who still see in it only the seeds of a soon forthcoming paroxysm of political fratricide and consequent dissolution. Most students of Soviet affairs, however, accept the idea that the system will not soon collapse from internal pressures. What then seems the most likely course of Soviet development in the next few decades?

Two major and rather polarized positions have come to dominate the discussion. At the one pole there are those who assert that what Stalin wrought was a kind of modern oriental despotism, even more effective than the earlier absolute states, such as traditional China, because the modern instruments of force, communication, and education facilitate even greater mobilization of the population in the service of the dictator. This group holds modern totalitarianism as developed in the Soviet Union to be unchanged and unchanging. Nothing, except the complete destruction of the system, can stop the drive toward dictatorship, and nothing can sway the dictator from the absolute exercise of power, from the total mobilization of the population for the ends of the state. In this system there is no such thing as a 'concession' to popular will. The dictator acts as he sees fit, now playing soft, now hard, but always according to his own plan—'from above.'

Published in *Antioch Review* (Summer 1958).

Alex Inkeles, author of *Public Opinion in the Soviet Union* and co-author of *How the Soviet System Works* and *The Soviet Citizen*, is Professor of Social Relations at Harvard University.

Classes are made and, when they grow too powerful, unmade. Institutions are created and, when they have served their purpose, dissolved. Police controls, censorship, terror, a dark struggle for power at the higher reaches are inherent qualities of the system. Indeed, even the leaders are powerless to change it. They must preserve all its essential features as a total unity. To compromise is to risk destruction, to lose the power which is presumably the main motive force for the leaders.

These theorists also hold that Soviet foreign policy is undeviatingly committed to the destruction of the free world, and that it is premised on this destruction being ultimately effected by force of arms. All treaties, agreements, arrangements, and understandings are purely tactical maneuvers to gain time or other advantage. The Soviet word cannot be trusted, the very idea of good intentions is alien to them, and negotiation with them can have no other useful purpose than to demonstrate our gullibility or our good intentions.

This rather grim picture must be set opposite a much more cheerful political landscape as sketched by others. They see the gradual democratization of Soviet society as inevitable, and indeed claim to have substantial evidence that the process is already far advanced. They maintain that Stalin's system was developed largely to meet the unusual conditions of forced draft industrialization and the threat of war. But in this process the country became industrialized, the farms mechanized. A large urban population was assembled and trained in the 'higher' culture of the cities. Education became very widespread. Most important, a large technically trained, responsible, educated middle class arose which had aspirations for a more sane and rational pattern of life. At the same time, the leadership itself was changing as more men whose experience lay in this new middle class themselves attained to positions of power and responsibility. Thus the needs felt by the leaders for rational, orderly, efficient processes, for higher labor productivity, for more spontaneous and intelligent compliance, joined forces with desires for a better life on the part of the population. Together they set in motion a retreat from Stalinist extremism, toward reform and liberalization of the system. These changes are assumed to be irreversible, and therefore are taken to promise the gradual democratization of the Soviet system.

With regard to foreign affairs, those who hold this position claim that the present Soviet leaders are genuinely interested in a peaceful, stable world order, within the framework of which they can engage in friendly competition with our democratic capitalist system for world leadership. It is assumed that they seek a reduction of international tension and a consequent reduction in the arms burden in order to free them for more effective action in this competition. The exchange programs they have undertaken are taken to be a genuine expression of their intentions in this direction. They are taken to be reasonable men amenable to reasonable argument.

As is so often true with such theories, one can find substantial evidence in support of both. The release of thousands from forced labor camps, the tremendous reduction of political arrests to the point where they affect only a small proportion of the population, the cessation of obligatory deliveries from the private plots of the peasants, the opening of the Soviet Union to foreign tourists and the permission for Soviet citizens to travel abroad, the numerous programs for the exchange of scholars and students—these and a host of other measures taken by the government all argue that a new style of governing has come to the fore after Stalin's death. In contrast to Stalin's time the system is more 'liberal,' and the process shows some signs of further development.

On the other hand, those who argue for the unchanging nature of the system can point to the fact that people are still arbitrarily arrested by the secret police—even if they are fewer in number—and are sentenced without open trial. The dark struggle at the top continues—as Beria and his associates were first to discover, and Molotov and company not so long after. The use of force on a mass scale against a whole population was amply demonstrated in Hungary to the horror of the entire world. Hence, in essence, they would argue, the system remains unchanged.

Both of these positions suffer from a certain degree of rigidity which makes them inadequate for an assessment of future Soviet development. They are rigid in that both assume that totalitarianism is an 'either-or' proposition rather than a matter of degree. Each of these contrasting views depicts one of the two sets of forces at work in the Soviet Union, one stemming from the nature of the totalitarian system established under Stalin, the other from the nature of the industrial society which has grown up beneath the totalitarian structure. The two sets of forces have already demonstrated some compatibility, and the pertinent question is not which will triumph but what the concrete resolution will be.

It seems highly unlikely that the Soviet system, any more than any other modern industrial society, can be, or indeed has been, unchanging. It may be true, for example, that the shift from mass terror to political arrest limited to a small group at the top is not a change in principle but merely in degree. Yet for the hundreds of thousands of Soviet citizens who now sleep more securely, without the continuous fear of the early morning knock at the door, the change is real enough. They would think us mad to argue that this was not a 'real' change. Yet such changes do not add up to democratization. Although few are arrested, no man is granted a true immunity from arbitrary arrest, and no one can assume that he will be protected by proper safeguards of due process if he is arrested. There is very little evidence of any deliberate move for the Communist Party to share power, or even to observe democratic processes within its own organization. The term 'liberalization' of the system seems granting too much if we insist on giving the word 'liberal' an even moderately strict limitation, and there certainly seems nothing inevitable about the process.

Indeed, inevitability is a rock on which most theories of history founder, Marx's theory being not the least notable example. We can assume neither the inevitable stability nor the inevitable democratization of the system. In any event, either designation is largely a label we apply to a social process. Rather than argue about the labels, we might do better to go directly to the social processes which the labels presume to describe. In doing so we need to keep distinct three aspects of the problem: popular feeling and opinion, the desires and aspirations of the middle ranks of Soviet leadership, and the intentions of the ruling elite.

With regard to the rank and file of the population, extensive discussions with former Soviet citizens, supplemented by recent travel in the USSR, point to the following conclusions:

1. Stalinist rule created a deep and long-lasting impression in the Soviet people and left a residue of bitterness and resentment against arbitrary, violent, and despotic patterns of governing with which all

subsequent governments must reckon. There is a widespread feeling that this was a terrible aberration, and a general determination that it must not happen again.

2. The prolonged depression in the standard of living associated with collectivization of the farms and the years of forced industrialization was a source of resentment second only to the terror, and a widespread basis for questioning the legitimacy of the regime. The same deprivations would not again be accepted without large-scale passive resistance and the generation of tensions which would threaten to become explosive.

3. While consciously resenting the deprivations which Stalinist rule introduced into their lives, most Soviet citizens were nevertheless strongly, albeit more subtly and unconsciously, influenced by the processes of social change which Stalin set in motion. These changes are to be measured not merely in terms of the usual census categories of increasing education and urbanization but more in terms of changed attitudes, values, and life patterns. The values of the peasant family rooted in the local community, devoted to the soil, and consecrated to the continuance of religious and social tradition have suffered enormous attrition. These patterns, though they still exist, now characterize only a minority of the population. In their place the culture of the cities, the values of the rapidly changing industrial order, have now been ensconced. The 'consumption ethic' has come to Russia as it has to other industrialized countries. Indeed, it may well be that this quality is almost as strong in the Soviet Union as it is in the United States. It is obvious that to manipulate the Soviet population the regime will be less effective if it uses force or coercion than if it juggles opportunities and rewards in the form of occupational advancement and other tangible and intangible goods.

4. Despite great hostility to the Stalinist rule of terror, and profound resentment against the depressed standard of living, the great majority of Soviet citizens seem to find much that is acceptable in the system. This applies particularly to the idea of government ownership and operation of industry, transportation, and most trade, and to the concept of the welfare state exemplified in government guarantees of work, medical care, and education. Opportunities for social mobility are sensed and appreciated, probably beyond what the actual situation warrants. There is great pride in the industrial attainments of the

society and in the apparent 'cultural' development of the country, as represented in the theatrical arts, music, literature, painting, sculpture, and, to a lesser degree, architecture, The performance of both the government and the people during the war and the period of reconstruction is a source of admiration and pride, tinged with a sense of wonder. The central position of the Soviet Union in world affairs is a source of gratification. 'The Soviet power' is a big thing, which no one takes lightly.

5. Resentment of the oppressive features of the Soviet system took, in some instances, violent and explosive form—a total or global rejection of everything 'Communist' and Soviet. However, for most people grievances tended to be highly concrete and specific. The main themes were 'end the terror,' 'slow up the pace of economic life,' 'improve the standard of living,' and so on. The execution of the program, rather than the conception itself, was deemed bad. Even though the essential disparity between the Soviet system as idea and as reality was grasped, there was still a woeful failure to generate alternatives which commanded respect or attention. The Soviet refugees often left with people the impression that there was not only little understanding but little need felt for the *strictly constitutional* apparatus of guarantees, rights, and safeguards which characterize the democracy of Western Europe. Good rulers, kind, considerate rulers, who 'cared' for people, did not terrorize them or push them too hard, would be quite acceptable, especially if they provided an increasing standard of living and opportunities for personal advancement.

6. Most Soviet citizens seem to have accepted the main outlines of the official image of foreign affairs disseminated by the official media. They see the United States government as dominated by powerful groups who seem committed to waging a war of destruction against the Soviet Union and other countries. They imagine a vast conspiracy by the West to prevent colonial and underdeveloped areas from attaining their independence and achieving their rightful national aspirations for peaceful economic development. There is substantial pride in Soviet strength and the image of the USSR as a leading world force. The Soviet government is believed to be a champion of peace and a defender of the small and weak. Soviet citizens are eager for peace and the smaller burden of arms a stable world order would yield. But they do not assume they understand the complexities of world politics, and they

incline overwhelmingly to leave these issues to the leaders 'who understand these things, and know best.'

After Stalin's death his successors acted with intelligence and forcefulness to eliminate or reduce most of the prime sources of popular resentment and discontent which Stalin left them as part of their political heritage. They did this by drastically reducing the application of terror, taking measures tangibly to improve living standards, and giving more meaning to the welfare state guarantees of free education, medical care, and old age security. They also reduced the intensity of the pressures put on intellectuals and the enormity of the controls placed on administrators and economic managers, and made substantial concessions to the peasant. No one of these concessions and grants to the people is necessarily 'permanent.' Neither do they represent 'permanent' solutions of the several social problems to which they were a response. Their significance lay mainly in the evidence they offered that the leaders were aware of the greatest sources of tension and the worst grievances in the system, and were willing and able to take effective measures to deal with the situation. This suggests, therefore, that even within the structure of the perhaps unstable Soviet oligarchy, there are greater capacities for change and adjustment than many have been willing to allow.

The leaders' capacity to make such adjustments argues well for the short-run stability of the system. It does not, however, insure its long-range stability, nor does it give us any sure guidelines as to what that long-range stability will be like.

The most crucial argument posed against the compatibility of the Soviet political system and its newly developed modern industrial order is that the very development of Soviet industry and the modernization of Soviet society—with its emphasis on rationality, its dependence on science and research, its ever-increasing corps of well-educated and well-trained engineers, managers, and other professionals —has made the usual Soviet pattern of operation unsuited to the needs of Soviet society and unacceptable to the new managerial class which ultimately holds power in its hands.

There is in this argument more assertion, or perhaps faith, than hard substance. To begin with, there is hardly much evidence to support the assertion that education by itself generates a love of freedom.

It was, after all, a country with one of the best educated populations and one with the largest groups of industrialists, engineers, scientists, and other educated men which treated us to the experience of Hitlerite Germany. And there are few who will deny the widespread, indeed pervasive, support he received among the educated classes in the military, business, industry, education, and other realms. In the second place, and perhaps more important, there is good reason to believe that the underlying principles of Soviet political control over the *ends* or goals of economic and administrative behavior are accepted by most Soviet engineers and managers, indeed are willingly supported by them. They accept these as 'political' decisions to be decided by political specialists. They are, in other words, largely withdrawn from politics, 'organization men' similar to their counterparts in the United States. Their main complaint in the past was not over the principle of directing the economy, but rather over arbitrary political interference in predominantly technical decisions, the unreasonably high goals often set in the face of insufficient resources to meet them, and the treatment of failures in judgment or performance by management as if they were acts of political defiance or criminal negligence. Since Stalin's death such abuse has been tremendously reduced. Soviet managers seem, on the whole, quite satisfied with the situation.

Of course, there is always the risk that the political leaders will overreach themselves, and in seeking to maintain their own initiative will violate the rights of the managerial class so flagrantly as to provoke retaliation. The facts of recent experience indicate such a sense of outrage is not easily aroused. The top political leadership has been able to effect massive changes in the formal structure of economic administration in the Soviet Union without any sign of major resistance or even disturbance. Indeed, even the outstanding military leader of the country has been dismissed summarily without apparent serious repercussions. While these very events were in progress, the Soviet Union successfully launched two earth satellites, which hardly argues that it is having great difficulty either in motivating its scientists and engineers or in organizing their efforts effectively around important governmental programs.

This conclusion should not be taken to mean that the regime will not make further adjustments in its domestic administrative arrangements in the interests of efficiency. Such changes may, on occasion, be popular with the technicians and administrators, may even be taken at their suggestion. But it would be unwise to see in such adjustments some kind of managerial revolution, the forerunner of some basic reorientation of Soviet policy.

There is, of course, one group which could reorient that policy—the ruling political elite of the Soviet Union. No one can, of course, assert with confidence that he knows the intentions of the Soviet leadership. Yet it is essential that we make some estimate. The following represents one such estimate:

1. Soviet leaders still believe that fundamentally there is an immanence in history, which requires that it progress through certain clear stages toward an eventual world condition in which all 'capitalist' societies, including what they call its 'bourgeois democratic' forms, will have been replaced by 'Communist' societies. They read recent history as validating this proposition, and they see the process of transition as in full swing. As Molotov expressed it, "All roads lead to communism."

2. The roads to communism are, however, not all straight or easy. The process is complex, and proceeds not only through wars and revolutions but through nationalism, economic crises, diplomatic maneuver, cultural exchange, and other means.

3. What advances this movement at any particular moment cannot be decided by chance, but rather requires a guiding intelligence and active support from some base of strength. The base of strength they assume lies in the Soviet Union, a conviction which makes it easy to identify and indeed even to confuse Russian national interests with those of the international Communist movement. The guiding intelligence is assumed to be provided by the leadership of the Soviet Communist Party, which makes it easy to blur the distinction between the domestic power interest of that group and the power interests of the leaders of Communist movements in other nations.

4. The Soviet leaders will take no action which seriously endangers either the Soviet home base or their position in command of it. This means that they will not undertake any action which they are reasonably certain would precipitate a global war with the newer weapons of mass destruction. It seems highly unlikely that they would risk a

surprise war, even if they had a substantial technological edge. Although here we cannot be so sure, it also seems unlikely that they would support another Korean-type action, that is, an action which meant putting troops across a major national border we have given fairly clear intention to defend, for fear of the extension of such conflict to the respective home bases.

5. At the same time, the campaign to spread Soviet influence, to weaken the Western world, and to capture additional areas for communism will continue unabated. The main front for action will be the former colonial and other underdeveloped areas in the Middle East, Asia, and Africa. The campaign will, however, continue to have a definite 'new look,' in which the national aspirations of former colonial people are seemingly supported, economic aid will be extensive, cultural exchange featured. The Soviets have, indeed, launched a massive campaign intended to create an image of themselves as the world's leading scientific, cultural, social, and humanistic force. This strains the Soviet system, however, and makes any safe reduction of the arms burden of substantial interest to them.

6. While this process of nibbling away at the periphery is in progress, it is essential to neutralize or minimize the extent of the opposition from the Western world and to soften it up as much as possible for its eventual fateful days of transition to communism. This demands: (a) Disarming the Western alliance by weakening its awareness of the ultimate threat to its way of life. The peace campaign is the main weapon. Intellectual, cultural, and other exchanges are part of this campaign, though not solely based on such considerations. (b) Weakening the Western alliance. This has the objective of weakening concerted action to resist Soviet expansion in the uncommitted areas and of reducing the extent of the active military threat to the Soviet home base, should something go awry and total war ensue.

7. Beyond this Soviet leaders have no clear program, since they clearly now entertain serious doubts as to the instability of the free societies of the West. They hope that while they work on the periphery, which can surely occupy them for two decades or more, the long-expected domestic economic crises in America and Europe may yet come to pass.

There are three main sources from whence a fundamental change in the pattern of Soviet development may spring, especially as it affects the Soviet impact on the rest of the world. One possibility is that the problem of the succession crisis will never be solved; eventually one of the struggles for power at the top will break out in the open, and in the process of resultant conflict the old order will be destroyed. Although the possibility certainly cannot be discounted, such an event is of a rather low order of probability, especially in the light of Khrushchev's recent ascendancy. Yet we would be unwise to assume that the inevitable outcome of such a struggle would be a democratic Russia. On the contrary, it is highly likely that whoever was the victor in such a struggle would in his turn impose the standard pattern of totalitarian rule, and probably with renewed vigor.

A second possibility is that a future breakup of the Soviet satellite empire, as exemplified by the revolt in Hungary and the relative defection of Poland, might have sufficiently serious repercussions within the Soviet Union to change materially the path of Soviet development. There are major sources of instability in the Soviet empire, or coalition, although it does not seem *markedly* unstable. But even if there were serious defections from Soviet control, there is no compelling reason to assume the response within the Soviet Union would be in the direction of democracy. On the contrary, there is great likelihood that, under such circumstances, there would be increased totalitarianism in an effort to recapture lost or ebbing control over the satellites.

A third prospect is that the industrial maturation of Soviet Russia, the mellowing of its social structure, will 'erode' the dictatorship and set in motion important processes of social change which will lead to a democratization of Soviet society, and perhaps also a transformation of its foreign policy. While such a transformation is to be hoped for, it seems hardly to be counted on. The Soviet system *has* changed. Yet the formidable challenge which faces the world rises not from the unchanging character of the Soviet Union but precisely from the fact that its present leaders have been able to make adjustments in the Soviet social structure which have adapted it to take account of the earlier development of the society. The crucial point is that they have done so without sacrificing the basic features of the system—the monopoly of power in the elite of the one-party system, the absolute dominance of the state in the control and direction of economic life, the limitation of freedom of opinion and expression to those few cases and to that degree which the regime regards as politically harmless, and the use of force or extralegal measures, however selective, to impose the will of the leaders in such a way as to make an ultimate mockery of the law and constitution. It is no less autocratic and certainly not *more* democratic, if by that we mean supremacy of law and individual rights. But such a society is more, not less, a challenge to the free world. The leadership may have lost some of its freedom of maneuver, in the sense that it can no longer so readily commit the whole nation to an assault on objectives the people do not support. But the regime is far compensated by the vastly increased popular support for the objectives to which it has committed the nation. And it presents an immeasurably improved façade to the world.

In the balance hangs the decision as to what the dominant cultural and political forms of human endeavor will be for the remainder of this century and perhaps beyond. It is, perhaps, only a little thing that separates the Soviet world from the West—freedom. Inside the Soviet Union there are some who ultimately are on our side. But they are a minority, perhaps a small one. Their ranks were first decimated by Stalin and later thinned by the refugee exodus. We had therefore better turn our face elsewhere, rest our hopes on other foundations than on the hope that the Soviet system will mellow and abandon its long-range goals of world domination. We must look for our defense to the capacity of our own social order to yield fuller, richer, more dignified life *under freedom* not only for ourselves but for the uncommitted, the half committed, the neutralists, and even those who have already cast their lot with the Soviet Union. If we are not equal to the task, we will leave it to the Soviet Union to set the pattern of human existence for the next half century.

Soviet-American Relations: Problems of Choice and Decision

HENRY L. ROBERTS

"It is only against a background of hard reality that choices count." This observation by Ben Shahn in *The Shape of Content* applies to much more than the world of the artist. Indeed, in the realm of international affairs I am increasingly impressed with the difficulties of discussing choices of policy without close and continuing touch with reality and without the burden of responsibility. This is not to suggest that discussion should be confined to governmental circles—any such limitation would be both impossible and undesirable. But just as it is hard for a person to understand the game of poker (unlike chess) unless he plays for real money, so the effort to discuss policy formation away from the point of decision where choice must be turned into action can lead to serious and possibly dangerous misconceptions.

At least three fallacies may be involved in making international policy decisions: the failure to think in context, the oversimplification of the problem, and the demand for omniscience and omnipotence. All three errors occur commonly in the area of Soviet-American relations, where the issues are incredibly complex and difficult, the stakes fearful, and self-evident answers not at hand.

There is nothing mysterious or unusual about the need to think in context. We do it all the time in making personal or family decisions. Any parent who has had to take an action concerning his child's health or education is aware of the distinction between a decision accompanied by the burden of responsibility and the advice or recommendation of an outsider, whatever the latter's qualifications or competence. It

Published in the *Texas Quarterly* (Summer-Autumn 1958).

Henry L. Roberts, author of *Russia and America: Dangers and Prospects* (New York, 1956) and other studies, is Director of the Russian Institute of Columbia University.

seems difficult, however, to transfer this distinction to the larger, more remote, and less personal spheres of national and international politics. The result is a characteristic type of policy proposal, often containing a fruitful or suggestive idea, which is presented as matter for choice or decision but which in fact is nothing of the sort. These proposals may originate in the press, in academic circles, or even in branches of the government itself; what they lack is not necessarily sobriety or insight but the sense of context.

For example, the proposal that the United Nations be given a monopoly of arms, or that the United States double its aid to underdeveloped countries, or that Germany be reunited by a mutual disengagement of NATO and Warsaw treaty forces, or that the United States support colonial peoples against the metropolitan powers (or vice versa)—while each concerns real problems and could conceivably be part of a program of action, it is not amenable to simple acceptance or rejection. It is not that the responsible policy-maker must be a cautious trimmer—at times neither caution nor hedging is possible—but that he must operate within a setting in which timing, the form in which particular issues emerge, the general state of domestic as well as foreign politics, and indeed his own personality and style of performance are an integral part of the act of decision. Neglect of this obvious fact only creates unwarranted hopes in panaceas, and a necessarily frustrated demand for 'bold new programs.'

The second fallacy represents an effort to reduce the 'hard reality' with which we are confronted to more manageable terms. Certainly it is useful to develop concepts and techniques that may bring at least partial order out of the chaos of international politics. The fallacy appears when we begin to play games with ourselves at the expense of our grasp of reality. Several examples come to mind. One is the attempt to proceed deductively from some such concept as 'the national interest': the term is defined and then national objectives and policies are expected to flow from it like Euclidean corollaries. Usually the 'national interest' turns out either to be a tautological or circular definition or to represent special pleading for a particular line of policy which was in mind at the beginning of the exercise.

A second device for simplifying a particularly ambiguous and intricate problem is that of setting up 'alternatives,' as though forming policies were like selecting one French pastry from a number on a tray. There is a deceptive modesty about this device. All sides are presented and the choice is left open. But even when the presentation is not stacked in favor of one alternative, there is a serious difficulty. How is one supposed to make the final choice? If there are additional and decisive considerations, they must be introduced, in which case one alternative may clearly be called for; if it is just a matter of flipping a coin, we are no longer in the area of serious political decision. Moreover, the pattern of alternatives, while perhaps attractive architecturally, frequently does not represent real choices open to the policymaker. In retrospect, 'containment versus liberation' appears to have been an untenable set of alternatives; the actual problems confronting the United States in Germany and Eastern Europe were such that we could not make a choice in these terms.

A third device for stating a complicated problem in manageable terms is the method of 'abstraction,' an effective tool of analysis in some situations, but liable to dispose of the baby along with the bath water in others. For example, to abstract Soviet political motivations while studying the economic objectives of Russia's foreign trade and aid activities would probably cause more confusion than clarity. Related to this procedure is the 'tentative hypothesis.' A year or so ago I encountered the suggestion that it would be good to study the requirements of American policy over the next decade under two differing assumptions: (a) that the Soviet regime remained strong and cohesive, (b) that the Soviet regime suffered internal strains and disintegration. Unfortunately, most of the problem lies precisely in these assumptions, and it is evident that the answers resulting from such a study would be of little use.

Finally, in attempts to simplify a highly complex situation there is the tendency to speak in terms of a 'calculated risk'—in the event of an uprising in Eastern Europe the United States should supply aid, as a 'calculated risk.' Whatever the merits of such an action, it is surely anything but a 'calculated risk' (unless we mean simply, it is risky and we know it). The likelihood of the various possible outcomes is demonstrably incalculable, as is the relationship between the odds and the size of the stakes. Risks may have to be taken in our dealings with the Soviet Union, but it adds nothing to introduce a spurious if comforting sense of mathematical precision. A statistician could demonstrate, quite rigorously, that such major political decisions simply do not lend themselves to treatment in terms of probabilities.

The third type of fallacy also arises from the complexity of Soviet-American relations. Those whose thinking is clouded by this fallacy, instead of oversimplifying the picture, fall into the opposite fault of demanding of those responsible for policy, usually by implication, omniscience and omnipotence.

Perhaps the most significant form of this fallacy is the capabilities-intentions analysis, which is useful in dealing with a limited and definable situation but which can get out of hand when applied to the Soviet Union. By this procedure we undertake to discover *what* our opponent wants to do and whether he has the wherewithal to do it; the combined estimate which emerges then provides the basis for our requirements. Unfortunately, the distinction between capabilities and intentions is not as clear-cut as it might appear to be. The meaning and significance of capabilities may depend upon the intentions behind them and may not even be usefully measurable without reference to those intentions. Conversely, certain intentions may not be directly ascertainable but must be inferred from the nature and growth of the capabilities. Beyond that, of course, Soviet capabilities and intentions are not independent variables; both are in constant interaction with American capabilities and intentions, and any estimate for the future must take account of the additional influence of this interaction.

But the real trouble with this line of analysis, in dealing with the Soviet Union, is that requirements of the type it assigns to the United States are, in the end, both limitless and without criteria for priorities. It is not hard to show that, if we try to devise a pattern of complete insurance against an opponent of equal present and future military, economic, and political capabilities, whose intentions may be to work against us with any available means—except perhaps those which are self-destructive—we have set ourselves an insoluble problem. The debate on the kinds of warfare we should be prepared to fight—general thermonuclear, conventional, tactical-atomic, brushfires, and so forth—has been plagued with this difficulty. Reliance on any one form of defense fails to take account of the potentialities inherent in Soviet capabilities and possible intentions; the attempt to develop military capabilities to meet all contingencies appears to involve an impossibly heavy burden. And, of course, the Soviet Union may prefer to stick to the 'peace' line and economic penetration.

In other words, we are in danger of being in the situation of an individual who tries to buy insurance policies against all eventualities, including insurance against bankruptcy from paying his premiums. If the second fallacy, that of oversimplification, attempts to get around the 'hard reality' of Soviet-American relations by avoiding some of the awkward features of that reality, the third, of which the capabilities-intentions analysis is only one example, suffers from the attempt to impose a total solution, a task which is probably not within the realm of possibility.

There is little doubt that these difficulties and frustrations have contributed to the periodic attempt to break through the uncomfortable and exasperating terms of the problem, either by demanding a 'forcible showdown'—though these demands have been less in evidence with the arrival of the ballistic missile—or by deciding that the Soviet regime is evolving into a more amiable and cooperative form of government, a pleasant thought but one for which there is no convincing evidence.

The answer, however, cannot lie in denying the question. We would do better to recognize that it is a 'hard reality' we face. It is not a 'game' to be played: the rules are not given and we cannot pull out and go home. It is not even a problem, properly speaking, since there is no given solution.

This does not mean, however, that rational decisions are impossible. Nor are we caught in an inexorable historical process against which our actions are in vain—though the Soviet leaders may think so. But, as in all human situations, the task is one of coping with, rather than solving, a series of concrete challenges which are never quite the same and never entirely different.

Probably the best approach to decisions under these circumstances is that of a continuing dialogue, or debate. Actually there are two debates going on simultaneously, one between us and the Communist leaders, an antagonistic debate, and one among ourselves, domestically and with our allies, a consultative debate. These debates, which include actions as well as words, both influence and are influenced by the development of Soviet-American relations, and at the same time provide the material for policy decisions.

It is important to realize that the relations between the Soviet Union and the United States are not fully reciprocal; the absence of symmetry in the motivations, goals, and organization of these two great states makes it quite inappropriate to regard their controversy as simply a 'great-power conflict.' Nevertheless, they constantly interact upon each other, to the extent that by now the political and diplomatic position of either is unintelligible without reference to the other. Both, in other words, are in part a product of their continuing encounter. This being so, it is to be expected that the policy decisions will be in the setting of this antagonistic debate, the terms of which will shift as the debate continues. The end of the debate is not in sight.

The domestic debate is in good part a response to the external debate, a constantly recurring effort to work out patterns of action that can meet the shifting requirements. The debate may follow party lines, or it may cross them. It is rarely conclusive, partly because the terms of the debate change, or appear to change, partly because neither line of recommended action may be feasible. Still, for all the uncertainty and lack of precision, choices are made, actions are taken.

If we review the course of the years since the end of the Second World War, we find that the pattern of debate—both domestic and foreign—has passed through several distinct stages, each raising different questions and each producing a different set of responses. The first of these, which lasted roughly from 1945 through 1947, was dominated by the confusion resulting from Russia's role as a wartime ally against Germany and its subsequent promotion of active Communist expansion. While the terms of our postwar relationship were being debated internationally in a series of increasingly hostile and sterile conferences, the domestic debate was expressed in the terms 'toughness versus cooperation.' For a time our national policy tried to combine the two—in Secretary Byrnes' phrase, 'patience with firmness'—but the hope for cooperation proved vain.

In the second period, from 1948 to 1953 or 1954, the terms of the problem were quite different: internationally the lines were drawn, the Iron Curtain was down, the cold war was in progress, accompanied by a shooting war in Korea. Domestically the pattern of debate was expressed in the terms 'containment versus liberation.' While the debate was exaggerated by polemical fireworks and while the choices were considerably more complex than is suggested by these two words, there was an important problem to be explored through this debate, a problem set by the existing international conflict. By this time there was general agreement that the Soviet Union was an opponent with hostile intentions, not just a suspicious war-ravaged power. The difference lay in the definition of our response. Put in simple terms, the position of 'containment' held that our national strategy should be to hold the existing line between the Communist and non-Communist spheres, work hard to strengthen and unite the free world, but not to press for a rollback of Soviet control and influence from areas of post-war expansion. While there were hopes that such containment might cause the Soviet system to fester internally, the principal argument was that our national security could be maintained by this means and without the threat to peace that a policy of 'liberation' appears to carry with it. The argument for liberation, which involved pressing Soviet power at least back to the Russian frontier, was that mere containment gave the advantage of initiative to the other side, would lead to an erosion of the free world, and would ultimately imperil our own security. Hence, even with a possibly greater chance of conflict, the areas of freedom had to be expanded when and where possible.

As it turned out, neither line of argument was able to produce very relevant answers to certain problems that our policy-makers had to contend with. Containment had little to offer with regard to a divided Germany; liberation faltered when it came to dealing with uprisings in the Soviet orbit. As a matter of fact, American policy, Democratic and Republican, contained elements of both positions, but not because any higher synthesis had been achieved.

The fact that neither containment nor liberation has much currency today would suggest that we have passed on to a new stage in our relations with the Soviet Union. One factor leading to this shift was that both earlier positions conceived of the division between the two systems as being a territorial line, at which you stood, or from which you retreated, or across which you advanced. But this linear concept, while corresponding to the existence of Communist and non-Communist states with frontiers between them, raised problems when it came to a divided state like Germany, and it didn't encompass such significant features of the international scene as the movement of ideas, broadcasts and propaganda, Communist and pro-Communist parties in the free world, and rifts within the Communist bloc. Perhaps even more significant was the advent of thermonuclear weapons and the ballistic missile. War and weapons could not be thought of in the same spatial terms in which they had been considered in the past. The terms 'containment' and 'liberation' seem increasingly inappropriate as we contemplate the fantastic revolution in the art of warfare that we, and the Soviet Union, are creating.

The death of Stalin and his successors' tentative experiments with some measure of 'decompression' also contributed to this shift in perspectives. The domestic Soviet 'debate'—in the peculiarly bitter and murderous setting of that political system—may have had a function analogous to those in our own. On the whole, however, events of the last few months, and especially the renewed campaign against revisionism, would indicate more continuity with Stalinism than appeared in prospect in 1955 and 1956.

The combination of these various developments since 1953 seems to have set the division between the Communist and non-Communist worlds less in terms of lines or curtains than in terms of zones or areas, not necessarily to be defined geographically. Perhaps this can be best illustrated by reference to two terms that now appear frequently in discussions of Soviet-American relations, 'disengagement' and 'exchange.' (It may be noted that neither is included in the theme either of containment or of liberation.)

Proponents of 'disengagement' feel that the *status quo* with its unresolved tensions will be increasingly precarious as time passes. They also proceed from the premise that the Soviet regime, for the foreseeable future, will remain intact and largely invulnerable to external influences. From this it follows that any arrangement for altering the *status quo* must be through mutual agreement. Among the terms of such an agreement might be a withdrawal of armed forces from their more advanced position, usually in conjunction with a reunified but neutral Germany. Under such an agreement the Communist and free worlds are to be separated, not by an Iron Curtain, but by a large, uncommitted area or zone, created by concessions on both sides. This line of argument derives in part from certain apparent lessons of the Hungarian revolt: that even such an explosion did not undermine the effective power of the Soviet Union; that the United States was unable to support the revolt without risks which it was unprepared to take; that such upheavals in the satellite area merely increase Soviet vigilance and could, if they threatened to get out of hand, lead to war; but that the Soviet Union may feel overextended in some regions and might consent to a partial withdrawal if the Western powers made some corresponding move.

Against this impulse toward disengagement there is a contrary one toward greater engagement. This may take the form of 'exchanges'—cultural, academic, technical, and economic—or, if one prefers a grimmer term, of 'in-fighting.' As with the position of disengagement, there is agreement that the Iron Curtain is increasingly porous and may not be the decisive point of contact in the future. But this position would have some confidence that the reasons for the changes that took place in Poland and Hungary may also, in time, be operative in the Soviet Union itself. Hence one accepts the challenge or risks of mutual interpenetration of the two systems, not with any simple hope of achieving neighborly relations, but in the expectation that this will foster, in some fashion and at some time, beneficial change within the USSR itself.

It is obvious that both approaches have their difficulties, and neither is able to guarantee the achievement of its objective. On the one hand, the Soviet leaders have given no sign that they are prepared to witness the de-Communization of an area that has once been Communized; on the contrary, they have stated explicitly that this is not to be permitted. Disengagement may be blocked by this formidable obstacle. On the other hand, the recently renewed emphasis on orthodoxy shows that the Soviet leaders are fully aware of the danger of ideological erosion or backsliding through contact with the 'imperialists.' This may effectively block the hoped-for consequences of exchange.

Whatever their prospects of success, these two approaches diverge in several respects from earlier policy and also emphasize some different and possibly incompatible lines of action. The diplomatic stance for a policy of disengagement, with its overtone of non-intervention and non-involvement, may not fit easily with the more active scrambling of closer engagement. And yet it is doubtful that a clear-cut choice of either is feasible, for reasons indicated earlier. Decisions must be made in context, whether in connection with negotiations on exchange of persons, or in meeting a Soviet proposal for a summit conference, or in gauging the significance of a new crisis in the Soviet orbit. The issue is not one between theory and practice, or between principle and expediency, but between relevance and irrelevance. Our actions must be relevant to the threat, challenge, or opportunity of the given situation. The function of these approaches is not to serve as blueprints for policy but to indicate avenues of possible action, to suggest the implications of particular acts, and to warn against certain pitfalls.

The emphasis placed in these pages upon the importance of concrete decisions by officials with the burden of responsibility does not mean that public discussion of foreign policy and general analysis of the international scene is a waste of time. This is certainly not the case. The argument here is not for policy-making by an exclusive group of officials nor for spur-of-the-moment decisions. While it may, in fact, be impossible for the United States to have a completely articulated foreign policy designed to cover all contingencies, and while many private citizens will continue to feel aggrieved at the failure of our administrations to come out with electrifying new programs, constant debate on these matters and the continuing effort to relate general principles to specific requirements are at the heart of the democratic process. Indeed, it may prove to be that this circulation of ideas, the creation of at least partial solutions from the play of divergent views, is a significant source of strength in our encounter with the Soviet Union. While the Soviet leaders, at times, display greater flexibility in their diplomatic tactics than we are able to do—a natural consequence of their governmental structure—it remains true that their great enemy is spontaneity, which, as events of 1956 and 1957 demonstrated, is always a danger to their political system. Their practice of alternating repression and relaxation may have some effect in stimulating and reviving, but, like artificial respiration, it is no real substitute for the natural breathing of a free society.

Changing Appreciation of the Soviet Problem

MARSHALL D. SHULMAN

Whether we articulate them or not, the assumptions that we make concerning the future development of the Soviet system are fundamental to our thinking about American foreign policy. The objectives toward which we can reasonably direct our efforts, the philosophy of our situation, are in a very large measure a function of the image we have in our minds of the changes we discern or anticipate in the character of the society and the government of the Russian people.

In recent years we have come to learn a great deal about aspects of the Soviet Union, certainly much more than is reflected in public discussion. But of the actual distribution of power within the Soviet system or of the laws governing the development of a modern totalitarian state, we still know very little. Necessarily, our thoughts regarding the changes which time can be expected to produce in this confrontation lead us into the realm of speculative projection from rather tenuous data.

The data at our disposal are, however, constantly increasing, and the assumptions on which we are operating require constant examination. It is evident that the present period is witnessing changes of a profound character in the Communist world, although it is certainly too soon to say with assurance what these changes signify, let alone to describe what they are. Even such fragments of information as are suggested by recent developments in the Soviet situation open up perspectives of the problem more profoundly challenging for American policy, both foreign and domestic, than have yet been faced in current discussion of these matters.

Published in *World Politics* (July 1958).

Marshall D. Shulman, a specialist in Soviet foreign policy, is Associate Director of the Russian Research Center at Harvard Univeristy.

1

Whatever one might think of the Soviet regime, the Soviet achievements in World War II made it necessary to think about it in a somewhat longer-term perspective than many had been accustomed to before the war. As Stalin justifiably boasted in his electoral speech of 1946, the Soviet Union could no longer be regarded as a transient phenomenon.

For the most part, the prevailing conception which was brought to this longer perspective was of the Soviet Union as a variant of the Western pattern of political and economic development. Those who were sympathetically inclined continued to see the Soviet Union as an advance in Western social development, and analogized from Western revolutionary experience in deriving their expectations of its future course. Projecting a normative life cycle for revolutions, they anticipated that time could be expected to bring about a diminution of its harsher aspects and that the social advance would remain in a domesticated form. To those who were more critically disposed, it was also possible to conceive of the Soviet order as an aberration from the normal, that is, the Western, pattern of development, the degree of aberration representing the extent of the contradiction between reality and the Soviet path of development. In this view it was anticipated that events would oblige the rulers of the Soviet Union to realize the error, if not the unfeasibility, of their ways, and in time to return to a more 'normal' pattern of development and of relationship with other nations. If the Soviet leaders persisted in their error, it was felt, they would in time be replaced by another and more realistic regime.

In his remarkable article "The Sources of Soviet Conduct," published eleven years ago, under the pseudonym 'X,' Mr. George Kennan proposed that the frustration of Russia's expansionist tendencies would be likely to lead either to the breakup or to the 'gradual mellowing' of Soviet power.[1] The argument was based upon the assumption that the Soviet Union was faced with powerful internal strains: economic weakness and imbalance, the exhaustion and disaffection of the population, the problem of succession, the difficulty of bringing the younger generation into the system of power, and other factors which added up to the

---

[1] *Foreign Affairs*, XXV, No. 4 (July 1947), 566-82.

strong possibility that the Soviet power bore within itself the seeds of its own decay in a less-than-ultimate sense. These strains would, if Soviet external pressures were met and blocked by counterforce, produce fundamental changes in the character of the regime, presumably moderating the features responsible for the situation of conflict with the rest of the world. Leaving aside the question of the validity of the general proposition, whose essential condition was only partly realized in the following period, the question involved here is what expectation was suggested by the concept of the 'mellowing' of Soviet power. What Mr. Kennan himself had in mind was more fully set forth in another essay, "America and the Russian Future," which he published in 1951.[2] There are many aspects of this landmark essay deserving of attention, but our interest at the moment is in the nature of the image it projected of the possible forms of development of the Soviet system.

Recognizing that the primary responsibility for enduring change in the Soviet system would have to come from within and that there were rather narrow limits to what could be achieved from abroad, Mr. Kennan set forth a course of action for the United States that he believed most likely to influence Soviet development in the desired direction. His emphasis was upon perfecting our own society, so that we might set an example of 'spiritual distinction.' He took for granted the mounting of military strength and cohesiveness in the Western world, the necessity for which had been generally accepted by this time, and said that the purpose of this policy should be "to convince the masters of the Kremlin that their grand design is a futile and unachievable one, persistence in which promises no solution of their own predicaments and dilemmas."[3]

Mr. Kennan believed it possible, but unlikely, that desired changes could come about by evolution, "by erosion from despotism rather than by the violent upthrust of liberty." Chiefly, this was because he felt that the modern police state, unlike the despotisms of the past, does not have behind it 'a driving political will,' does not concern itself with the well-being of the people over whom it rules, does not recognize an obligation to the future, relies chiefly upon terror and coercion to maintain its power. He saw not only a dichotomy but a smoldering

[2] *Ibid.*, XXIX, No. 3 (April 1951), 351-70.
[3] *Ibid.*, p. 370.

hostility between the small ruling group and the Russian people, and expressed faith that any such system, "based on the evil and weakness in man's nature," could never achieve genuine stability.

It was no use, Mr. Kennan warned, expecting Russia to become capitalist and liberal-democratic, with institutions like our own. We had to anticipate a continuation of the collective tradition, although in agriculture, which he saw as the Achilles' heel of the Soviet system, one could anticipate voluntary cooperatives instead of forcible collectives. Three minimum changes were required, however, for Russia to become the kind of a country we could live with in peace: abolition of the iron curtain, elimination of imperialist expansion and oppression, and elimination of totalitarian controls over the Russian population. These apart, the Russian people should be allowed to work out their internal problems in their own manner.

Subsequent thinking on the possibilities for change in the Soviet system has been substantially influenced by two developments: first, the death of Stalin and the transfer of power to his successors have been handled by the regime not without incident but, so far at least, without the upheaval that many had anticipated; and, second, Soviet economic and technological progress has continued at an extraordinary rate and has, so far at least, managed to surmount agricultural, transportation, and other vulnerabilities as problems rather than as crises.

Perhaps the highest degree of optimism in the period following the death of Stalin was to be found in the writings of Mr. Isaac Deutscher, who argued that economic progress and the spread of literacy in the Soviet Union made possible—indeed, had already begun to produce—a transmutation of the Soviet system to a form of social democracy.[4] Although few other writers went as far, many began to explore the implications of the impact of industrialization upon Soviet society and speculated on the ultimate effects of the emergence of a middle class, of a class of bureaucrats and technicians, with varying expectations.[5]

[4] *Russia—What Next?* (Oxford, 1953).
[5] E. H. Carr, "The Structure of Soviet Society," *The Listener*, LIV, No. 1379 (August 4, 1955), 167-68, and a letter by Hugh Seton-Watson to the editor of *The Listener* on the above article, *ibid.*, No. 1380 (August 11, 1955), pp. 222-23; Barrington Moore, Jr., *Terror and Progress — USSR* (Cambridge, Massachusetts, 1954); Carl J. Friedrich, ed., *Totalitarianism* (Cambridge, Massachusetts, 1954).

Even before the appearance of the Soviet earth satellite brought this point home forcibly and perhaps traumatically to the American public, it had become evident to students of Soviet affairs that the remarkable Soviet economic and technological progress made obligatory a revision of any expectations of a collapse of the regime resulting from the unsoundness of its economic base.

In 1956, for example, Mr. Henry Roberts, in his excellent summation of the Soviet problem, based upon a two-year study by a group of prominent Americans, indicated the impact of these developments on our thinking. "There is no question," he wrote, "but that the Soviet regime has made some remarkable achievements, and has been able to exploit the potentialities of twentieth-century technology and organization to a degree greater than we might have thought its cumbersome and doctrinaire outlook would permit."[6]

And when, in 1957, Mr. Kennan returned to the subject in his Reith lectures over the BBC, now published in the United States as *Russia, the Atom, and the West*, he began his series by acknowledging freely that Soviet economic progress had surpassed anything he had thought possible at the time of the 'X' article ten years before.

However, he is concerned lest we exaggerate the significance of this fact. In a part of his analysis which has received less public attention than other sections of the series,[7] Mr. Kennan endeavors to strike a new balance of the strengths and vulnerabilities of the Soviet system, and its prospects for change. He points to the imbalance of the Soviet economy, particularly in agriculture, and cites the familiar assurance that the Soviet rate of growth is likely to slow down as it runs out of the advantages of backwardness and begins to experience the problems common to other advanced industrial societies. In any case, material progress is not everything. The Russians, he finds, are inclined to be 'Babbitts' about their economic growth, just as we were some years ago, and they will become more mature about it in time. Despite Mr. Khrushchev's challenge, we are not in a contest between the two economies; rather we should welcome each advance of the Soviet economy. As to its effects upon the Soviet power position, Mr. Kennan is inclined to

[6] Roberts, *Russia and America: Dangers and Prospects* (New York, 1956), p. 20.
[7] *Russia, the Atom, and the West* (New York, 1958), pp. 2-31.

deprecate this concern, since "the danger is already so great that variations in degree do not have much meaning."

Mr. Kennan's equanimity about Soviet economic progress is strengthened by his estimate of the deepening crisis of Soviet political life. He holds that the Communist Party is in an unstable situation because of the existence outside of the Party of groups and interests that do not find, under the present system, representation in the political process. Another source of instability lies in the pressure of Soviet intellectuals, artists, and students for 'complete intellectual and cultural freedom,' which the Communist leaders cannot grant without undermining their own rule.

Mr. Kennan suggests, although he does not explicitly say so, that his expectations of an evolutionary pattern of development in the Soviet system are somewhat greater than they were at the time of his earlier writings, and he expresses the wish that "Russia's progress toward more mature political institutions might proceed with as little violence and trouble as possible."[8] In the meantime, as he has urged before, the chief means of countering the Soviet threat will be found in remedying our own failings: the racial problem, urban developemnt, education, and so forth.

The impression this suggests is that, in his anxiety to counteract errors of emphasis in the public mind, Mr. Kennan has unbalanced his argument in the other direction. He is out to dispel the overmilitarized and frenetic cold warrior in us, and to induce instead a state of dignified composure and moral perfectibility. The posture he evokes is appealing, but the question is whether it represents an appropriate or an adequate response to the problem in its present form.

2

What we know about the events of the past few years in the Soviet Union, fragmentary and inconclusive as the evidence may be, is suggestive of a much more complex and disturbing image of the pattern of development of the Soviet system than we have yet acknowledged. Although not necessarily contradictory of all that Mr. Kennan and

[8] *Ibid.*, p. 14.

others have been anticipating, the changes which seem to be in process lack some of the benignity and promise connoted by the term 'mellowing' and, instead of bringing us closer to a 'normalization' of our relations, seem more likely to effect our defeat.

Whereas ten years ago our policy proceeded on the confident assumption that 'time is on our side,' it is now the case that, unless we respond more adequately than we are doing to the situation created by Soviet internal and external developments, the reverse assumption appears the more probable.

Indeed, many things have happened in the Soviet Union in recent years which may in time turn out to have been part of a 'progress toward more mature political institutions.' But if the changes that have taken place turn out to be more than the cyclical alternations which have characterized Soviet policy from the beginning, the 'maturity' they adumbrate represents a greater rather than a lesser challenge, different in character perhaps from the one we are accustomed to, but more profoundly threatening over the course of time.

Ferment has been reported among Soviet students, artists, and intellectuals, and the intermittent widening and narrowing of the latitudes of discussion and of creative activities which have been permitted by the regime suggest an experimental approach to the question of the limits to be accepted. While a lessening of the degree of Party control over the arts would constitute in that measure progress toward a less totalitarian society, it is not necessarily a question of absolute control or absolute freedom, as is suggested in Mr. Kennan's image of the pressure from these quarters for 'complete intellectual and cultural freedom.' Insofar as one can judge from the outside, the pressure of the intellectuals appears to be directed chiefly at a reduction in the interference by the Party in cultural matters, and does not imply a widespread political dissidence toward the regime or an espousal of an alternative form of government.

The administrative decentralization, apart from its other significance, may permit a degree of local initiative, although ample means for central control remain through Party and planning channels. The elimination of the Machine Tractor Stations not only may portend a change in the collective farm system but, even more importantly, reflects a greater pragmatism in dealing with the organization of agriculture than would have been thought possible a few years ago. In responding to trouble in the satellites, the regime seems to be involved in a critical experiment as to the degree of variation in local patterns it can accept within its sphere, providing the adherence of the area to the Communist bloc is not in question. The somewhat greater emphasis on the production of consumer goods, the reported reduction in reliance upon military and administrative tribunals in the legal system, the less overt use of police surveillance, and the possibility of greater travel abroad and of more widespread cultural contacts with the non-Communist world —all these elements may portend a refinement and a modification in the nature of Soviet totalitarianism, although it would be disproportionate to regard these measures as 'democratization' in any Western sense of the word.

While it is possible, as some writers maintain, to picture these measures as reluctant concessions by the leadership to threatening pressures from within, it is at least as plausible to suggest that the easing of controls in certain areas of administrative and cultural life is possible because the fundamental allegiance of the population can be taken for granted, and that the interests of efficiency are better served by reliance upon voluntary service to the interests of the state. Such samplings as exist of present or former Soviet citizens indicate substantial dissidence only among the peasantry,[9] whereas the predominant view of the population as a whole appears to be one of acceptance of the regime because it 'works,' because it provides opportunity for individual advancement, some improvement from year to year in living conditions, and has had external successes. If a smoldering hostility exists between the Russian people as a whole and the Soviet regime, it is not reflected in the evidence available abroad.

Further, the Communist Party has shown skill in identifying and absorbing potential interest groups outside itself, and thus in preventing the growth of independent power elements in the society. As the Roberts study pointed out to those who count upon the army or the managerial elite to threaten the position of the Party, "while the Communist regime has been bureaucratized, the bureaucracy (including

[9] R. A. Bauer, Alex Inkeles, and Clyde Kluckhohn, *How the Soviet System Works* (Cambridge, Massachusetts, 1956).

the military) has been Communized."[10] In a recent study of the position of the Party, Professor Merle Fainsod comes to the conclusion that, at least to the present, the Party has shown a capacity for adaptation and growth, and that this has assisted it to maintain its primacy in Soviet society. "Better educated than their Stalinist predecessors, more technically oriented in their training and experience, the present-day Party functionaries have had to learn to balance zealotry with the pragmatic skills required to manage a complex industrial society."[11]

Although he feels that the authority of the present ruling group in the Party rests upon a precarious equilibrium which will be tested by the next succession crisis, Professor Fainsod finds no evidence in recent Soviet experience to suggest that the interests of the men who run the factories cannot be accommodated within a framework of totalitarian Party control without yielding them political power. "There is no iron law," he says, "which dictates incompatibility between one-party rule and a highly-developed industrial society."[12]

In considering the consequences of Soviet economic growth, while it might be unseemly, as Mr. Kennan instructs us, to groan each time the scoreboard shows a Soviet advance, it would be foolhardy to ignore the dangers for us in the relative statistics. At the very least, we cannot afford to ignore the dilemma that, while Soviet economic progress may over the long run present the hypothetical advantage of having certain desired effects upon Soviet society, it results in the meantime in a threat which is not hypothetical of a significant improvement in the Soviet power position relative to our own.

It may very well be true that, to the extent the Soviet regime commits itself to the production of consumer goods, this may over the long period circumscribe the freedom of action of the Soviet leadership in disposing of the nation's resources. So far, however, it must be said that the Soviet leaders have been able to make enough of a concession in the direction of consumer goods to have a beneficial political effect, domestic and foreign, without significantly reducing their capabilities in heavy industry and defense.

[10] Roberts, p. 27.

[11] "The Party in the Post-Stalin Era," *Problems of Communism*, VII, No. 1 (January-February 1958), 13.

[12] *Ibid.*

It may also be true that there are factors in the Soviet situation which may lead to a slowing of the rate of industrial growth, and indeed this may already be the case, but the comfort this affords is small, considering that the rate of growth of gross national product still remains and seems likely to remain something on the order of double our own. It is a milestone of enormous portent that the steel production of the Sino-Soviet bloc for the first time surpassed that of the United States in the first quarter of this year, according to the Director of the Central Intelligence Agency.[13]

That this is not just a matter of being outpointed at some game devised by Mr. Khrushchev is soberly documented in the account presented by Mr. Allen Dulles of the ways in which the advances in the Soviet economic and technological capabilities are leading to a strengthening of the relative power position of the Soviet Union in the world.

What is involved is not simply the production of a larger quantity of weapons, which Mr. Kennan perhaps rightly feels would not alter the situation a great deal, but a number of other uses of Soviet economic power which would indeed alter the situation qualitatively and for us disastrously. Apart from the possibility of a technical breakthrough in weapons development—which becomes ever more possible, given the increased Soviet capabilities in this direction—the more direct and immediate danger is the use by the Soviet Union of economic means to affect the political orientation of other countries. It is already the case that both advanced industrial areas and economically underdeveloped areas have shown susceptibility to the appeal of Soviet trade credits, and other instruments of economic penetration. It does not require an exercise of the imagination to anticipate the possibility of a number of areas of strategic importance becoming not necessarily communized but oriented toward Soviet policies and away from our own, as a result of the increased capabilities of the Soviet Union in the economic realm. The influence of the Soviet system as a model of rapid industrialization is reported as a tangible political factor by all who visit Asia and Africa. Technical breakthroughs by Soviet science and technology in matters that bear upon the living conditions of these

[13] Allen W. Dulles, speech to the U.S. Chamber of Commerce, *The New York Times*, April 29, 1958, p. 8.

populations would further contribute to the expansion of Soviet influence and power.

There is another point which should be mentioned in this connection. In his lecture on "The Soviet Mind and World Realities,"[14] Mr. Kennan finds one of the sources of conflict in the persistent misunderstanding by the Soviet leadership of the motives of the West. Distorted by the Marxist-Leninist ideology, their perceptions of "the things that make our life tick as it does" mislead the Soviet leaders and tend to perpetuate the situation of conflict. Presumably this error can be eradicated only by confronting the Soviet leadership over long periods of time with situations which will require them at last to make an adjustment in their mode of thought.

But what seems more to the point is not so much their understanding of our *motives*—a subjective factor which the Communists have been inclined to dismiss—as the extent to which their analysis of the dynamics of our political and economic system appears to them to have validity. And here it must be said that the events of recent years seem more likely to strengthen than to weaken the faith of the Soviet leadership in the validity of their conception of the dynamics of our society. Writing at this moment, under the impact of dramatic Soviet technological and economic achievements, contrasted with the current recession in the American economy, there may be a tendency to over-emphasize this consideration, but even before sputnik and the recession, the contraction of American power and influence cannot have appeared to the Soviet leaders to have contradicted their expectations. Soviet ideology has shown resilience in many respects, particularly in the realm of the tactics of transition to communism, and Soviet ideologists did experience some difficulty in explaining the high rate of industrial output in the United States; but the central element of the ideology, which rests upon a Marxist interpretation of the dynamics of our economic system, has for the most part survived the four decades of Soviet experience intact. What is most difficult for us to face is this: that events do not appear to have contradicted the conviction of the Soviet leaders that their directed economy has competitive advantages over the free market economy of the West in an age of advanced industrialism.

[14] Kennan, *Russia, the Atom, and the West*, pp. 21-24.

Nor, barring fortuitous developments in our behalf or a substantial change in our policies, do they appear likely to do so in the future.

What this brief reference to current trends in the Soviet system suggests is the possibility of a pattern of development toward a form for which we have neither the conceptual framework nor a nomenclature. Bearing in mind always that imponderable and fortuitous factors may influence the course of development of the Soviet system in ways that we cannot anticipate, we are obliged to face the hard implication of the direction pointed by present trends. There is at least the possibility that the Soviet system shows signs of development toward a more highly differentiated and stabilized state, perhaps less totalitarian in the degree of intervention of the Party in all aspects of the society, but still collectivized, authoritarian, and heavily centralized under the direction of a single party, which encompasses within itself the pluralist interests of a complex industrial order. There does not appear to be reason to believe that this development will be accompanied by a process which can be described as the 'normalization' of its external relations, in the sense that it involves a diminution of the Soviet commitment to the ultimate emergence of a Communist world system. On the contrary, it seems more probable that the Soviet system, evolving in its own terms, strengthening its military and economic capabilities, may represent an increasingly effective challenge for world influence with the passage of time.

Luck, of course, may be with us, and this picture may turn out to have been too dark. It is always possible, in a situation containing so many imponderable factors, that difficulties impossible to anticipate may rise up to alter the balance radically, but we cannot base our planning on a less sober estimate of the Soviet challenge than these indications present.

If this is the assumption on which we can reasonably base our thinking about the future, what follows from it? One thing certainly is that, separate from the plane of moral judgment, it is necessary for us to take the full measure of the Soviet system as an alternative form of the organization of society in the age of industrialism. That is to say that the pursuit of virtue in our democratic life, although by no means irrelevant, is not a substitute for the effective utilization by our society of its human and material resources. Questions of the ultimate values

of our society are, of course, involved; the word 'effective' immediately raises the question 'Toward what ends?' But the implication
of this challenge is that the validation of our convictions regarding
the values of a democratic society will depend on whether we are able
to relate them to the conditions of a highly advanced industrialism.

Beyond the problem of maintaining some kind of military equilibrium
with the Soviet bloc over a long period of time under conditions of a
rapidly changing military technology, and of countering Soviet political
and economic maneuvers, there is the more difficult and more fundamental question of whether over the years we shall be able to find ways
of expressing a national sense of purpose in the utilization of our resources more effective than the centralized planning and direction of
the Soviet system. It is likely that the measure of effectiveness in this
confrontation will be taken in terms of national power in the broadest
sense, military and nonmilitary, tangible and moral, including the satisfaction of the needs of the respective populations.

The ultimate question, in short, is not merely the wisdom of our
policies, but the adequacy of our institutions for the conduct of our
affairs both at home and abroad.

3

In the mood of collective introspection which the Soviet earth satellite
induced in the American people, many aspects of American life have
been looked at as though they had never been seen before, from professors' salaries to automobile tail-fins. But even before the general
public was aroused by this dramatic Soviet technical achievement,
here and there isolated sectors of the discussion over foreign policy
problems opened heretical chasms for examination.

In a study entitled *Foreign Policy and the Democratic Process*, the
British writer Max Beloff takes note of the "sustained and serious
debate" going on in the United States, and observes that it is "bound to
continue to probe until it calls into question the most fundamental
of all American beliefs: that of the absolute validity of the American
philosophy of government and of the institutions in which it has become
embodied."[15] The question to which Mr. Beloff addresses himself is the

---

[15] *Foreign Policy and the Democratic Process* (Baltimore, Maryland, 1955), p. 12.

adequacy of democratic processes for the conduct of foreign policy in the face of the Communist challenge, and in the light of the advantages possessed by a totalitarian society for concentration of effort, secrecy, and speed of action.

Another writer—also British, as it happens—Mr. G. L. Arnold, has invited our attention to the question "whether democratic politics can in time produce agreement on the degree of public planning necessary to preserve the social health of the non-Communist world." In a sketchy and neglected book entitled *The Pattern of World Conflict*, Mr. Arnold defines the cold war as "competitive attempts to alter the balance of power without overt resort to force,"[16] and urges upon us a planned international investment policy, providing for the interrelated needs of the advanced industrial and the economically underdeveloped areas of the non-Communist world.

Mr. Arnold is a member of what he describes as "the new hard-bitten generation of post-totalitarian liberals [which] is distinguished by a reluctant acceptance of the need for more centralized power."[17] In his analysis, totalitarianism is merely a perverted expression of the impulsion toward centralized state control provided by the industrial revolution. The answer to it is to be found in democratic planning—national and, for the non-Communist world, international. Mr. Arnold doubts the capacity of private investment and the free play of market forces to offer much competition to communism's efforts to integrate itself with the nationalist movements in the underdeveloped areas of the world.

Doubtless the debate has only begun, and, if the American economy and the Soviet leaders combine to administer further traumatic shocks to the American public, the national self-inquiry is likely to go forward with that zeal which characterizes all pursuits of American public opinion. The outcome of this period of inquiry involves as many imponderables as the question of the future of the Soviet system; indeed, some of them are the same.

Certain elements of the problem appear evident, although just to enumerate them plunges one immediately into a painful awareness of the conflicts they involve. Certainly some more effective form of

---

[16] *The Pattern of World Conflict* (New York, 1955), pp. 228-35.
[17] *Ibid.*, p. 15.

expression of a sense of national purpose in the use of our resources will need to be found, as the anomalies and irrationalities resulting from leaving matters to the interplay of private interests are contemplated by the American public.

Just as certainly, it is not in the nature of our society to follow doctrinaire solutions, and what is most likely to occur is a period of pragmatic development and expansion of the many instrumentalities already available to us. This may lead us to direct our attention to the quality and effectiveness of the administrative agencies we have developed, a revision of procedures for the selection and responsibility of administrative personnel, review procedures, and measures to ensure a greater degree of political responsibility of these agencies. Perhaps at this conjuncture the politics of administration becomes a critical sector in considering the adequacy of our institutions to meet the problems of an increasingly complex industrial society under competition from a centralized and controlled society.

This is of course the central dilemma: whether we can accept the need for a higher degree of centralization in certain areas of our national life to provide for a more rational and effective use of our resources, and at the same time vigilantly distinguish and preserve the pluralist values of our society in the cultural and spiritual realm. The full measure of political genius of the American people will be needed for the task.

We have enormous advantages in this competition. Our resources and technology are a source of strength; even more so, the limitless potentialities of our free society. But the quality of our leadership may be the decisive factor, for this is less a matter of devising new and different institutions than of suffusing the ones we have with a sense of national purpose.